ORDINARY CHRISTOLOGY

Explorations in Practical, Pastoral and Empirical Theology

Series Editors

Leslie J. Francis, University of Warwick, UK,
Jeff Astley, North of England Institute for Christian Education, UK
Martyn Percy, Ripon College Cuddesdon and The Oxford
Ministry Course, Oxford, UK

Theological reflection on the church's practice is now recognized as a significant element in theological studies in the academy and seminary. Ashgate's series in practical, pastoral and empirical theology seeks to foster this resurgence of interest and encourage new developments in practical and applied aspects of theology worldwide. This timely series draws together a wide range of disciplinary approaches and empirical studies to embrace contemporary developments including: the expansion of research in empirical theology, psychological theology, ministry studies, public theology, Christian education and faith development; key issues of contemporary society such as health, ethics and the environment; and more traditional areas of concern such as pastoral care and counselling.

Other titles in the series include:

The Ecclesial Canopy
Faith, Hope, Charity
Martyn Percy

Shaping the Church
The Promise of Implicit Theology
Martyn Percy

Engaging with Contemporary Culture
Christianity, Theology and the Concrete Church
Martyn Percy

Ordinary Theology
Looking, Listening and Learning in Theology
Jeff Astley

The Faith of Girls
Children's Spirituality and Transition to Adulthood
Anne Phillips

Ordinary Christology

Who Do You Say I Am? Answers From The Pews

ANN CHRISTIE
York St John University, UK

ASHGATE

Published by
Ashgate Publishing Limited
Wey Court East
Union Road
Farnham
Surrey, GU9 7PT
England

Ashgate Publishing Company
Suite 420
101 Cherry Street
Burlington
VT 05401–4405
USA

www.ashgate.com

British Library Cataloguing in Publication Data
Christie, Ann.
   Ordinary Christology : who do you say I am? Answers from the
   pews. – (Explorations in practical, pastoral and empirical theology)
   1. Jesus Christ – Person and offices. 2. Faith.
   I. Title II. Series
   232–dc23

Library of Congress Cataloging-in-Publication Data
Christie, Ann.
   Ordinary christology : who do you say I am? : answers from the pews / Ann
   Christie.
       p. cm. – (Explorations in practical, pastoral, and empirical theology)
   Includes bibliographical references (p.   ) and index.
   ISBN 978–1–4094–2535–9 (hardcover) – ISBN 978–1–4094–2536–6 (ebook)
   1. Jesus Christ – Person and offices – Miscellanea. 2. Salvation – Christianity –
   Miscellanea. 3. Theology, Doctrinal – Popular works.
   I. Title.
   BT203.C473 2012
   232–dc23   2011052190

ISBN 9781409425359 (hbk)
ISBN 9781409425366 (ebk)

Printed and bound in Great Britain by the
MPG Books Group, UK.

Contents

Acknowledgements

This book is based on my doctoral thesis which has been reworked and updated for publication. Additional data from further research carried out under the auspices of the North of England Institute for Christian Education (NEICE) has also been incorporated. The first person I therefore want to thank is my PhD supervisor and the Director of NEICE, Jeff Astley. Anyone who reads this book will see that it is heavily indebted to his work on ordinary theology. I count myself extremely fortunate to have had Jeff as my PhD supervisor, and my debt of gratitude to him as supervisor, then colleague and now friend is immense. His theological wisdom and gentle kindliness are always to be relied upon, and for that I am very thankful.

There are also many others who have helped make this book possible and I am particularly grateful to the church members who so generously gave of their time, and more importantly themselves, to participate in the project. Without them there would be no book. I want to thank them for letting me listen to their ordinary Christology and for trusting me with it. I am also grateful to the two incumbents who allowed me to carry out the empirical research with members of their congregations.

Without the encouragement of colleagues at York St John University I doubt that this book would ever have seen the light of day, so to them, as well as Jim Francis who has always been a great supporter of the project, I offer my thanks.

Finally, I would like to thank my family and friends for all their love and support, especially over the last few years. They have been a constant source of strength and without them I would never have been able to get to the point of turning the thesis into a book. My gratitude to them is beyond measure.

Chapter 1

Introduction

'Who do you say I am?' Jesus is reported to have asked his disciples. This book asks the same question of a group of ordinary churchgoers. Who do they say that Jesus is? What significance do they attach to him? These questions have traditionally been discussed in Christian theology under the heading of Christology. Christology is the branch of Christian theology which studies the person and work of Christ, investigating who he was (or is) and what he did (or does). So this is a book about *Ordinary Christology*, defined here as the account given by ordinary believers of who Jesus was (or is) and what he did (or does). It aims to identify and critique the ordinary Christologies of a group of ordinary believers. Ordinary believers, by the definition employed here, have not studied Christology as an academic subject. Their Christology is non-academic and non-scholarly. This study of ordinary Christology is based on the data from in-depth interviews conducted with 45 Anglican churchgoers in rural North Yorkshire. It therefore makes a contribution to Anglican studies and rural theology, as well as ordinary theology. Ordinary theology is a growing field within the discipline of practical theology due in large part to the pioneering work of Jeff Astley. His book *Ordinary Theology* argues for ordinary theology to be taken seriously and since its publication in 2002 ordinary theology has become an established term within practical and empirical theology. So far, however, only a few worked examples of ordinary theology have actually been published. Most notable among these are the empirical studies by Andrew Village (2007) on ordinary hermeneutics and Mark Cartledge (2010) on ordinary pneumatology. This book is the first to be published on ordinary Christology. The main research findings are presented in Chapters 3 to 7, and for the sake of clarity and convenience I have maintained the distinction that is usually made in academic Christology between Christology and soteriology. Ordinary Christology (who Jesus was/is) is discussed in Chapters 3 to 5 and ordinary soteriology (what Jesus did/does) in Chapters 6 and 7. The last two chapters of the book address generic issues arising from the research, such as the characteristics of ordinary Christology and the ongoing hermeneutical process at its heart, before concluding with some reflections on the vexed question of how to respond to ordinary Christology. In this opening chapter I want to prepare the groundwork for the analytic chapters that follow by outlining the doctrinal norms against which ordinary Christology must be tested (much more detail will be added later in dialogue with the data); and set out the main questions to be asked of the interviewees, before finishing with some brief reflections on the learning of ordinary Christology. The methodological issues will then be fully discussed in Chapter 2.

Testing Ordinary Christology

Ordinary Christology cannot just be described. It must also be subject to careful theological analysis and critique in the same way that academic theology is.[1] It must be tested against doctrinal norms and questions asked about its adequacy. 'Is it orthodox?' is one question that will have to be asked. The Christological dogmas of Nicaea and Chalcedon are the touchstone for all orthodox Christology and the doctrinal norms against which ordinary Christology must be tested. These Christological dogmas affirm two key beliefs, namely that Jesus is both truly God and truly human. The Chalcedonian dogma can also be said to act as a rule of Christological speech: Jesus is the one person who can be spoken of as both God and a human being. So, if one is to speak with the orthodox Church, one must talk about him in two ways – as both God and man. The Christological dogmas of Nicaea and Chalcedon (also referred to as classical Christology) are intimately related to the doctrine of the incarnation (and the doctrine of the Trinity). One of the problems with using the doctrine of the incarnation as a Christological norm is that the meaning of the word incarnation in relation to Jesus can be variously understood. For the purposes of this present study, I will assume the following understanding, commonly accepted as the traditional understanding of the doctrine of the incarnation – that God the Son was incarnate in the particular individual Jesus of Nazareth, so that Jesus of Nazareth is 'unique in the precise sense that, while being fully man, it is true of him and of him alone, that he is also fully God,

---

[1]   This is discussed in more detail in Chapter 2. See pp. 25–6.

the Second Person of the co-equal Trinity' (Wiles 1977a: 1; 1979: 12, n4; cf. Crisp 2007: 160–1).[2] Incarnation, on this understanding, involves an ontological identity between the person of Jesus of Nazareth and the Second Person of the Godhead. Jesus in some literal sense 'is' God. As Brian Hebblethwaite, a staunch upholder of this understanding of incarnation, puts it:

> The doctrine [of the Incarnation] expresses, so far as human words permit, the central belief of Christians that God himself without ceasing to be God has come among us, not just in but *as* a particular man, at a particular time and place. The human life lived and the death died have been held quite literally to *be* the human life and death of God himself in one of the modes of his own eternal being. Jesus Christ, it has been firmly held, was truly God as well as truly man. (Hebblethwaite 1987: 1–2; cf. 2005: 118)

The doctrine of the incarnation is often shortened and simplified to the doctrine that Jesus is God. It is this latter doctrine that I primarily use to test the Christological orthodoxy of the sample. The Amsterdam Confession of the World Council of Churches states that the World Council consists of those 'Churches which acknowledge Jesus Christ as God and Saviour'. Similarly, the Athanasian Creed (dating from the fifth century) explicitly states that 'the right faith is that we should believe and confess that our Lord Jesus Christ, the Son of God, is equally both God and man'. The main question to be asked of the sample is whether they believe and confess Jesus Christ as God and saviour? Do they adhere to the Church's teaching about Jesus – that he is both God and man and saviour of us all?

The doctrine that Jesus is God is commonly used as a way of determining whether a person is orthodox and therefore 'really Christian' or not. It acts as the shibboleth for distinguishing orthodoxy from heresy. But, as James Mackey points out, whenever the bald statement 'Jesus is God' is made in the literature of the early Church, it 'must surely be understood in the context of the elaborate explanations of that conviction to which that same literature devotes a considerable amount of its space', so that the statement Jesus is God must be explained further if it is not to be misleading. The basic formula Jesus = God is a simplification of

---

[2] The assumption that there is such a thing as 'the traditional doctrine of the incarnation' has not gone unchallenged. See Sykes 1979: 115–27.

what Christian tradition has claimed and many professional theologians would not accept it without qualification (Mackey 1979: 212). But it has proved itself adequate for our present purposes, in that the question, 'Do you consider Jesus to be God?' has helped uncover the doctrinal stances adopted by the interviewees in respect of Christology. But what about soteriology?

Although it was soteriological concerns that drove developments in classical Christology, the Church has never formulated a dogma for salvation in the way it did for Christology. Salvation has always been understood to be grounded in the life, death and resurrection of Jesus, but how Jesus functions as saviour has never been precisely specified. However, from New Testament times to the present day, the Christian tradition has always put the passion and death of Jesus at the centre of the whole process of salvation. It is the cross which has entered history as the primary symbol of Christianity and the cross which is central to any Christian understanding of salvation. It was for this reason that I focused on the death of Jesus in the interviews. The main soteriological aim of the interview was to explore what meanings, if any, the interviewees attach to the death of Jesus and the claim that Jesus is saviour. The theology of the cross or atonement theology, like incarnational theology, is highly complex. The 'traditional' theology of the cross (about which there is much debate) is, in summary, that we are saved or redeemed from sin and death by Jesus, through his death on the cross, which atoned for or expiated our sins. The idea of atoning for, in the sense of expiating or 'wiping away' sin, originates in the cultic atonement and sacrificial rituals instituted in Leviticus. In these rituals, scapegoats and sacrifices are used to 'atone for' or 'expiate', that is, 'wipe away' or 'cover over' sins and thereby bring forgiveness. In the New Testament, Jesus' death is interpreted in the framework of these rituals. It was the apostle Paul in particular who interpreted Jesus' death in the light of both the ritual of atonement, depicting Jesus as the scapegoat which carries away the sins of the world, and in the ritual of expiatory sacrifice, depicting Jesus' death as an expiatory sacrifice which dealt with sin once and for all. The questions for this study are: Do the sample adhere to the traditional theology of the cross? Do they consider Jesus' death to be an atonement for human sin?

Some of the many New Testament metaphors associated with the death of Jesus have been developed into theories of atonement; some of which will be discussed later in relation to the data. Atonement theories attempt to give an account of how reconciliation between God and humanity is realized through Jesus. They seek to explain what Jesus' death achieved and how it is salvific. It is said that the satisfaction or Anselmian theory of atonement has been of primary importance in western Christianity. Elizabeth Johnson goes so far as to say that this theory of atonement 'was never declared a dogma but might just as well have been, so dominant has been its influence in theology, preaching, devotion, and the penitential system of the Church, up to our own day' (Johnson 1994: 5; cf. Ruether 1998: 97–8). The questions relevant here are: Do the sample adhere to this or any other theory of atonement? Can they give an account of how the cross is salvific?

Throughout most of Christian history the Christological dogmas and the doctrine of the Trinity have been 'the unquestioned – and unquestionable – touchstone of truly orthodox faith and teaching' and classical Christology is still the official teaching of almost all denominations of the Church (Pelikan 1999: 58). However, ever since the Enlightenment classical Christology has been challenged on a number of fronts and in the academy today it continues to be under pressure. This, says Peter Hodgson, is because the traditional models for interpreting Jesus as the Christ 'are perceived as ethnocentric, patriarchal, misogynist, anti-Judaic, exclusivist and triumphalist' (Hodgson 1994: 234, 236–43). Every area of challenge has generated a multitude of new Christologies (see Schweitzer 2010, 2–4; Lassalle-Klein 2011). And in the academy today, classical Christology is being reconstructed with varying degrees of radicalness. Some wish to remain true to the so-called 'governing intention' of Chalcedon and their 'orthodox reconstructions' give great import, if not normative status, to the dogmas of Nicaea and Chalcedon. Others, however, propose abandonment of the classical dogmas altogether and a complete reform of Christology. Since Christology and soteriology are intimately related it should not surprise that soteriology too, has been the subject of fierce debate in recent decades. Satisfaction atonement in particular has come under severe pressure. Liberal theologians have always criticized this approach for compromising both the biblical view of God's love and mercy, and a moral view of justice. And in recent decades a whole host of other theologians (for example, pacifist, black, feminist and womanist) have all joined them to challenge (on various grounds) this understanding of atonement.[3] This empirical study explores the world beyond the academy, and seeks to find out whether classical Christology

---

[3]   Some of these voices will be heard in Chapters 6 and 7 in dialogue with the data.

is intact in the pew. Do ordinary believers still adhere to the ancient dogmas or is classical Christology under attack there as well? Do ordinary believers also challenge the traditional understanding of atonement?

Doctrinal orthodoxy or right belief has always been of great importance for Christianity, but it is 'a very Christian assumption that *belief* is central to religion, an assumption that does not hold good for most other religions' (Gellner 1999: 13). It may be that for ordinary believers doctrinal orthodoxy or right belief is not that central to their religion. We shall see. H.M. Kuitert says we must not exaggerate doctrine's importance. 'Doctrine is a wafer-thin layer, a meagre residue, that certainly tells us what people *needed* to think, but hardly what they really thought, what they really desired, and where their passions really went, as believers' (Kuitert 1999: 119). Clearly doctrine is not everything and it cannot say all there is to say about Jesus. This is why it is so vital that the soteriological question, 'How does Jesus help you?' is asked of ordinary believers, as well as the Christological question, 'Who is Jesus?' Finding out what Jesus *means* to people is arguably more important than finding out who they think he is.

Learning Ordinary Christology

Believers learn their Christology. They are not born with it. And it is learned primarily, but not exclusively, from the tradition. The way of learning about 'the Christian thing', says David Kelsey, 'always goes through some tradition, that is, through a complex of beliefs, truth claims, practices of worship, stories, symbols, images, metaphors, moral principles, self-examination, meditation, critical reflection, and the like' (Kelsey 1992: 109). Or as Lucien Richard puts it, 'The Christ-event is mediated through the particular historical form that the Christian church is. Thus, the church as tradition is the way for the organization of human experience as Christian' (Richard 1996: 147). Believers are socialized into a religious tradition or culture and their Christology is shaped, but not fully determined, by that tradition. It is important, therefore, to say something at the outset about the particular tradition to which the interviewees belong. All of the sample, at the time of the interviews, were regular members of one of four Anglican churches in a rural deanery in North Yorkshire. (All four churches have pews, justifying the sub-title of the book!) The style of Anglicanism in all four churches is best described as 'middle-of-the-road', with liturgical services being the order of the day. Nearly all of the sample were brought up in Anglican or Methodist Christianity as children. Most, but not all, stopped going to church in teenage years or early adult life and only resumed the practice later on in adult life, usually as a result of moving to the area and wanting to be part of the local community. Six of the sample have been socialized into evangelical Christianity and, as we shall see, this makes a considerable difference to their Christology.

Some would say that the community of faith 'shapes, forms, and structures an individual's faith not only by its belief system but also and principally by its action which is the more vital expression of its faith' (Haight 2001: 33). Thus what the community does as well as what it says helps define the shape of ordinary Christology. Indeed all Christian activities, 'from behaviour in the pews prior to a service, through ritual, music and church architecture, to reading church noticeboards and budget decisions may be said to serve as a medium of implicit Christian learning' (Astley 2002: 9). Much Christian learning is implicit, unconscious, informal and unstructured. It occurs via the 'hidden curriculum' of the tradition, that is, 'a set of experiences through which people learn very effectively, but which are not explicitly labelled as *learning* experiences, and which normally are not consciously intended as such'. And the hidden curriculum of worship, it has been said, 'is arguably the most important medium of implicit Christian learning' (Astley 2002: 9; cf. 1996: 244–5; see also Percy 2010: esp. 1–14). For Anglicans, liturgy is said to be the primary medium of Christian learning, and in the liturgy 'the story of the incarnation is repeatedly rehearsed and implied' (Sykes 1979: 119). It is through the liturgy that Anglicans learn how to think, feel and act Christianly. In this context, learning to become and be Christian is a whole person activity. A person's Christology, similarly, is not just a matter of cognition, but of affect also. It involves the heart as well as the mind, with an affective ('feeling') dimension as well as a cognitive ('thinking') dimension. When we take into account the dimension of practice, Christology may truly be said to be multidimensional, involving ideas/concepts, feelings/ experiences and actions. It is a cognitive, affective and conative ('lifestyle') affair. Learning Christology cannot therefore be a cognitive matter only; there must be affective and conative learning here too. In other words, learning Christology is not just a matter of learning *beliefs-that* about Jesus. It also involves learning those affects that properly accompany the *beliefs-that*. Dean Martin argues that, 'without such things as fear, contrition, and increasing love of God', the concept of God has not been fully understood and that 'God is genuinely known only when God's identity is established in a manner that includes one's passions' (Martin 1994: 190). Jonathan Edwards similarly placed considerable stress on the affective dimension of religion, claiming that 'true religion in great part consists in the affections' and 'he that has doctrinal knowledge and speculation only, without affection, never is engaged in the business of religion (Edwards 1961: 27, 30). *Belief-in* Jesus encompasses both *beliefs-that* about Jesus and affective states such as trust in Jesus and other pro-attitudes towards Jesus (see Price 1969: 447–54; cf. Astley 2002: 29–33). Learning to feel these accompanying attitudes and emotions, and learning to behave in a manner appropriate to the beliefs and affects that have been learned through worship, is part and parcel of learning Christology. Unless a believer learns to positively value Jesus, consider him worthy of worship and desire to follow and obey him, then he or she cannot be said to have fully learned a Christology. Having said this, the focus in this study will be on the cognitive dimension of Christology, partly because the affective and conative dimensions of Christology are much harder to measure. What does it mean to 'follow', 'obey', 'trust' or 'honour' Jesus? There are few objective criteria for measuring religious commitment, or the extent to which beliefs are embraced and expressed in action. It is easy enough to observe overt behaviour, but more difficult to be clear about the extent to which such behaviour is motivated by or expresses a person's Christology, without discussing it with the subject. The interviews did generate some affective and conative data, but this was incidental rather than major. It does not follow from this that the affective and conative dimensions of Christology are less important; as we shall see, they are arguably the more important aspects of ordinary Christology.

A believer's Christological thinking, feeling and acting may be learned primarily from the tradition, particularly from the liturgy, but it is not learned exclusively from there. It is learned from other sources too. Sources mentioned by the sample included other people (parents, teachers, clergy, other Christians), significant events (doing the Emmaus course, the birth of a child, going on pilgrimage), books and films, television and radio programmes, art and sacred music. Clearly, a multitude of factors can and do shape a believer's Christology. Several of the sample (all women) mentioned Franco Zeffirelli's classic film *Jesus of Nazareth*, when speaking about Jesus' death. It is possible that a believer may not have read or heard read the passion narratives as recorded in the gospels, so that their own narrative of Jesus' death is based primarily on secondary sources, such as film. Film (unlike the New Testament?) is a powerful and accessible medium: the film is '*really captivating*', whereas the New Testament is '*something I ought to spend more time reading*'.[4] Film can reach where the scriptural word might not.

One factor which has *not* influenced or shaped the Christology of the sample is academic theological study. As was indicated at the outset, none of the sample have received any formal academic theological education, with one exception. One of the sample had undertaken a course of academic theological study as part of her lay-reader training, but whether she learned much theology is questionable, if learning is defined as a change in a person brought about by experience. Consider this extract from her interview.[5]

A *I am just interested to know if, in any way whatsoever, doing the bits of theology that you have done on the lay-reader course has had any impact at all on the way that you think about God and Jesus?*

X *They frustrate me more than anything. No, I mean doing stuff like the filioque, I couldn't care less. It leaves me completely cold. It doesn't bother me at all whether it was this or it was that. I don't know if it has changed my view of God. No, no I don't think so.*

A *For some people doing theology is a kind of life-transforming event.*

X *No. I wouldn't say it was that. I suppose the way I was looking at it was, I've got to get through this and I hope it is not going to change me too much. You know, in the sense that it was going to ... my worry was that it might take away rather than build up.*

---

[4] Interviewee comments are always printed in italics in this text.

[5] Longer interview extracts are also always printed in italics. 'A' stands for Ann (the interviewer) and 'X' stands for the interviewee. To prevent this interviewee from being identified in subsequent chapters, I have not used her pseudonym here. The notation, ... , denotes a pause in speech. The notation, [...], (used in later chapters) denotes an omission of some of the interview text. All interview extracts are in quotation marks, apart from passages of continuous dialogue such as this one.

So academic theological study does not necessarily impact on a person's Christology. It is worth noting here that 20 of the sample had attended an Emmaus course and of these 20 people, 13 are housegroup members. (Neither of these contexts is considered to be 'academic theological study'). It may be that more Christian learning, including Christological learning, goes on in housegroups than in any other context. Here the Bible is read and studied, often in some depth. Some of the housegroup members, the evangelicals mainly, try to read the Bible daily; but the remainder of the sample rarely, if ever, read the Bible for themselves, still less study it. They hear scripture read in church; that is all. This may not be untypical. The results from a survey of Bible-reading practice among regular Anglican worshippers have shown that, in the sample surveyed, the majority of Anglicans do not have the habit of reading the Bible, evangelical Anglicans excepted (Fisher 1992: 382–93; see also Village 2007: 43).

Christological doctrine and Christological learning are clearly both complex subjects. In this opening and introductory chapter I have done little more than set the scene for the rest of the book. The detail will come later in the analytic chapters, after the methodological issues have been discussed. It is to this task that I now turn.

Chapter 2

Studying Ordinary Christology

Empirical Theological Research

Studying ordinary Christology requires both empirical and theological work, which locates this study in the discipline or field of practical theology. The extent to which practical theology incorporates empirical research varies, but many practical theologians are now integrating empirical data into theology. Gerben Heitink is one such: he argues that, 'A practical theology, which chooses its point of departure in the experience of human beings and in the current state of church and society' must be 'characterized by a methodology that takes empirical data with utter seriousness'. But also, 'If practical theology really wants to be theology, it cannot be content with only an empirical approach, as is customary in religious studies. It must also deal with the normative claims embedded in the Christian faith tradition'. In other words, practical theology must have both an empirical and a theological perspective. Thus Heitink opts for a 'an empirically orientated practical theology' that is rooted in the actual experiences of people and the situation of Church and society, uses empirical methods and is set within a hermeneutical framework (Heitink 1999: 7, 220–1). What I am doing in this study is not dissimilar. I too am engaged in an empirically orientated practical-theological study that takes Christian experience seriously and requires both an empirical and a hermeneutical perspective. However, unlike Heitink, I do not primarily understand my practical-theological research as praxis-based or action research. My underlying concern is not with changing the situation, although the results of this study clearly do have implications for both Christian mission and Christian education.

A leading exponent in the field of practical-empirical theology is Johannes van der Ven. He too advocates a model which has a hermeneutical foundation and requires empirical methods. The term empirical theology was actually coined by him to highlight the perspective from which he approaches practical theology.

Van der Ven argues that theology itself should become empirical, that is, it should incorporate social scientific methods into its own methodology. Theology should 'expand its traditional range of instruments … in the direction of an empirical methodology' (van der Ven 1993: 101). He proposes an *intradisciplinary* model for empirical theological research, in which theology provides an overall framework that incorporates social science methods to further its own work. In this approach, the empirical-theological cycle begins with the development of the theological problem and goal followed by theological induction, theological deduction, empirical-theological testing and theological evaluation.[1] William Kay and Leslie Francis (1985: 64–7), on the other hand, opt for an *interdisciplinary* approach to the study of empirical theology. Their model is based on a looser connection between the social sciences and theology. They might start with a sociological or psychological model and apply this to a theological problem or issue, rather than always start with a theological issue or problem to which empirical research is then applied, as in the intradisciplinary approach. Both these approaches to empirical theology could be used to study ordinary Christology, but they are most suited to research aimed at testing theological hypotheses.[2]

This study is essentially a descriptive-exploratory one, rather than a hypothesis-testing one; that is, it follows an inductive rather than a deductive method. However, all empirical research, of whatever type, is 'a conscious process of comparing and evaluating' and therefore 'contains inductive as well as deductive moments, and the inductive and the deductive methods in research therefore never exclude each other but rather make room for each other' (Heitink 1999: 233; cf. van der Ven 1993: 115–8). According to Heitink, in its simplest form a practical-theological study consists of the following elements: description, interpretation, explanation and action. The basic hermeneutical path that my research follows is very similar: that is, description – analysis – theological reflection – (limited) suggestions for action. My formula, like Heitink's, grossly simplifies what is a highly complex process. The different elements in the formula 'call for each other in a reciprocal way' and show the need to interrelate the theological, empirical and

---

[1]   For a worked example of an empirical-theological study using van der Ven's method, see Cartledge 2002; especially chapter 2.

[2]   A succinct summary of the various approaches to the relationship between theology and the social sciences can be found in Cartledge 2003: 11–16.

hermeneutical dimensions.[3] Each phase of the study presents aspects that touch on theology as well as on the social sciences and hermeneutical theory. So an empirically orientated practical-theological study of this kind can be theological, empirical and hermeneutical all at the same time as the following section will illustrate.

Descriptive Research: A Hermeneutical-Phenomenological Approach

Descriptive research aims to give as full a description as possible of the topic under study on the basis of the empirical data. As mentioned above, it usually characterizes the first phase of an empirical-theological research project. One major research tradition that may be classified as descriptive research is phenomenology. The phenomenological research tradition seeks to describe the phenomena under study in as accurate a fashion as is possible. The outcome of an effective phenomenological investigation is a 'thick' description of the life-world or experiences of the individual or group being studied.[4] The goal of phenomenology is often described as seeking the 'essence' of the phenomena. Understanding the 'essence' of a phenomenon comes through empathic indwelling of the phenomenon (*Verstehen*). In order to achieve *Verstehen*, the process of *epoche* or 'bracketing out' must be used. This process involves setting aside personal biases, values and prejudgements about the phenomenon under investigation in order to see the phenomenon as the research participant sees it.[5]

The 'purely descriptive' approach marks out phenomenology as a distinctive discipline, but in doing so makes it vulnerable to the charge of 'hermeneutical naivety', since description is never neutral, value-free or 'pure' (Erricker 1999: 82). For the practical theologian Don Browning, description is always hermeneutical, involving an interpretive dialogue or conversation between the researcher and

---

[3]   The account given here is a modified version of that given by Heitink 1999: 228.

[4]   The term 'thick description' was introduced into the social sciences by the anthropologist Clifford Geertz (who took it from the philosopher Gilbert Ryle). It is used by social scientists to denote a multidimensional, nuanced and complex account of a situation in its context. See Geertz 1975: chapter 1.

[5]   For a full account of the phenomenological research tradition, see Moustakas 1994; Erricker 1999: 73–104.

the subjects being researched. On this account, the researcher brings her pre-understandings into the dialogue 'with the practices and meanings of the subjects', rather than setting them aside, as in the phenomenological tradition. Descriptive research is thus a hermeneutic conversation between the presuppositions of the researcher and the practices and meanings of her research subjects. Proponents of the hermeneutic view of descriptive research believe that detachment is impossible; 'both researcher and subjects are influenced and changed by the research itself', and even listening is a hermeneutic act (Browning 1991: 47–8, 64). As Browning puts it:

> When we listen, we do not simply receive information passively. We listen in order to describe, and the description comes from a particular perspective. We hear, listen, and empathize out of a particular social and historical dialogue. Listening is the first part of conversation and dialogue. Listening is never perfectly neutral, objective and internal to what the other person or group is saying. The listener's attempt to get deeply into the internal frame of reference of the other is transitional and partial. We understand the other largely in analogy to our own experiences, although even here, as in all experience, new elements from the other's experience occasionally break through our fore-concepts. (Browning 1991: 286)

Browning's thought is heavily influenced here by the hermeneutical philosophy of Hans-Georg Gadamer who proposed that understanding was like a dialogue or conversation where we actually *use* our prejudices and prejudgements in the understanding process (see Gadamer 1982). Describing someone else's theology is thus a hermeneutical process, involving an interpretive dialogue or conversation between the theological pre-understandings of the researcher and those of her interviewees. The researcher must bring her theological pre-understandings into the dialogue (she can do no other) and use them positively rather than set them aside. Indeed, if her theological pre-understandings were wholly bracketed out and set to one side then she would not be able to understand the other person's theology at all. Her theological presuppositions are essential for understanding the theology of the other person. They provide her with the reference point from which she can view the theology of the other person and they open up the meaning of the other person's theology to her. Her theology is the lens through which she views the theology of others. This hermeneutical approach recognizes that the researcher's own theology is a conversation partner in descriptive theological research; and that the researcher's own horizon of understanding, the perspective from which she sees things, always enter into the interpretive process and shapes the final description. As Astley puts it:

> The point is this: even in describing your theology I am implicitly engaged in a conversation between my theology and yours, at least to some extent. My perspective influences what comes to my attention as I listen to you talk about, and see you practise, your faith; indeed it influences what it is that I am capable of seeing and hearing, and what I take seriously in what you say. (Astley 2002: 109)

Whilst pre-understandings are necessary for interpretation, however, they must not be allowed to dominate or to distort the process. After all the aim is to give a description of the interviewees' theology, not the researcher's! But the hermeneutic model of a conversation shows that any description of another person's theology will always be at least partly dependent on the theological pre-understandings of the researcher. In Gadamer's phrase, descriptive theology involves a 'fusion of horizons' between the researcher's own theology and that of her interviewees. The personal, religious and cultural history of the researcher, including her theological commitments and preoccupations, are all relevant to what she sees and hears in her conversations with her research subjects. In describing their theology, she must therefore not omit to describe her own, which is what I will now do.

Anything to Declare?

I am a white, middle-class, middle-aged English female, who is already shaped by what I aim to interpret, having been a life-long churchgoer. Like every Christian, I have a Christology. I am an insider, researching an aspect of the religious tradition to which I belong and to which I feel bound.[6] I was brought up as a

---

[6] On the advantages and disadvantages of being an insider, see Hopewell 1987: 88–9.

Roman Catholic, but am now an Anglican. This change of tradition came about as a result of becoming involved in evangelical-charismatic Anglicanism while at university. Evangelicalism taught me to embrace the faith and be embraced by it and for that I will always be grateful, but its theology became increasingly problematic. In my mid 30s I embarked on an academic course of theological study for the first time in order to explore some of the theological issues that were bothering me, which included Christological issues such as atonement and exclusivism. This research has arisen out of an ongoing existential concern with Christological questions and I should admit that, in part, its focus included that of resolving these concerns. Both atonement and exclusivism – key loci of debate for Christian apologetics – are addressed here. My interest in the phenomenon under study is thus not disinterested. This enquiry is also heuristic in that it forms part of my own personal search to understand the meaning and significance of Jesus Christ for my own and others' faith and life. In one sense, then, it is as much a self-enquiry as it is an enquiry into the Christological beliefs and believing of others. Now, a Christological quest can be approached in various ways. After having undertaken a module in Christology as part of a taught MA, I was intrigued to know how ordinary believers interpreted Jesus. What did they make of him? The module had focused on what academic theologians thought about Jesus, not on what ordinary believers thought about him. I was curious to know something of what Christology in practice might actually look like. What significance and meaning did ordinary believers attach to Jesus? This question became the focus of my PhD and subsequently of this book. Studying ordinary Christology has helped me to resolve some of my own Christological questions. It has helped me to become a self-confessed liberal. I openly declare it, acknowledging that this shift in perspective, from the evangelicalism of my 20s to the liberalism of my 40s and now 50s, has been partly shaped by and has partly shaped the present work. Hence, this study is inevitably influenced, but hopefully not distorted, by my own liberal theological predilections. I have had to work particularly hard not to let my own interests adversely affect the way in which I describe and critique the Christology of the small number of evangelicals in the sample.

Another interest which I must declare is my relationship to the interviewees. The researcher of ordinary Christology has several methodological choices to make, one of which concerns the choice of research participants. Whose ordinary

Christology should she study? Thirty of the interviews (those for my PhD thesis) were conducted in 2002–2003 with members of my then-husband's three Anglican congregations in rural North Yorkshire. The remaining 15 interviews were conducted in 2006 with members of another rural congregation in the deanery.[7] There was the potential for 'personal reactivity' (also called 'interview bias'), as a result of the 'vicar's wife' factor, to be a major source of error in the PhD interviews but this proved not to be the case.[8] It is also worth noting here that the data from the later interviews added no new themes or patterns and served primarily to confirm the results of the earlier PhD research. This suggests that the ordinary Christology described in this book might be typical for rural Anglicanism.

Choosing an Empirical Research Method

The researcher of ordinary Christology has to decide which of the social-scientific method or methods she is going to use to carry out her empirical research. Empirical research can be divided into two categories: quantitative and qualitative research. Both of these approaches can be used to study ordinary Christology, and the strengths and weaknesses of each approach have been well rehearsed.[9] Empirical theological research has been carried out using both quantitative and/ or qualitative research methods, and van der Ven's empirical theology relies on both methods. Choosing a research strategy depends partly on the purpose of the research. Since the purpose of this research was to obtain as 'thick' a description as possible of ordinary believers' Christological beliefs and believing, a qualitative approach was adopted. A small-scale qualitative approach necessarily sacrifices the 'hard' data made available by a large-scale quantitative study, but it gains in 'digging below the surface and revealing the texture of religious feeling and

---

[7] These interviews were carried out under the auspices of the North of England Institute for Christian Education.

[8] See Christie 2005: 31–2. On 'personal reactivity', that is, the possible effects of the personal and social characteristics of the researcher on the research participants, see Hammersley 1998: 85–7; cf. Bailey 1994: 175.

[9] For a summary of the differences between quantitative and qualitative research, and their respective strengths and weaknesses, see Heitink 1999: 222; McLeod 1994: chapters 4–6; Astley 2002: 97–100.

experience which surveys miss altogether' (Ahern and Davie 1987: 12). Empirical theological research through quantitative methods is generally considered to be unsuitable 'if one wants to penetrate to deeper levels of consciousness' (Heitink 1999: 232; cf. Martin 2003: 2–3). It is widely acknowledged that qualitative methods offer the best chance of acquiring depth insights into the character and shape of a person's religious beliefs and believing. James Hopewell (1987: 88) writes, 'What expresses the faith of a congregation is not numerical data but rather the stories that the numbers only grossly approximate.'[10] But qualitative research is not without its problems as we shall see. It inevitably draws on small samples only and is highly selective. Such research is also frequently criticized on the grounds that the researchers 'merely find what they knew already'. The charge is that the researcher 'has done little more than gather information to support her pre-existing biases and prejudices' (McLeod 1994: 98). This is partly why Browning insists on the researcher giving some signals about her cultural and religious history in order to show how personal and historical factors have shaped her research findings. Awareness by the researcher of the ideological nature of description reduces the chances of the data being distorted, as does methodological transparency.

A variety of qualitative research tools are available. My choice was partly pragmatic. 'In real world research you have to use the methods that are *possible*' (Gillham 2000: 5). The in-depth interview was the tool I felt most competent to use. It is in fact one of the most widely used research tools for obtaining qualitative data.[11] The qualitative research interview provides a first-person in-depth account of what the phenomenon under study means to the participant. David Hay and Kate Hunt (2000: 9) prefer to call the research interview a 'research conversation' rather than an in-depth interview, because they 'were interested primarily in understanding what people had to say rather than testing a hypothesis'. The term 'research conversation' also has the added advantage of signalling that the research interview is set in a dialogical and hermeneutical framework which 'recognizes the irreducible significance of the interpreter' (Astley 2002: 112).

It is worth noting here the 'curious fact that people are, in general, far more willing to devote an hour and a half to an interview (even of no benefit to

---

[10]   See also Towler 1974: 158 and Jenkins 1999: 33–4.

[11]   For an overview of the different methods that have been used in gathering qualitative data, see McLeod 1994: 79–9.

themselves) than to give 15 minutes to the completion of a questionnaire'. It has also been observed that 'large sections of the population are not comfortable with *any* kind of written response. And people, as a whole, find it much easier to talk than to write, even if the writing doesn't amount to much' (Gillham 2000: 15, 17). Several of my interviewees expressed concern about filling in a questionnaire for exactly this reason. Others expressed more sophisticated concerns, suggesting that a questionnaire, even an open-ended one, would not be able to capture the complexity of their believing in the way that the interview had. A face-to-face interview allows for meanings to be clarified by both the researcher and the interviewee, but with questionnaires the interviewee can only respond to what is written on the page and the data show that people understand the meaning of religious language and phrases in different ways. They may understand the same question in different ways or alternatively they may give the same reply to a particular question but mean different things by it.

The Qualitative Research Interview

First some theoretical considerations: in empirical theological research the theological (and hermeneutical) perspective is operational from the outset. As we have seen, the interviewer does not come to the interview theologically empty-handed. She comes with her own theological presuppositions and theological perspective which she needs if she is to hear her interviewees theology as *theology*. She also comes with a specific theological aim(s) in mind, having selected a particular theological theme for investigation. Selection operates at every stage of the research process, and both interviewer and interviewee select. All description, be it the interviewees' description of their own Christology, or the interviewer's description of the interviewees' description of their Christology, involves selection and therefore subjectivity. The interviewer is looking and listening with 'theological' eyes and ears both during the interview and afterwards as the data is analysed for aspects of ordinary Christology, selecting what is significant at least partly on the basis of what she takes to be significant. The theological researcher is thus not an innocent listener. She is continually listening out for theology and exploring theology. Theology is her focus and it is this focus that distinguishes her approach from that of the sociologist or anthropologist (see Astley 2002: esp. 109–10, 14). Theological listening and theological exploration characterizes the interview stage of the research process. As has already been said, the researcher's aim in the interview is not to impose her own Christological beliefs or ideas on her research subjects or to evaluate their beliefs against her own, rather it is to hear them put into speech their Christological beliefs and perspectives. The aim is to explore and understand their Christological world. Obviously nothing as complex as a person's Christology can be entirely captured in words, either by the person themselves or by the researcher. Maybe much of Christology is actually unsayable. Every individual believer has their own conscious and unconscious thoughts and feelings about Jesus which one interview cannot hope to capture. But through the judicious use of questions, probes and prompts in a conversational setting, it is not impossible to gain some insight into another's Christological world.

Now for some practical considerations: the research sample was not self-selecting across any of the four churches. All the research participants were purposefully selected to provide a representative sample (across ages, educational backgrounds and occupations) from the adult research population of around 130–140 churchgoers (the total from the four churches). Forty-seven people (around 2:1 female: male) were approached. Only two people from the last church refused to be interviewed, although several of the women from across the churches did express concern, prior to the interview, that they would have very little to say. It is well documented that even people with a formal religious commitment are reluctant to talk about their spiritual lives (Hay and Hunt 2000: 7; cf. Hopewell 1987: 90). Every interviewee was told in advance what the aim of the research was and permission was sought to tape-record the interview and to quote from it in any report under a pseudonym. The interviews generally lasted from 60 to 90 minutes.

There are different approaches to structuring qualitative research interviews.[12] As there were certain themes that I wanted to explore with the research participants (as outlined in Chapter 1) I adopted a semi-structured approach. In the semi-structured (also called the focused or guided) interview, the interviewer selects in advance the various themes into which she intends to inquire. The themes I selected were subject to modification and refinement as the research progressed, as

---

[12]   On the qualitative research interview, see Bailey 1994: chapter 8; McLeod 1994: 79–84; Oppenheim 1992: chapter 5; Kvale 1983: 171–96; Gillham 2000.

were the questions I used to explore the themes. It is a feature of many examples of qualitative research that the research questions are allowed to grow and change as the research advances. Proponents of 'grounded theory' qualitative research argue that the researcher should be allowed to revise and adapt the research question as the data collection progresses. Margot Ely writes:

> For most of us, the questions shift, specify and change from the very beginning in a cyclical process as the [data] grow, are thought about, analysed, and provide further direction for the study. This is certainly different from positivistic research in which questions are posed at the start and do not change. (Ely 1991: 31)

In the semi-structured interview the questions are open-ended. Open-ended questions allow respondents to answer in their own words, whereas closed-end questions require respondents to choose from a limited number of fixed alternatives. Open-ended questions make it possible for research subjects 'to organize their own descriptions, emphasizing what they themselves find important' (Kvale 1983: 173; cf. Bailey 1994: 118–23). Robert Bellah argues that the research interview (he calls it the 'active interview') has advantages over the survey questionnaire based on fixed questions, because the latter 'produces data that take on the aura of "natural facts" rather than meanings taking shape within an ongoing historical conversation' (Bellah 1985: 305). The semi-structured interview allows questions to be tailored to suit the needs of the situation, with probes, or follow-up questions, being used to achieve as full and complete an exploration of a theme as possible.[13]

In ordinary theology research, the interview is essentially a theological discussion with people 'not given to that sort of talk' (Hopewell 1987: 90). So to encourage the discussion I usually began with an open question inviting people to share their thoughts, feelings, beliefs about Jesus, or else I invited them to talk about their churchgoing as a way in to exploring their Christology. According to Gillham, 'In interviewing you start off with a question, the opening shot; where it goes from there may be unpredictable but you have to follow, controlling the direction' (Gillham 2000: 4). For a novice interviewer this can be disconcerting. But learning how to follow the respondents' lead, structuring the interview

---

[13]   On the use of probes, see Bailey 1994: 189–90.

into shape and giving it direction, does becomes easier with practice and as the interviewer becomes increasingly familiar with the likely range of discourses to be encountered. The interview conversation, however, must always be controlled and managed by the interviewer. Without the structure provided by the interviewer, 'the interview could degenerate into a worthless exercise in which questions are asked at random and neither the interviewer nor the respondent knows what the interview is supposed to achieve' (Bailey 1994: 200).

Ethical considerations also have to be taken into account when interviewing. Oppenheim's view is that 'the basic ethical principle governing data collection is that no harm should come to the respondents as a result of their participation in the research' (Oppenheim 1992: 83). The data is 'thin' in various places precisely because ethical concerns always have to take precedence over the pursuit for rich data. The interviewer must be non-judgemental, affirmative and respectful at all times. Interviewing, in these circumstances, takes on some aspects of the character of a pastoral activity. Ottmar Fuchs (2001: 239–47) describes the qualitative-empirical theological encounter as a pastoral encounter, arguing that the depth quality of the data depends to a significant degree on the pastoral quality of the empirical research. The research interview requires 'pastoral-theological qualities' if interviewees are to feel sufficiently secure to bring up their experiences and conflicts about their religious beliefs in an open and honest way.

The interviews I conducted were not perfect. They never are. But every research conversation, without exception, yielded a surprising richness of data, with doubts and uncertainties, as well as heartfelt convictions, being readily expressed. One aspect of the qualitative research interview is that it can be a positive experience for the interviewee and several of my interviewees reported that it was. Hopewell comments that 'so accustomed are members [of congregations] to being told what they *should* believe that to be asked what they in fact *do* believe may prompt unprecedented communication' (Hopewell 1987: 91). Most of the interviewees seemed to appreciate the opportunity to talk about and explore their beliefs and generously engaged in the process, generating a wealth of rich, personal and detailed data for analysis. What seems to matter most is that the interviewer is a good listener, the sort of person people will talk to. I trust that I was.

Data Analysis

'Qualitative data are often difficult to handle and report on, and the researcher who adopts this approach will frequently feel swamped by her data' (Astley, 2002: 99). This has certainly been my experience. Each interview generated around 15 to 20 pages of (single-spaced) transcript which then had to be analysed properly. One disadvantage of qualitative research is that it is very time-consuming. Every hour of interview tape generated approximately six hours of transcribing. Analysing the interviews takes even longer. Methodological choices face the researcher at this stage of the research process too, as a range of different strategies can be applied in qualitative data analysis. Phenomenologists, for instance, are 'careful, often dubious, about condensing' interview transcripts. 'They do not, for example, use coding, but assume that through continued readings of the source material and through vigilance over one's presuppositions, one can reach the "*Lebenswelt*" of the informant, capturing the "essence" of an account' (Miles and Huberman 1994: 8; cf. Davies 2000: 16). Grounded theory research, by contrast, relies on 'a series of well-articulated analytic steps', including extensive coding and categorization, often impossible without the use of computer-aided techniques (McLeod 1994: 93–7; cf. Glaser and Strauss 1967).

It is clear that qualitative data analysis is a complex and often idiosyncratic business. As John McLeod (1994: 89) observes, it is reasonable to claim that 'no two researchers approach the task of qualitative data analysis in quite the same way'. According to Clark Moustakas, every method in human science research is open ended. He writes, 'Each research project holds its own integrity and establishes its own methods and procedures' which facilitate the flow of the investigation and the data collection (Moustakas 1994: 104). Certainly, there are varying degrees of transparency about methodological issues in qualitative research. Some researchers prefer 'intuitive, relaxed voyages through their data', whilst others opt for 'thoroughness and explicitness', insisting that the reliability and validity of findings derived from qualitative data depends on explicit, systematic methods 'that are credible, dependable, and replicable in *qualitative* terms' (Miles and Huberman 1994: 2, 5).

Various stages are said to occur during any type of qualitative analysis, namely, immersion – categorization – data reduction – interpretation (see McLeod 1994:

89–93; Miles and Huberman 1994: 9–12). My approach to data analysis followed this general pattern. First, every interview was transcribed and then coded – this is the process of categorizing qualitative material. The researcher systematically works through the transcript assigning coding categories and identifying themes within the text. At the same time she is immersing herself in the data, trying to enter, in an empathic way, into the Christological world of the interviewee. The process of coding is essentially one of data reduction. Data reduction occurs continuously throughout the life of the project until the final report is written up. It is a form of analysis 'that sharpens, sorts, focuses, discards, and organizes data in such a way that "final" conclusions can be drawn and verified' (Miles and Huberman 1994: 11). The data were analysed as they were gathered, enriching the quality of the data from subsequent interviews. All the while the coded data were being scrutinized and interrogated, sifted and sorted through, to identify repeating phrases, patterns and themes, as well as differences and commonalities. The researcher is constantly analysing and interpreting and taking the findings out into the next wave of data collection. Matthew Miles and Michael Huberman draw attention to the cyclical nature of the analytic process. Their model for qualitative analysis consists of three concurrent flows of activity: data reduction, data display and conclusion drawing/ verification. These three streams of interpretive activity, together with the activity of data collection itself, form an interactive cyclical process. 'The researcher steadily moves among these four "nodes" during data collection and then shuttles among reduction, display, and conclusion drawing/verification for the remainder of the study.' Thus qualitative data analysis is 'a continuous, iterative enterprise' (Miles and Huberman 1994: 11–12). It is, of course, also a complex hermeneutical one. Hay and Hunt (2000: 10) describe the research method as 'a spiral, with the texts being revisited on numerous occasions and themes emerging and developing as the process continued'. It must be noted here that assessing the validity, that is, the 'truthfulness', of my conclusions/interpretations, by asking the interviewees to comment on them, was not really possible as the analysis was conducted at a theological level they would not readily recognize.[14]

---

[14] On the vexed question of validity in qualitative research, see Merriam 2002: chapter 2.

Theological Analysis

I would agree with Geoffrey Ahern that 'trying to identify explicit and implicit models from the total context of what was said has been not far short of a methodological nightmare' (Ahern 1984: 15). But identifying patterns and processes of Christological believing is not the end of the study for the researcher of ordinary Christology. She must also offer a theological critique of ordinary Christology as well as a description and analysis of it. This final stage, which includes writing up, is by far the most demanding and stressful part of the whole enterprise. It involves a great deal of theological work and involves a shift in emphasis from description and analysis to theological reflection and critique. According to Astley, ordinary theology must be subject to an analysis and critique of 'the language and forms of argument that people use when speaking of God and religion' and 'it must also embrace the evaluation of theological beliefs from the standpoint, and using the resources, of the normative theological criteria derived from Christian scripture, doctrine and ethics' (Astley 2002: 104). This is a demanding task indeed, involving as it does both philosophical and theological work. Similarly, for Browning, descriptive theology, as the first movement in what he calls a fundamental practical theology, must later be related to the second and third movements, namely the normative texts of historical theology and the critical and philosophical questions of systematic theology. And there must be a critical hermeneutical dialogue between all three movements (Browning 1991: 47–54).

So the researcher of ordinary Christology must attempt to test the Christological beliefs of her sample against doctrinal norms and ask questions about how far ordinary Christology is faithful or unfaithful to 'the Christian thing'. Are their Christological construals 'true'? (Kelsey 1992: 206–7). In order to do this she must bring ordinary Christology into a critical conversation with doctrinal Christology and academic Christology. The literature here is enormous. Academic Christology encompasses doctrinal Christology and includes numerous other sub-disciplines, such as New Testament Christology, patristic Christology, the history of Christology and contemporary Christology. If she is also to critique the language and language use of ordinary believers when they speak of Jesus, then the philosophy of religious language must become a conversation partner too. A tall order indeed!

The analytic chapters which follow are best viewed as an offering in which the critical conversation is necessarily limited. But before the ordinary Christologies of the sample are described, analysed and critiqued, I want to draw attention to some other methodological problems surrounding the study of ordinary Christology.

Some Methodological Problems

With hindsight I can now appreciate how theologically demanding the interviews were. I was asking quite searching questions about the identity and function of Jesus Christ to interviewees who had had no formal theological training and who, more importantly, had not often spoken about or even thought about Christological questions before. Michael Hornsby-Smith reports that, 'Not infrequently ordinary Catholics, in our interviews with them, gave the impression that they were confronting questions about their religion to which they had never previously given any thought' (Hornsby-Smith 1991: 110). Such a situation is considered problematic by Robert Towler, who argues that in this situation, answers to questions are often misinterpreted as 'people's ideas' when in fact they are no more than 'the spontaneous formation of religious ideas'. He illustrates how the response to the question 'Do you believe in any sort of after-life?' may actually be a response to a different question, namely 'When you stop to consider it, even though you have never done so before, do you believe in any sort of after-life?' He suggests that responses, therefore, 'should be interpreted as reactions to stimuli, and treated accordingly, not naively accepted as rationally thought-out answers to simple questions'. He draws on the work of Jean Piaget to illustrate how responses to questions may not be ideas that have previously been thought-out, but are ideas spontaneously formed in response to a particular stimulus (Towler 1974: 159–60). The same point is made by Martin Stringer with regard to Victor Turner's reliance on the ritual specialist Muchona. He writes, 'It also becomes clear that a large amount of what is being said by Muchona is being made up on the spot, simple because the questions, and the ideas that they generated, had never occurred to him before' (Stringer 1999: 64).

But there is counter-evidence to suggest that asking people about a subject for the first time 'often evokes a deep, but hitherto unarticulated conviction that they *already* hold, rather than some superficial non-answer that masquerades as an answer. Many people will find themselves, whether in public discussion or private reflection, saying in effect, "Now that I think about it, I realize that I do believe *a* and *b*, and I don't believe *c* and *d*"(Astley 2002: 103). Beliefs can be held without being expressed and questions can help bring previously unarticulated beliefs to expression 'provided they were both long-standing and available to consciousness' (Bailey 1997: 52). A belief may be thought of as a mental state of which we become aware, or a disposition to say, do, feel and think something. So through the interview people may come to discover what they have believed but not 'thought' (occurrently and explicitly). Hay and Hunt report that the research conversation 'forced [interviewees] to look at their own lives in a different way, many discovering what they actually believed as a result (Hay and Hunt 2000: 10; cf.15–16).

Similarly, the research interviews I carried out forced many people to stop and consider what it was that they actually believed about Jesus. Their Christological beliefs were thus coming to expression for the first time. People were discovering their beliefs as they said them. Before her interview Jill said, '*I might not have much to say to you. You don't often formulate things like that until someone asks you*' and, tellingly, '*I don't know what I think until I say it.*' Others, like Richard, talked about the interview provoking them into thought and helping them '*to look deeper and just confirm what you believe*'. There is ample evidence to suggest that some people, at least, came to discover what they believed about certain Christological themes through the interview process. Sometimes there would be an evolution of thought during the interview, with beliefs being modified or changed. This is an acknowledged feature of the qualitative research interview. Steinar Kvale writes, 'During the interview the interviewee may himself have discovered new aspects by the themes he is describing, and he may suddenly see relations which he has not been conscious of earlier' (Kvale 1983: 177; cf. Bailey 1998: 53). And, of course, the process of being interviewed may produce new insight and awareness for the interviewer, as it does for the interviewee.

But how can we be sure that what is being brought into speech for the first time during the interview process is an accurate verbalization of a previously unarticulated belief, and not a belief that is just being made up on the spot (and, perhaps, will soon dissipate)? Towler suggests that questions should be so phrased that they allow for a variety of *negative* responses (Towler 1974: 159–60). Edward Bailey addresses this problem by telling the interviewees at the start 'that the purpose was to discover what they already felt and thought, and not to think up answers to questions on which they had no views' (Bailey 1998: 46). Following Bailey's lead, I encouraged interviewees at the start of their interview to decline to answer questions on which they had no views; they duly obliged. Thus they would quite happily admit to having no opinion about something and frequently did so. Phrases such as '*I've not thought about it before*', '*I don't know*', '*I haven't really thought this out*', litter the interviews, especially of the women. Perhaps women are more honest? Or it could be that the questions being asked demanded analytic or abstract thought, which is a style of thinking preferred by men rather than women? There is a gender and/or psychological type issue here which requires further empirical investigation.[15]

What is clear is that people were more than willing to say that they had not thought about certain questions before, suggesting that already-existing beliefs were coming to expression. The idea that people 'make up' Christological beliefs in an interview seems less likely. There is a risk, of course, that respondents might feel constrained to give the 'right' answer, to reply in terms of the accepted orthodoxy, while what they actually believe is not what they profess to believe. But this is unlikely, given that the data show that most people do not actually know what the 'right' or orthodox answer is. They willingly, if hesitantly, share their beliefs, unaware that the beliefs they hold are often unorthodox. There is no evidence in the data to suggest that the interviewees tried to be anything other than open and honest. Tom sums up the general attitude when he says, '*I mean there is no point agreeing to talk to you if I don't tell you what I really think.*'

The problem discussed above is one aspect of the larger practical problem associated with empirical studies, namely 'the hoary problem of how the observer is to avoid imposing his own frame of reference, or his own way of thinking about a topic, on his subjects' (Towler 1974: 158). Whilst the interview is open, enabling interviewees the space and time to speak about their own Christological beliefs and understanding, it is structured by the theological questions which

---

[15]   On this issue, see Slee 1999: 126–7; cf. Astley 2002: 77–82.

the interviewer asks. And these questions are her questions. It is her theological agenda that sets the framework for the discussion, not the interviewees. Callum Brown draws attention to this dynamic in oral history interviews. He writes:

> The interviewer poses questions, setting the agenda and, most importantly, providing the vocabulary and conceptual frameworks within which informants are invited to respond. This is literally a process of 'putting words into the mouth' of the interviewee, a process which can simplify or alter the vocabulary of the interviewee. (Brown 2001: 117)

There is a danger that the subject being studied gets reduced to the pre-set categories of the researcher and that the respondent alters their replies to fit in with these categories. Brown says that this should not be looked upon merely as a problem, but as an opportunity. The disjunctions between interviewers' questions and the interviewees' answers provide clues about the two ways of understanding the subject. The transcript discloses as much about the 'discursive domain' of the interviewer as of the interviewee (Brown 2001: 117). The transcripts from this research show that my 'discursive domain', unlike that of the interviewees, is shaped by the categories of thought of academic Christology. I come to the research conversation with academic Christological concerns in mind. To give an illustration: the identity of Jesus is a key academic Christological concern. It was one of my concerns. But disjunctions between my questions about Jesus' identity and the interviewees' answers reveal that this topic is not of key concern to ordinary believers. Academic Christology is concerned to understand how Jesus relates to God, or how Jesus can be both human and divine; again, however, this concern is not shared by (most) ordinary theologians. They have beliefs about Jesus, but are not concerned or interested in exploring the theoretical/metaphysical implications of these beliefs.

In general, the questions which concern academic theologians do not usually concern ordinary ones. This is not a criticism; it is an observation. One of the difficulties is that most people have 'little time for the intellectualizations of doctrine ... that are so beloved of the religious professionals; they respond only very poorly to abstract concepts and verbal formulations' (Momen 1999: 455). This particular characteristic of ordinary Christology will be discussed further in

Chapter 8. My point here is merely to draw attention to the fact that disjunctions and negative responses can both be vitally important sources of information. Although the methodological problems mentioned here are important, they should not be made too much of. The semi-structured interview provides ample opportunity for interviewees to put their own stamp on the interview and most did, making it quite clear where their Christological priorities lay and what was important to them.

But it has to be acknowledged that understanding what people meant was not always easy. It is inevitable that people use the language and vocabulary of the tradition to express their Christological beliefs. They have learnt an idiom and they use it, sometimes repeating set phrases from the tradition. But what do they mean by this? What inferences can legitimately be made from the observation that some respondents do little more than repeat received information and are unable to elaborate on a particular theme? Understanding the meaning attached to the language and verbal categories that people use to express their religious beliefs and attitudes is notoriously difficult. The language of faith is capable of different interpretations. One of the aims of the researcher of ordinary Christology must be to uncover, as best she can, the 'depth grammar' of peoples' speech. The depth grammar of a word or sentence is its real significance, as shown in its usage; the 'surface grammar', by contrast, is its appearance, which can often mislead us (Wittgenstein 1968: § 664). It is important, therefore, that any criticism of what people say be directed to its depth grammar (what people actually mean), and not to its surface grammar (what people might appear to mean). We must look at how language about Jesus *works*, how it is used, if we are to understand Christological beliefs. What this means for an empirical-theological study is that an accurate description of what people are really saying must be based on the evidence of the implications or conclusions that people actually draw from the language they are using (see Astley 2002: 121–2). Hence identifying the implications that people draw from the Christological language they use must be one of the key tasks for the researcher of ordinary Christology. I have attempted to do this at various points (see especially, pp. 163–76), but the analysis is limited as it was not always possible to question the interviewees in the required depth.

Having addressed the main methodological issues in this Chapter, it is now time to move on to the analysis and critique of the ordinary Christologies operating in the sample. Three main Christologies have been identified.[16] I will begin with what I have called functional Christology.

---

[16] For a summary of these three Christologies, see Christie 2007.

Chapter 3

Functional Christology

One of the most surprising and unexpected findings from the data was the discovery that the majority of the sample (around 30) do not consider Jesus to be God. They do not appear to have learned this doctrine, or the related doctrines of pre-existence and the immanent Trinity. They do not conceptualize Jesus' identity in the belief that he was both God and man. They can be said to affirm a doctrine of the incarnation understood as the incarnation of God's creative, revelatory and salvific power in the person of Jesus Christ; but not a doctrine of the incarnation understood as the incarnation of God the Son, Second Person of the Trinity. This group has a functional rather than an ontological Christology. In this chapter I will present each strand of the evidence in turn with a view to building up a doctrinal picture of how this group views the identity of Jesus of Nazareth.

Absence of a Doctrine of Pre-existence

In response to a question about pre-existence, along the lines of, 'Would you think of Jesus in any way existing before his birth?', the responses were always negative:[1]

Eleanor
A   *Would you think of Jesus existing before he was born or ...*
E   *Oh crikey. I don't know. I think I just thought he was born, because that was what God wanted for the world.*

---

[1]   I am fully aware that the wording of this question can be criticized. Strictly speaking it is not Jesus who pre-existed but the Word/Logos (see below, pp. 72–3). But many academic theologians use this language and the experience of talking to ordinary believers shows that too fine a distinction would be confusing for interviewees.

Diane

A   *The other thing around this is ... um ... would you think of Jesus existing in*
      any sense ... um ... before he was born?

D   *I must admit, I never have thought that. I accept that, you know, the coming*
      of Christ at Christmas, is when Jesus was born.

Marion

A   *Do you think of Jesus as, like, existing before his earthly life?*

M   *No, not really. I think that he was born.*

However, the data on pre-existence was often ambiguous. Pre-existence could not be entirely ruled out on the basis of this evidence alone because this group would also use phrases that might appear to imply pre-existence, talking about Jesus being sent by God or coming from God. If God sent forth his Son, must not that Son have already been in existence? But many scholars argue that talk of God sending someone does not in itself imply any form of pre-existence of the one sent, otherwise we would have to ascribe pre-existence to John the Baptist and the prophets in the Old Testament, who were also 'sent' by God. 'Sending' texts and language may imply pre-existence, but they can be read otherwise.[2] Macquarrie (1990: 56) writes, 'God's metaphorical "sending" of his metaphorical "son" can be understood in ways that do not imply pre-existence, once we accept that the language is metaphorical and not literal'. Drawing on the work of various New Testament scholars, he argues that nearly all the biblical texts which seem to entail a doctrine of the pre-existence of Jesus do not in fact do so, and that they can be understood without recourse to the idea of a pre-existent divine being. But this does not mean that all thoughts of pre-existence have to be done away with. The texts are perfectly compatible with, and probably demand, says Macquarrie, 'the idea that Jesus pre-existed in the mind and purpose of God'; so Jesus pre-exists, if at all, in this way only – as an idea in the mind and purpose of God (Macquarrie 1990: 56–7, 388–92). This kind of pre-existence is implied in the following statements:

---

[2]   See, for example, Mackey 1983: chapter 6, esp. 56; Macquarrie 1990: 55–9, 388–92; O'Collins 1995: 128. See also Küshel's comprehensive study of pre-existence Christology, 1992.

Eleanor

'*... that was what God wanted for the world.*'

Tom

'*God chose to put Jesus on this earth.*'

Hilary

'[Jesus] *was part of God's plan.*'

According to Macquarrie, this is the only kind of pre-existence that one should look for. He writes, 'If one wants to go beyond this and claim that Jesus Christ had prior to his birth a conscious, personal pre-existence in "heaven", this is not only mythological but is, I believe, destructive of his true humanity' (Macquarrie 1990: 57). That this group have no sense of pre-existence, other than in the sense outlined above, and must therefore be using the language of 'sending' and 'coming down' metaphorically is confirmed by the responses they give to other questions about the creed and the Trinity. At no point is there ever any suggestion of a second divine 'person' or hypostasis distinct from God the Father and from the historical Jesus before Jesus was born. They do not draw this implication. The depth grammar of their language here is metaphorical. The majority of this group never seem to self-consciously acknowledge that they are using the language of 'sending' metaphorically. They just use it, like they do their mother tongue, and do not stop to consider its status. But the metaphor of 'sending' seems to express their conviction that the person and work of Jesus are completely the work of God's initiative; it acknowledges that 'All this is from God.' James Mackey argues that we have no choice but to use this kind of language if we wish to speak, as it were, from God's side of any person, thing or event in our world of time and space (Mackey 1983: 63–4; cf. Knox 1967: 3–4). That this group have no belief in any more metaphysical notion of pre-existence is further confirmed by their responses to questions about the Trinity.

Absence of a Doctrine of the Immanent Trinity

If Jesus is not thought by these respondents to pre-exist his birth, they would be unlikely to have a doctrine of the immanent Trinity. This is what we find: this group are economic Trinitarians. They do not have a doctrine about God being three in essence. No one was unfamiliar with the word Trinity, however. They recognized it and gave similar responses to questions about it: either they named three 'things', namely God, Jesus and the Holy Spirit; and/or they said it is 'three-in-one'

> Hilary
>
> *'If someone said to me in terms of your belief, what is the Trinity, I would say it is God, the Holy Spirit and Jesus. So I understand what it means, but I don't think it is ... it is not something I would use in my vocabulary ... It is just not a term that I would use.'*

> Suzanne
>
> *'It's the three things isn't it? Jesus, God and the Holy Spirit. I don't think of it a lot. Am I right with those three things?'*

> Marion
>
> *'It's not something that I have delved into a great deal. I'm not that knowledgeable about it really* [pause]. *We say Father, Son, Holy Spirit don't we?'*

> Rose
>
> *'I just think ... Trinity ... three-in-one ... or whatever* [laugh]. *No, I don't know. I haven't thought about that. I'm not sure* [pause]. *Perhaps I don't think enough about it.'*

These kinds of comments were repeated many times over. The word 'Trinity' is seen as a technical term – part of the Church's, not the individual's, vocabulary. It appears to have little relevance to the ordinary believer other than as a trigger for naming three 'things', namely God, Jesus and the Holy Spirit. Threeness was what the word Trinity most seemed to convey and there was a general assumption that three 'things' should be named. Geoffrey Ahern (1984: 16) says that 'it is linguistically understandable that [the word Trinity] should suggest threeness more than three-in-oneness'. That threeness should be associated with the Christian God is not unexpected since the Christian God is named as Father, Son and Holy Spirit. This threefold naming permeates both liturgy and hymnody and is deeply rooted in Christian consciousness; but the ability to name God in this way cannot be regarded as constituting a doctrine of the Trinity. What this group have is a story, which has a Trinitarian structure, rather than a doctrine about an eternally triune God. They know that the Christian story of God has three 'characters' in it – God the Father, Jesus the Son and the Holy Spirit – and that these three are intimately connected with one another. They also know that the story proceeds in a certain way: first there is God the Father, then the Son, and then at the Son's 'departure', the Spirit comes. The main character in the story is God the Father, because he sends both the Son and the Spirit. Trinity is the three-fold name for these three 'characters'.

The results from my study concur with those of Ahern. He reports that only a few of his sample (5–10 out of the 30) seemed to have a fairly explicit idea that the Godhead is triune in essence:

> Not very many directly identified the threeness of the concept Trinity as the triune Godhead. The threeness appears usually to have been located somewhere 'outside' the 'inmost' Godhead. This is to use the spatial metaphor that implicitly seems to have lurked. The threeness was very often perceived as in some way at a remove, or askew, from the final transcendence of 'God'. (Ahern 1984: 16)[3]

This particular group in my study, similarly, do not ascribe Trinitarian identity to the Godhead itself. Indeed, Godhead is not a word they would use. They talk only of God, together with Jesus and the Holy Spirit. God is one in essence, not triune and this one God makes himself known through Jesus and the Holy Spirit. The threeness is associated with the activity of the one God in relation to the world. What we have here, in doctrinal terms, is economic Trinitarianism. This, of course, is not an analysis that this group would adopt for themselves. They do not have the language to make such a statement.

---

[3]   Similar findings are reported by Cartledge in his study of ordinary Pentecostal theology. See Cartledge 2010: esp. 48–9, 174.

The New Testament itself may be said to bear witness to economic Trinitarianism. Certainly, it does not have an explicit doctrine of God as Trinity. As the report of the Doctrine Commission of the Church of England (1987: 105) states:

> Even Paul's familiar grace in 2 Cor.13:14 is not Trinitarian in this stricter sense:
> 'the grace of the Lord Jesus Christ and the love of God and the fellowship of the
> Holy Spirit' clearly indicates that 'God' here means the Father alone, despite the
> close (but theologically unclarified) juxtaposition of Son and Spirit.

Similarly, much of the liturgy is 'economic' in shape, as in the Greeting, the Prayer of Preparation and the Prayers of Penitence.[4] Even the Nicene creed 'does not have an explicit doctrine of the Trinity spelled out systematically: the three "characters" in the story are described and implicitly related to one another, but the word Trinity is not used, and there is no exposition of the doctrine of God as Three-in-One' (Young 1991: 5, 56). The creed states the essential components of the doctrine of the Trinity, but does not spell it out conceptually.

When this group speak of *God* they mean the Father only. The word God doubles up for Father, so that there is a one-to-one correspondence between the two words. To speak of God is to speak of the Father:

Marion
'*God is God. He is my Father when I want to talk to him.*'

Maureen
'*... the Father ... well that is obviously God himself.*'

Elizabeth
'*... the Holy Spirit, Jesus and God being, you know, God the Father.*'

Jürgen Moltmann complains that most Christians in the West, be they Catholic or Protestant, are really only 'monotheists' where the experience and practice of their faith is concerned (Moltmann 1981: 1; cf. Church of England 1987: 104–5). Karl

---

[4]   See *Common Worship: Services and Prayers for the Church of England* 2000: 167–9.

Rahner has similarly remarked that 'Christians, for all their orthodox profession of faith in the Trinity, are almost just "monotheist" in their actual religious existence' (Rahner 1966: 79). If this is the case, it is not surprising that many, if asked to describe 'God', give a description of the Father only. To be a Christian monotheist is to think of God as one in essence rather than triune. The concept that God is eternally triune is not a concept that this present group seem at all familiar with. They have not learned or assimilated this doctrine, so that their thinking about God cannot have been shaped or informed by it. Suzanne, for example, said that the idea of a triune Godhead *'does not fit my picture at all'*, *'is beyond my understanding'*, *'a bit startrekky'*; and she adds that she liked things *'very simple'*.

Friedrich Schleiermacher also understood Christianity as a monotheistic mode of belief. He saw the Church's doctrine of the Trinity as secondary, because (as Moltmann describes his position) it is 'a mere web of different statements about the Christian self-consciousness; it does not alter Christianity's monotheism at all. Consequently it is enough to talk about the one God, by talking about one's own Christian self-consciousness. The doctrine of the Trinity is superfluous' (Moltmann 1981: 3; cf. Schleiermacher 1928: 738–51). Certainly, for this present group, the doctrine of the Trinity appears to be superfluous. They manage perfectly well without it and have no obvious need for it. Moltmann (1981: 3) criticizes Schleiermacher's view, claiming that failure to hold to the Church's doctrine of the Trinity results in 'abstract monotheism'. But we may argue that for the Christian the threefold naming of God mitigates against any descent into abstract monotheism. The word God may denote the Father, but it also connotes Jesus and the Holy Spirit. To think of the Father is to think of the Son and/or the Spirit as well. This threefold naming ensures a dynamic and relational, not a static and monadic, view of God. But the threefold naming need not, and from the data obviously does not, necessitate a doctrine of an eternally triune Godhead in which 'there are united three "persons" ("hypostases"), who are distinguishable only by number and relation to one another, and inseparable in their activity' (Church of England 1987: 105).

It is therefore axiomatic for this group both that God is one *and* that threeness in some way applies to this one God; but they do not concern themselves with what can be inferred about God's own immanent, eternal being from the threefold pattern of God's activity in relation to the world. They do not abstract from the story of God's action to God's being. This is what academic theologians do. Ordinary theologians are content with story and tend not to engage in speculative thinking (see below, pp. 149–59). This group have learned the basic 'rules' which govern the use of the Trinitarian language of Father, Son and Holy Spirit, so that they know, for example, that it is wholly inappropriate to say 'God the Father died on the cross'. But proficiency in operating the basic 'rules' of Trinitarian discourse, is not the same as acknowledging God as Trinity (cf. Church of England 1987: 104–5).

What impact, if any, does the absence of a belief in God as eternally triune have on the doctrine of the person of Jesus Christ? If God is God, then who is Jesus?

Jesus is Not God

Out of this group of 30, whom I have distinguished as possessing a functional Christology, around 23 were unwilling to make the bald statement 'Jesus is God.'[5] Various reasons were given, but all hinged on the simple logic that God is God, and therefore Jesus cannot be God. In response to a question about whether the interviewee considered Jesus of Nazareth to be God in any way, the responses were always negative: some expressed incredulity at the suggestion, while others were more hesitant and qualified their denial. Examples from the range of responses are given below:

Eleanor

A   *But ... would you look on* [Jesus] *as being God?*

E   *No. Because God isn't a person. God's just ... no I mean God isn't a person.*

Richard

A   *So ... to confirm ... you wouldn't look on* [Jesus] *as God?*

R   *No. I look at him and believe that he embodies God and God lives through him. God is a ... God is not another being ... It's a spirit. It's a ... it's a power*

---

[5]   The seven exceptions all had modalist tendencies. See below, pp. 57–60.

Bruce

A   *And you wouldn't look on the historical Jesus as God in any way?*

B   *Well how ... how ... how could he be if he was the Son of God ... unless you have got ... multiple gods. Do you see what I mean?*

If you have one God, which is what we sort of profess, then if he is the Son of God, he can't be God otherwise you have multiple gods. If Jesus is a God and God is a God, then you have got two gods. That's the way I sort of see it. If you say that Jesus is God, then you have got the problem then of two gods.

Marion

A   *So ... you wouldn't necessarily say [Jesus] was God?*

M   *No. I don't think of Jesus as God. Oh no. I think God is God and Jesus is his Son or whatever and he's a different person. I certainly don't believe that Jesus and God are the same. Should I?*

I mean I think he was God's Son, but I don't see Jesus as God. To me he was a ... person who lived in that period of time and lived a very, you know, good life and um ... a big example to everybody around. But no, I don't think ... I think God ... well who is God, where does he come from? I don't know, but God is ... God. I mean he created this earth. He may have created other earths. We don't ... know that [laugh] ... But I don't see Jesus as God. No. To me he is a ... separate person.

Diane

'I have never actually thought of him as being God, but he is part of God.'

Edward

'God exists in different forms if you will. And I think Jesus was one form of God, but I wouldn't say Jesus was God.'

The New Testament itself (and the liturgy) is also very hesitant about saying Jesus is God. Jesus is hardly ever called 'God' in a direct straightforward way in the New Testament and every instance in the New Testament in which it is said that Jesus is called God is hotly debated by scholars. Rudolf Bultmann contends that 'Neither in the Synoptic gospels nor in the Pauline epistles, is Jesus called God; nor do we find him so called in the Acts of the Apostles or in the Apocalypse.' Bultmann insists that the only clear case in which Jesus is called God is the confession of Thomas (John 20:28) and he judges that to be an existential, even an emotional or an exclamatory utterance, not a metaphysical or ontological one (Bultmann 1955: 275–6; see also 277–90). John V. Taylor similarly argues that the New Testament writers instinctively avoided naming Jesus as God. He too cites the exclamation of Thomas, 'My Lord and my God', as the only real exception, but claims that this is 'an impulsive avowal of personal adoration rather than a theological statement' (Taylor 1992: 287, n.24). Other scholars, however, do not take such a negative view. Raymond Brown, for example, claims that 'in three clear instances and in five instances that have a certain probability, Jesus is called God in the New Testament' (Brown 1968: 28–9; see also Wainwright 1962: 53–74; Cullman 1959: 306–14; Macquarrie 1990: 46–7). But it is generally agreed that such an apparently central Christian affirmation as 'Jesus is God' is only minimally supported by the New Testament.[6]

This group always identify Jesus through the appellation Son of God and claim that he is the one and only unique Son of God. Now, for the academic theologian, such a claim raises various questions, such as, 'What does it mean to say God has a Son?' and 'In what way(s) is Jesus unique?' Such questions, on the whole, do not concern ordinary theologians. This helps to make writing up how such people view the identity of the historical Jesus so problematic, as they do not present with fully worked out Christologies.[7] Rather what is given are snatches, glimpses into their thinking about the identity of this person who is affirmed as being the one and only unique Son of God. Although none of this group consider Jesus to be God, there is a deep assumption that there is *some sort* of identity between Jesus and God, an assumption which is expressed in various ways. The data are complex, as various models were employed in the struggle to articulate the relationship between Jesus and God and some of the interviewees adopted more than one model. Edward sums up the difficulties of many when he says, '*There is clearly some connectivity between the two of them, but I'm not ... I'm struggling to define exactly what that is*'.

---

[6]   This issue is discussed further in the next chapter. See below, pp. 64–5.

[7]   But then neither do all the New Testament writers. Macquarrie (1990: 81) suggests that Mark's Christology, for example, is not well developed or coherent.

Perhaps the best way to begin is at the beginning with the conception of Jesus. This event is highly significant for the majority of this group, as it marks not only the point in time when God created Jesus, but also when Jesus' life as the Son of God began.

Virginal-Conception Christology

Apart from the accounts given in the gospels of Matthew and Luke, there is no other mention of the virgin birth in the New Testament. 'In the letters of Paul, the earliest documents of the New Testament, there is no more than a terse mention, without any names, of the birth of Jesus "from a woman" (Gal. 4:4) but not "from a virgin"', and the earliest gospel, that of Mark, has no birth narratives but begins immediately with John the Baptist and Jesus' public life and teaching. This leads, according to Hans Küng, to the momentous conclusion that the virgin birth cannot be regarded as original or central to the Christian message (Küng 1993: 43–5; cf. Macquarrie 1990: 392–4). Yet this belief was incorporated into orthodox Christian faith and is affirmed in the Nicene creed. Adherence to the doctrine of the virgin birth is therefore, not unexpectedly, seen by many today as a test of orthodoxy. It is something that you have to believe. Around 23 of this group take this position:[8]

> Elizabeth
>
> *Well I think there are certain things you just have to believe if you are a Christian. You've got to believe it and I think that that's an instance that you do. I mean it is chronicled in the Bible. The Angel Gabriel coming down and telling Mary and I think that you have just got to accept it … I think it is central to the whole story.*

The virgin birth (more accurately, the virginal conception) is seen as central by most of this group, because this was the point in time when God created Jesus through the power of the Holy Spirit. Many talk about Jesus as God's creation, using phrases such as, '*God produced Jesus*', '*God created Jesus*', '*Jesus was God's creation*'. The birth narratives tell the story of how Jesus, God's Son, was created and

---

[8]   Around five 5 of this 23 admit to finding the virgin birth a very difficult belief to accept, but insist that it has to be believed.

born. His was '*a special creation*', because he was not created in the same way as we are. Jesus was conceived without male procreation, through the action of the Holy Spirit. What we have here is a 'virginal-conception Christology' (see Schwarz 1998: 236–40). Jesus' existence as the Son of God is regarded as starting at his conception/birth.[9] It affirms that already at the moment of his birth Jesus was God's special Son, born through a special act of God, and that here lies the difference between Jesus and other human beings, who could also be called sons and daughters of God (Schwarz 1998: 240). Several talk about the virgin birth marking Jesus out as somebody who was different or special. Edward, for example, says that '[Jesus] *was created by God*' and '*his creation came about via a different means from everybody else's creation*', and that '*clearly Jesus was ... was different from his conception. Right from the beginning.*'

The virgin birth narratives convey the claim that the coming of the Holy Spirit at Jesus' conception makes that conception a virginal conception, and makes the one conceived God's Son. In the story the Holy Spirit is cast in the role of the male parent, but there is never any suggestion that the Holy Spirit actually acts as the male partner or father in the conception of Jesus. That would make the birth of Jesus too much like that of some semi-divine beings in other ancient myths who were conceived by the mating of a god with a human female (Mackey 1979: 276; Küng 1993: 43). The conception of Jesus takes place, by contrast, 'without any intercourse between God and human beings, in a completely unerotic, spiritualized context' (Küng 1993: 43). There was never any suggestion in the interviews that those who believed in the virgin birth believed in a physical divine Sonship of any kind, but probing on this was difficult. Many talked about Jesus being God's Son because God created him, and the kind of creation they seemed to have in mind was of an *ex nihilo* kind:

Marion

M   *Well, he was God's Son, wasn't he? And I suppose if God created the world in all its majesty, then creating a child from ... in a virgin ... would be dead-simple to God wouldn't it, after all the other things he had created, if you look at it like that.*

A   *So you would definitely tend to think of God as creating Jesus and ...*

---

[9]   Wolfhart Pannenberg writes that, according to the legend of Jesus' virgin birth, 'Jesus first *became* God's Son through Mary's conception'. See Pannenberg 1968: 143.

M   Yes. The same as he created the world.

A   You said he was God's Son ...

M   Well, I suppose it would be a son wouldn't it, if he created him. He's not
     Joseph's son, because he didn't create him.

Suzanne

'I mean, God created Jesus didn't he, so the virgin birth is possible isn't it? And
he made the earth, so everything is possible.'

James Mackey is instructive here. He asks, if we do not wish to think of the Holy
Spirit acting as the male principle in the conception of Jesus, then just what do
we understand the role of the Holy Spirit to be in the conception of Jesus and
of Jesus' subsequent divine sonship? He hazards a guess that the Spirit of God
must have supplied what was necessary to the embryonic Jesus by an act such as
creation out of nothing. Jesus is God's Son as a result of this act, just as Adam,
who is called 'the son of God' by Luke in his genealogy of Jesus (Luke 3:38),
was created by God out of nothing (or out of 'dust') and not derived in the normal
way from parents. This explanation, says Mackey, would mean that the term Son
of God is being put to a unique use in the Luke text, which has little in common
with its meaning in other Christological contexts where it primarily refers to God's
salvific activity in Jesus (Mackey 1979: 272–80, esp. 274–6). Many in this group,
similarly, seem to put Son of God to this kind of use. Jesus is God's Son because
God created him. '*He's not Joseph's son, because he didn't create him ... He's
God's Son because he was born of God.*' Filial language is appropriate language
because Jesus '*was created by God for us in the form of a man*'. As Suzanne puts
it, '*I think of him as his Son, because he was created to be like us.*'

The virgin birth narratives affirm that God is at work in bringing Jesus into the
world as his own Son. They convey the sense that Jesus derives from God; that he
is 'of God' in a way that no one else is. Jesus thus has a unique status. Only he is
the Son of God, created through a special act of God, and for many this is the crux
of the Christian faith. As Diane put it, '*The whole Christian faith is pinned on that
isn't it really? If you don't believe that you are not really a Christian.*' A few of this
group, however, understand the term Son of God in its more usual biblical sense:

as serving the Christological purpose of pointing to the unique filial relationship between Jesus and God:[10]

Bruce

'[Son of] *signifies a very special relationship. A very special person.*'

Edward

'[Son of] *is just a phrase ... I think it is simply a matter of somebody trying to put into words that relationship.*'

Not all those who adopt a functional Christology are so wedded to the doctrine of the virgin birth. Around seven of this group of 30 are willing to accept that it could have happened, but for them it is not crucial.

Bruce

'*I think it is actually possible. I just don't find it a big issue to be honest.*'
'*And I suppose at the end of the day it is a good start to the story really. It helps the story.*'
'*It is like the star and the three wise men. It is all part of saying here is somebody special.*'

Three others firmly reject the idea of a virgin birth.

Valerie

'*I don't believe she was a virgin. To me, it's all about having a gift from God, having a baby. So that's my reading of it. It is a gift.*'
'*It's not important. The important thing was that God provided somebody on earth in human shape ... um ... to make us understand him better. Whether he came from a virgin ... actually I would be horrified to think that he came from a virgin. I would much prefer it to be a normal birth. It is a normal baby, created*'

---

[10]   Academic theology, unlike ordinary theology, constantly debates the meaning of the Christological title 'Son of God'. See, for example, Küng 1993: 56–9; Macquarrie 1990: 42–3; Dunn 1980: 12–64.

*in the normal way, which I think is a fine example of one of God's gifts. I don't
think it is a problem.'*

Valerie goes on to talk about Jesus becoming God's Son later in his life, as did
Percy, the other member of this group who did not believe in the virgin birth.
Valerie says:

'[Jesus] *was given such a gift that he became that mouth-piece that God had
intended ... Quite how that miracle happened, I can't explain ... But somehow
or other, he was significantly special so that he could actually become that Son
of God on earth. And I can't explain how.'*

This last Christology can be classified as adoptionist. Adoptionism is said to be
the earliest and most primitive form of Christology (see Knox 1967: esp. 5–18).
Its basic thesis is that Jesus was a man who because of his obedience to God
was adopted as God's Son or Messiah. This adoption may have taken place some
time during the ministry of Jesus (as in the extract above) or, more usually, it is
declared to have taken place at the resurrection. Adoptionism has no doctrine of
pre-existence or divine initiative in the birth of Jesus. Jesus 'lives an obedient life
and is then made God's special person, his Messiah' (Kysar 1976: 28).

One question which arises from the data in this section is, in what way(s) was
Jesus *'significantly special'* or *'of God'?*

Spirit Christology

All of the present group asserted that Jesus was either 'of God' or that he enjoyed
a unique filial relationship with God. The most frequently cited reason people gave
for Jesus being *'of God'* or *'more special than anyone else'* was that Jesus was
full of divine power, this was what marked him out. Here are just a few examples
which could be repeated many times over:

Suzanne

'[Jesus] *had the power of God to be able to do the things he had to do.'*

Diane

'[When we look on Jesus] *we are seeing somebody human, but we know that God is there as well.'*

'You don't really sort of see him as his own. You know there is a greater power. A power as great ... behind Jesus.'

Eleanor

'[Jesus was] *an ordinary human being but with extra gifts. He alone had God's power.'*

Elizabeth

'He was part human but he had an extra dimension you see because he was the Son of God and he could do things that ordinary humans couldn't do.'

Tom

'If [God] *chose to put Jesus on this earth, then he had to give evidence to the people that he is the Son of God. He had to give him power to do the miracles, otherwise he is no different to Joe Bloggs, you know.'*

Hilary

'He was able to perform miracles and nobody else has been able to do that ever.'

The majority of this group lay a heavy stress on the supernatural qualities ascribed to Jesus and draw attention to the miracles (both nature miracles and healing miracles) as evidence that Jesus was who he claimed to be, namely the Son of God. This kind of Christology is reminiscent of that found in Mark's Gospel. Mark regards Jesus as a man, but no ordinary man, since he was filled with supernatural powers. Mark's Jesus is 'a superman or even a divine man' and can be classified as a spirit Christology (Macquarrie 1990: 78–81; see also Hooker 1983: esp. chapters 1 and 3). Macquarrie (1990: 393) is critical of this kind of *theios aner* Christology, which he says 'still lingers in some quarters today', arguing that it is 'the wrong kind of Christology' because it 'demeans Christ by turning him into a wonder-worker'. If we consider that 'God as Spirit refers to God ... at work, as active, and as power, energy, or force that accomplishes something', then it does not seem unreasonable to classify most of this group as having a spirit Christology of sorts, albeit of a somewhat rudimentary and unformed kind (Haight 1999: 447). God as Spirit, as power, is active and at work within Jesus. This is both implicitly and sometimes explicitly stated:

Hilary

'[Jesus was] *imbued with divine powers. A very strong sense of the Holy Spirit. The ability to perform miracles. The ability to lead as well.'*

Jill

'*I do feel that God poured himself into Jesus for us.'*
'*Jesus was set apart and sent specifically, filled with God.'*
'*Jesus is full of God.'*

Richard

'[Jesus] *embodies God and God lives through him.'*

Many implied that God's Spirit as power at work within Jesus was not confined to the miraculous, but manifested itself through his whole life. In his words and deeds, suffering and death, indeed in his whole person, Jesus proclaimed, manifested and revealed God's will and ways. Many modern writers have developed spirit Christologies, believing them to be simpler and more intelligible than the classical Christology. They are Christologies of God's presence in Jesus.[11] Such Christologies raise questions about whether God's presence in Jesus was different in degree or kind and what it might mean to say 'Jesus is divine'. The data from this group raise both of these issues.

---

[11] See, for example, Lampe 1977. Haight also proposes a spirit Christology and favours talking about Jesus as symbol of God. See Haight 2001: 135–9; 1999: 12–15. See also Borg 2006.

Jesus is Divine?

None of this group confess the divinity of Jesus in the precise form that considers him Son of God incarnate and as such equal with the Father. It is often assumed that when people say Jesus is divine, they are saying that Jesus is God, but the data from this study clearly indicate that this is a false assumption to make. When this group acknowledge the divinity of Jesus they are not confessing him to be God.[12] Several people were actually very hesitant and uncertain about applying the word 'divine' to Jesus at all. They were not sure what such a designation might mean. Consider this extract from Hannah's interview. She asks:

> *How do you read divine?* [long pause]. *Well I don't know how they ... I mean are they going ... do they mean the divine is God or do they mean divine as a divine quality?*

She opts for the latter sense, saying that she can agree with the statement Jesus is divine if by that Jesus is understood to possess the divine qualities, such as love, forgiveness, tolerance, understanding. She says that Jesus possesses these qualities to a much greater extent than anyone else. Others say that Jesus is divine because he was perfect or because he was God's Son. John Hick argues that the word divine is being used adjectivally in these instances. When they say that Jesus *is* divine, they are using the *is* of predication and not the *is* of identification. Hick says that theologically, this treats divinity adjectivally, 'and suggests that the quality of divinity is something which may be present in varying degrees in different human beings, Jesus Christ being marked off from the rest of mankind in that he possessed this quality in a greater degree than other men' (Hick 1973: 154–7; see also Cupitt 1979a: 36).This can only result in a *degree Christology*. On this view, incarnation, understood as the embodiment in a human life of a certain quality of divinity, is something that is capable of degrees and approximations, so that Jesus is different in degree not kind from the rest of humanity (Hick 1973: 157). There are examples of this kind of thinking in the data. Jill thinks that there

---

[12]   Ahern, in analysing his data, seemingly fails to acknowledge this point. His groupings only make sense if the assumption is made that when people say 'Jesus is divine' they mean 'Jesus is God' and the data from this study has clearly shown that this is a false assumption to make. See Ahern 1984: 14–19.

is more of God in Jesus than anyone else, and that Jesus is '*a closer relation*' to God than anyone else. Richard says that Jesus is divine, because '*he embodies all the qualities of God in much more detail*' than anyone else.

There has been much discussion as to whether Jesus should properly be called unique in degree or kind.[13] John Robinson argues that whether Jesus had 'more of everything' than the rest of humanity is not the issue. When the New Testament writers make their claims for the uniqueness of Jesus, by speaking of him as God's only Son, 'it is not his moral qualities they are exalting, but his unrepeatable relationship to the Father' (Robinson 1972: 210). Edward makes the same point when he says:

> *I think I would have difficulty in making a comparison by saying there was more of God in Jesus than anyone else, in the sense that I don't regard those relationships as comparable. To say that there is more of God in Jesus than in other people, you are comparing the two relationships and I don't feel they are comparable. I suppose a lot of people have relationships with God of different sorts. But I suppose I just regard Jesus' relationship with God as in a different category somehow.*

The data demonstrate that a range of ways of understanding the divinity of Jesus are operating, as indeed is the case with academic theologians. Geoffrey Lampe and Roger Haight, for example, who both put forward spirit Christologies, disagree about what it means to say that Jesus is divine. Lampe acknowledges Jesus as divine, 'adverbially' rather than substantively;[14] whereas Haight (1999: 455) argues that the presence of God in Jesus should be construed as 'more than a thin functional or adverbial presence', but as truly 'an ontological presence because where God acts, God is'. Undoubtedly the divinity of Jesus can be construed in various ways and all statements to the effect that Jesus is divine need to be

---

[13]   John Robinson finds himself tempted to ask at this point, 'Is the difference of kind itself a difference of degree or a difference of kind?' See Robinson 1972: 209, n.123.

[14]   Lampe (1972: 124) writes, 'Spirit christology cannot affirm that Jesus *is* "substantivally" God ... An interpretation of the union of Jesus with God in terms of his total possession by God's Spirit makes it possible, rather, to acknowledge him to be God "adverbially"'.

weighed very carefully, and their depth grammar uncovered, if false conclusions are not to be drawn.

Functional Christology

This group talk about the relationship between Jesus and God using relational, revelational and functional language. They talk about what Jesus does and what function he performs: he reveals God in the world and he acts for God in the world. They use language related to action and doing rather than being, speaking about Jesus as '*God's mouth-piece*', '*God's messenger*', '*God's spokesperson*', '*God's representative*', '*God's helper*', '*God's assistant*'. Jesus is God's agent, not God:

> Eleanor
> '*He was specially sent. A sort of messenger.*'

> Lesley
> '*He came to do God's work on earth.*'

> Richard
> '*He's assisting in the conveyance of the meaning of God.*'

> Suzanne
> '*Jesus is God's way of reaching out to the world.*'

> Valerie
> '[Jesus] *appeared on earth to act and speak God's will.*'

Jesus is functionally related to God if not functionally identical with God in the New Testament (Mackey 1979: 213). Paul Fiddes writes, 'the three earliest gospels (Mark, Matthew, Luke) and earliest letters of St Paul understand the sonship of Jesus as a "functional" oneness with God: Jesus is one with the Father in action and relationship acting for God and being totally obedient to him'. Jesus was 'one' with the Father in function, since God revealed himself through this man and acted through him, and in this sense he was indeed 'Immanuel – God with us'. As the agent of the Father, 'all his actions and teaching were inspired and empowered by the Spirit of God, the dynamic power of God himself reaching out and affecting people' (Fiddes 1989: 53–4). Morna Hooker-Stacey argues that New Testament Christology is essentially theocentric. It is God who reconciles men and women to himself through his Son. The initiative lies with God and the Son is his agent: God is the origin, Christ the agent (Hooker-Stacey 2001: 298–302). According to Robert Kysar, agency Christology in the New Testament declares that God took the initiative to send a personal agent to perform a revelatory and saving function. He takes the birth narratives of Matthew and Luke to be essentially expressions of a form of agency Christology. He writes:

> In this case, the agent is more than just a man. His being is shaped by God's special action in one way or another. Still, whether the nature of the agent is that of a specially chosen person or an extra-human being, his function is to be an agent, a representative, or, if you will, a diplomat. (Kysar 1976: 28–9)

This group all assert a functional and/or revelational and/or relational identity between Jesus and God: Jesus reveals God, he represents God, he functions as God, he is God to and for them. Robinson (1972: 113–4) talks about Jesus being 'a man who in all that he says and does as man is the personal representative of God: he stands in God's place, he *is* God to us and for us'. Or as Frances Young (1977: 39) puts it, 'He is "as-if-God" for me'. And among more ordinary theologians, we may cite Valerie who talked about Jesus *'acting as God'* and performing *'a role for ... as God on earth'*. She went on to say, *'I think* [Jesus was] *almost the same as God'*. Or as Lesley put it, *'it's all like Jesus is God and it is all the same thing'*.

Many modern Christologies opt for a functional rather than an ontological Christology. Whatever their differences might be, functional Christologies all claim that Jesus was functionally equivalent to God. This can be worked out in various ways, but they all share the same basic premise: Jesus is not God, he is God's agent or representative. But Macquarrie and others argue that even the simplest of Christological affirmations, such as 'Jesus is God's agent', have ontological implications. Every functional statement about Jesus conceals 'ontological mysteries' so that ontology cannot be avoided in Christology (Macquarrie

1990: 81; see also 7–9; cf. Crisp 2007: 162). Robinson, however, insists that the functional way of representing reality is 'an equally serious way' and is sufficient for Christology. He says, 'The issue is not where [Jesus] comes from or what he is made of ... The issue is whether in seeing him men see the Father, whether, in mercy and judgement, he *functions* as God, whether he *is* God to and for them' (Robinson 1972: 182–5). This issue will be mentioned again at the end of the chapter. All I want to say here is that some kind of ontological identity between Jesus and God was implied in many of the statements made by this group, but this was never couched in terms of the incarnation of God the Son. Instead, various vivid pictorial models were used to envisage the link between Jesus and God:

Elizabeth

'Jesus is more really an offshoot in a way.'

Suzanne

'[Jesus is] Part of God. A limb. Reaching out. Sort of an arm of God I suppose.'

Edward

'Jesus is an aspect of God. One limb of God if you like.'

Some of the early Church Fathers used the same kind of imagery to talk about the immanent activities of God. Thus Irenaeus wrote about the Word and the Spirit as the two hands of God, both being instruments of the divine activity. For Tertullian, God in his transcendence was invisible, the Logos which proceeds from God was able to make God visible. The Logos was like a ray projected from the sun, an offshoot which could mediate the transcendent (Young 1991: 37, 39). The use of such imagery by the interviewees suggests that they too, like Irenaeus and Tertullian, want to assert that it is truly God (the Word, the Logos) present and active in Jesus.[15] As we saw earlier, Haight would argue that this is an ontological presence because where God acts, God is.

---

[15] Hick uses the image of an amoeba and its pseudopodium to illustrate how we might say that Jesus was 'wholly God', but not 'the whole of God'. For a full discussion of how Hick utilizes these ideas to conceptualize the Chalcedonian claim that Jesus was numerically identical with God, see Hick 1973: chapter 11, esp. 159–60.

One must not forget that the interviewees' reflections and thoughts about the identity of Jesus of Nazareth are made in the context of belief in his resurrection and ascension (as are those of the New Testament and traditional theology). Jesus is exalted by God and raised into the glory of the Father. Or, as Küng (1993: 56) puts it, 'this crucified one … has entered into the true, eternal life of God. He is alive – however that is to be explained'. The resurrection raises Jesus to the realm of God's own transcendence, so that Jesus and God become inseparable after this. In traditional pictorial language, Jesus is now 'at the right hand of the Father'. The story puts Jesus with God, so that now, as those who live after the story and by the story, Christians cannot help but put Jesus with God. Putting Jesus with God is what they do in their imaginations. '*Jesus and God can't be separated*'. '*Jesus and God are in the same team*'. '*Jesus and God go together*'. '*When I think about God I'm thinking about Jesus too*'. Küng (1993: 34) suggests that with statements of faith, such as belief in the virgin birth, or the resurrection and ascension of Jesus, 'many people do not so much have definitions of belief as pictures of belief in mind'. Their theology is pictorial rather than conceptual. This characteristic of ordinary Christology will be discussed further in Chapter 8.

Arianism All Over Again?

I wish here to make some final remarks on the adequacy or otherwise of the Christology of this group. The orthodox doctrine states that there is no inferiority within the Godhead. The Son is co-equal and co-eternal with the Father and the Spirit. Any Christology which considers Jesus to be God's Son created by the Father to be his agent in the world may be classified as subordinationist and effectively Arian (that is, as unorthodox). The language of creating implies inferiority. The Father who creates is greater than the Son who is created; the Father alone really counts as God and the Son is subordinate ('in second place') to God. Hierarchical and subordinationist thinking is widespread amongst this group. Such thinking can also arise as a natural product of theism: God as the sovereign monarch (see Inbody 2002: 44). Several people talked about God being '*the ultimate*', '*the boss*', '*the ruler of the universe*':

Bruce

'I do see it as, sort of, God being at the top and Jesus being at the right hand-
side or just below, however you want to describe it.'
'I would see [Jesus] *as something slightly less than God.'*

Eleanor

'I think, I think of God as being the ultimate benefactor. Oh, that sounds awful.
I didn't mean that. But as the ultimate. Jesus was just like you and me, but just
interpreting his word. I mean, go straight to the top. Why bother with the middle-
man? [laugh].'

Elizabeth

'God is Almighty. He put Jesus there and it's all from God; the whole creation;
everything from God.'

God is the source of all, including the Son. The Son is derivative of the Father.
There are obvious links here with Arianism, although it would be a mistake to
label this group as Arian, since Arius, when he talked about the 'creation' of
the Son, was talking about inner divine processes within the Godhead and the
'creation' of a pre-existent Son in eternity. This sample, however, when they talk
about the creation of the Son, talk about a creation in time, in history. Having
said this, there are obvious affinities between the two ways of thinking. Arius was
concerned to emphasis the total transcendence of God: God is the one and only
source of all created things; nothing exists which does not ultimately derive from
God. The Son therefore is created; a creature deriving from the will of the Father,
albeit the first and greatest of all the creatures. He is 'divine', but his divinity is of
a lesser kind than that of the One, the true God, who alone is unoriginate. The Son
is 'divine', one might say, but not God, as God is God. Arius wanted to safeguard
his monotheism 'by insisting, on the one hand, that the one God had no equal and,
on the other, that the divinity of Jesus was of a separate and totally subordinate
kind, the divinity, by some kind of participation, of one who was *par excellence*
in the image of God' (Mackey 1979: 229–30). This group are not thoroughgoing
Arians, however, because they claim (at least some of them do) that it is truly God
present in Jesus, not a pre-existent divine being distinct from God and less than

God.[16] It is perhaps legitimate to say that they are *effectively Arian*.[17] Certainly many will say that Jesus is both human and divine rather than that Jesus is both God and man and, according to Hick, this sort of language gives rise to an Arian rather than a Chalcedonian Christology.[18] It is worth noting here that in the rural popular religion of Latin America, 'while Jesus is seen as divine and not really of human estate, he is not considered quite the same as God' (Schreiter 1985: 128). This is a view with which this group would seem to concur.

Modalist Tendencies

The doctrine of the Trinity enables 'full divinity' to be asserted for the three Persons without at the same time compromising the oneness of God. The paradox of the doctrine can be dissolved by making two possible mistakes:

> One is to collapse the three Persons into one by making Father, Son and Holy Spirit simply characteristics or attributes of one Person; the other is to emphasize the distinct reality of the three Persons to the point of excluding the oneness of God – that is, of making three distinct gods of the three Persons. (Hogan 2001: 29)

Lapsing into tritheism is not a danger for Christian 'monotheists'. The danger for them is that the 'full divinity' of the Son and the Spirit is denied through subordinationism/Arianism, or else that the Son and the Spirit are considered to be different ways or modes of self-revelation of the one and only God, that is, there is a lapse into modalism. It is these modalist tendencies that concern us here.

Nicholas Lash writes, 'In so far as the scheme of one drama with three acts is allowed to shape the sense of our relationship to Father, Son and Spirit, it draws us back towards some version of the oldest of all families of Trinitarian heresies, known as "modalism"'. Modalism preserves monotheism through its insistence that the Son and the Spirit are different manifestations of the one God: the one God

---

[16]   See the discussion on Arianism in Mackey 1979: 210–40, esp. 232–5. Cf. Young 1991: 45–7; Wiles 1976: 28–37.

[17]   Young (1991: 76) says that, 'Much popular Christianity is effectively Arian or Eutychian rather than Chalcedonian'.

[18]   For the philosophical argument underpinning this claim, see Hick 1973: 155–64.

is revealed as Father, as Son and as Spirit. 'For the modalist, the three ways we know God are of the nature of appearances, transitory forms, "beneath" which the divine nature, unaffected stands.' Christian orthodoxy, on the other hand, states that 'the distinctions between Father, Son and Spirit are distinctions truly drawn of *God*, and not merely of the way that God appears to us to be, or of the way that – for some brief span of time – he was' (Lash 1992: 30–31). As we have seen, Moltmann argues that in the West there has always been a tendency in Christian thought to subordinate the doctrine of the triune God to the doctrine of the One God. He writes, 'Ever since Hegel in particular, the Christian Trinity has tended to be represented in terms belonging to the general concept of the absolute subject: *one subject – three modes of being*'. He goes on to say that the concept of God as absolute subject can never satisfactorily accommodate the doctrine of the Trinity because 'the unity of the absolute subject is stressed to such a degree that the Trinitarian Persons disintegrate into mere aspects of the one subject' (Moltmann 1981: 17–18). There are examples of this kind of modalist thinking within this group.

Jan, for example, starts off from the premise that *'obviously God is one'*. She gives a more sophisticated response to the trigger of 'Trinity' saying *'we are told that the whole Godhead is God the Father, God the Son and God the Holy Ghost'*. She then says, *'here you are speaking to me and you are a theology student and you haven't ceased to be a mother, a wife. You are still all those things, but this is the thing that you are doing now. So it is possible to hold different things in tension and other aspects come to the fore'*. From this passage alone it might be supposed that Jan holds a doctrine of the triune God, but the rest of the data does not support such a view. She has no concept of the pre-existent Son and is completely confused by the idea that God the Son became incarnate. It is God, the absolute subject, who becomes incarnate, who exists in the 'mode of being' of God the Son. Rahner (1966: 79–80) comments that 'the average Christian' who professes faith in the incarnation does not go any further in their understanding of the doctrine than this, drawing no more from the doctrine of the incarnation than that God became man. This appears to be Jan's position. Just as I am one individual, who plays different roles, so God is one individual able to perform different roles. God the Father, God the Son and God the Holy Ghost are different roles that the One God plays; in other words they are different aspects of the

One God. Many other comments were made by members of this group which lend themselves to a modalist interpretation. All emphasize the oneness of God and tend to dissolve the distinctions – in other words, there is a distinct tendency towards 'monotheism':

Lesley

'How do you separate it all out? It's one thing really isn't it?'

'It's one thing.'

'[God, Jesus and the Holy Spirit are] *facets of the one thing.'*

Percy

'I don't see any separatism, distinction between them at all. And it never occurs to me to do that. One way or the other. What do they call it? Monotheism. There it is. One God. That's all there is.'

Richard

'I see the Trinity as being one entity as opposed to three separate discrete parts.'

'I see them all ... perhaps it is just me ... I can't sort of split them into three separate areas. I find that a little bit too prescriptive really. I'd rather keep it simple, for want of a better word, in my own mind.'

'I see the Godhead as being just one ... one sort of God who embodies himself in lots of different ways.'

Edward

'God exists in different forms if you will. Jesus was one form of God.'

'[Jesus] *was a manifestation of God.'*

'[Jesus] *was one aspect of God.'*

Moltmann is highly critical of Christian 'monotheism' and its accompanying modalism, claiming that they threaten faith in Christ. 'Christ must either recede into the series of the prophets, giving way to the One God, or he must disappear into the One God as one of his manifestations' (Moltmann 1981: 131). Several of this group talked about Jesus *'dissolving back into God'* or *'not really existing anymore'*. But it does not follow from this that their faith in Christ was any less.

Indeed, some of the despised Christian 'monotheists' were, from my perspective, the most inspiring interviewees of all.

Assumptions of Orthodoxy

This group will typically say that the Nicene Creed '*sums up what I believe*'. '*It's putting it in a nutshell really*'. '*I can agree with it all. This is what I believe*'. They will say that they '*totally and utterly*' believe in the Creed, but what they actually believe in is not Nicene orthodoxy. Graeme Smith claims that versions of Arianism and Pelagianism are commonplace inside the churches. 'Jesus might be called divine, but he is often thought of as a super-special creature. He is not really man, in any recognizable sense, nor is he God (the Father).' He claims that 'these beliefs are held illicitly. Church members recognize that they are theological contraband, so it takes some time to discover them' (Smith 2002: 15). But this is not the case here. This particular group of believers do *not* realize that the beliefs they hold concerning the identity of Jesus fall short of Nicene orthodoxy. They think they are orthodox, that what they believe is what the Church teaches. We shall have cause in Chapter 8 to discuss in more detail how this group are interpreting the language of the Nicene Creed. Now I want to say something about the supposed 'falling short' of functional Christologies.

There are those who would say that functional Christologies should be rejected as inadequate versions of Christianity. Klaas Runia, for example, surveys and evaluates the functional Christologies of many leading Roman Catholic and Protestant scholars in his book *The Present-Day Christological Debate* and finds them wanting, claiming that they do not say enough. To refuse to go beyond such general affirmations as 'God was in Christ' or 'Jesus is the decisive and definitive revelation of God' is, in his view, to say less than Nicaea (Runia 1984: 92–115). Gerald O'Collins is similarly dismissive of what he calls 'soft' or 'neo-Arian' Christologies. To say that Jesus is God's revealer, embodiment or representative is, in his view, to claim too little. How could Jesus be the supreme revelation of God, he asks, without himself being equal with God? He insists that Jesus cannot function for us as God without actually being God. Only an ontological Christology will do (O'Collins 1995: 224–9).

But many modern writers do prefer to talk about Jesus in functional rather than ontological categories. The liberal tradition that springs from Schleiermacher, who speaks of incarnation primarily as the presence of God or God's activity in Jesus Christ, has sought hard to find a functional equivalent of Nicaea and Chalcedon. What counts as a functional or 'an allowable equivalent' for the Christological statements of the Nicene Creed or the Chalcedonian Definition is highly contested (Houlden 1977: 132). According to the liberal theologian Maurice Wiles, 'there must be some ontological truth corresponding to the central characteristic of the structure of the myth' of the incarnation. He suggests that the profound inner union of the divine and the human at the heart of the human personality may be the ontological reality at the centre of this myth, rather than an identity between the personhood of Jesus and the Second Person of the Godhead (Wiles 1977a: 161).[19] But he acknowledges that identifying such ontological truths is not at all easy. 'For one thing if the ontological truth were one that could be expressed with full clarity and precision there would be less need for the myth' (Wiles 1977a: 161). About Jesus he is prepared to say:

> He was not just one who had taught about God; he was not just one who had lived a life of perfect human response to God. He had lived a life that embodied and expressed God's character and action in the world ... The impact not merely of his teaching but of his whole person communicated the presence and the power of God with an unprecedented sense of directness and finality. (Wiles 1979: 24)

Many of this group make these kind of claims for Jesus. Some academic theologians would say that Wiles, in his own language, is reproducing the essentials of the traditional Christological teaching.[20] Others would strongly disagree.[21] Debating this point any further lies beyond the scope of this study. All I wish to say here is that many modern forms of Christology do interpret the incarnation 'in

---

[19] For a critique of Wiles' view, see Sykes 1979: 115–27, esp. 116.

[20] See, for example, Macquarrie 1990: 8. Macquarrie thinks that the claims Wiles makes for Jesus Christ may fairly be called ontological claims and that these claims do not assert any less than the traditional language asserted.

[21] See, for example, Hebblethwaite 1987: esp. chapter 1.

the language of will, purpose, spirit, activity, presence, grace or initial aims of God', and these are accepted by many as 'allowable equivalents' for the Nicene and Chalcedonian language (Inbody 2002: 56). They are not considered to 'fall short' of orthodoxy. To say that 'God was in Christ' or 'Jesus is God's revealer, embodiment or representative' is not to say too little. All of this present group of interviewees are at least saying this much. They are effectively liberals in their Christology without realizing it. If Christological orthodoxy has to be confessed only in terms of a recognition that Jesus is the pre-existent Son of God incarnate, and as such ontologically equal to the Father, then none of this group can be considered to be orthodox. But once it is accepted that Christological orthodoxy can be confessed apart from substantialist categories, in functional 'equivalents', then the orthodoxy of this group can be affirmed.

What is clear from this group is that most people in the sample have learned monotheistic rather than Trinitarian Christianity. They have learned the 'common sense' version of Christianity. Harvey Whitehouse (2004: 62) observes that much 'popular religious thinking will err in the direction of simpler, more "naturalised" concepts (often to the great annoyance of religious experts and authorities)'. Clearly, a 'functional' Jesus and a 'unitary' God are easier to understand. They also appear to be sufficient for the religious needs of this group: they have no soteriological need for Jesus to be God. Why would they need Jesus to be God when they have a perfectly acceptable God already?

But before we turn our attention to the soteriologies of this group, the other Christologies operating in the sample must first be analysed.

Chapter 4

Ontological Christology

Jesus is God

Around nine[1] of the sample hold the doctrine that Jesus is God. They all use the ontological language of orthodoxy, rather than adopting any species of functional language, and claim that '*Jesus is God*', '*Jesus is fully God*', '*Jesus was God*', '*Jesus is both God and man*'. Such confessions are regarded by this group as synonymous with being a Christian. '*You have to believe that Jesus is God to be a Christian.*' But if adherence to this doctrine is used as the normative criterion for what counts as Christian, then around two-thirds of the total sample cannot be classified as Christian since they do not hold this doctrine. The data thus call into question the commonly held descriptive assumption that Christians are people who believe that Jesus is God, since so few of the sample actually do. Why is it that these nine have learnt the orthodox position whereas the functionalists have not?

The data are insufficient to fully answer this question, but it turns out that two of the three non-evangelicals in this group have read some academic theology books and the suggestion is that they have learnt their orthodoxy from there.[2] Interestingly, the six evangelicals in the sample make up the rest of this group and they seem to have learnt their orthodoxy during the socialization process into

---

[1] This figure could be increased to 16, if the seven with modalist tendencies who can make the statement 'Jesus is God' were included. But since these seven do not have a doctrine of the triune God or of pre-existence they are included with the functional group rather than this group. They could be said to have a *hybrid christology*, falling between both groups.

[2] Some might say that reading an academic theology book counts as receiving some academic theological education, and therefore these two interviewees cannot be classified as ordinary theologians. But by my definition (see above, p. 1) they are ordinary theologians, because they have not studied theology as an academic subject or received any formal theological education. My definition may need revising, but this is not an issue I want to pursue here. On the problems of defining ordinary theology, see Astley 2002: 55–8.

evangelical Christianity. They have been explicitly taught '*classic evangelical thinking*', that is, '*the concept that Christ died on the cross for my sins and the fact that Jesus was not just a man, but he was also God*'.[3] The data from the functionalists show that without such explicit teaching people do not, on the whole, learn these Christological beliefs; they do not, for example, learn them from worship.[4] Evangelical Christology acknowledges the dogmas of Nicaea and Chalcedon as normative, but is said to appeal primarily to the New Testament, and particularly the Gospel of John, as the foundation for its Christology.[5] As we saw in the last chapter, there are certain passages in the New Testament that can be interpreted as saying 'Jesus is God'. There are also other passages, most significantly in the Gospel of John, where Jesus appears to claim to be God, as in the 'I am' sayings and other statements such as 'I and the Father are one' (John 10:30) and 'He who has seen me has seen the Father' (John 14:9). The data imply that the functionalists interpret these passages in the same way as they do the *homoousion* phrase, that is, as indicating a relational and revelational not an ontological identity between Jesus and God. James Barr offers them support in writing, 'When Jesus says in John 10:30 that he and the Father are "one", he does so in the context of numerous other sayings which make it clear that "one" does not betoken congruence or identity'(Barr 1984: 57). But the evangelicals read this passage in a different way, as if it does signify ontological identity: '*Jesus says he is God in the "I am" passages in John*'. Barr argues that if the idea that 'Jesus is God' is present in the New Testament, it is very definitely a minor rather than a major emphasis and that it is characteristic of the dominant presentation of Jesus by the main New Testament sources 'that Jesus is not presented as divine or as God, and does not so present himself'. He claims that the evangelical and fundamentalist understanding of Jesus, 'which insists on the definition of him as being God, is actually based on a highly selective and rather thin (or possibly non-existent) line of New Testament evidence and ignores the main line' (Barr 1984: 55–6). The functionalists take the main line and the evangelicals the minor one. Of course, it does not follow from this that the evangelicals are thereby simply

---

[3]   The evangelicals were all self-identifying and relative newcomers into the congregations.

[4]   This issue is discussed further in Chapter 8.

[5]   For an overview of evangelical Christology and evangelical writers on Christology, see Inbody 2002: 70–4. See also Greggs 2010.

'wrong', but it does mean that their view of Jesus 'depends on a selection and ordering of the biblical evidence, and a selection and ordering that actually takes its lead from a minority trend and suppresses the suggestions that arise from the majority trend' (Barr 1984: 60). The heretics in the classic formative periods of Christology 'contended to the last that orthodoxy was a misrepresentation of the given of Scripture' (McIntyre 1998: 15). What is clear is that the evangelicals and the functionalists see Jesus differently. The evangelicals see Jesus as God and think he claimed to be God, whereas the functionalists see Jesus as the Son of God and do not think he claimed to be God.

A couple of the evangelicals used the C.S. Lewis apologetic, which argues that someone claiming to be God must be either mad or bad or God; and since Jesus was evidently not mad or bad he must have been God. But this popular form of apologetic, still used in the Alpha and Emmaus courses, is undermined by historical-critical research which challenges the assumption that Jesus claimed to be God. Before the rise of the historical-critical study of the gospels, belief in Jesus as God incarnate was assumed to rest firmly on Jesus' own claims to divinity as recorded in the gospels, especially the gospel of John, but now 'there is scarcely a single competent New Testament scholar who is prepared to defend the view that the four instances of the absolute use of "I am" in John, or indeed most of the other uses, can be historically attributed to Jesus' (Thatcher 1990: 77; cf. Hick 1993: 28). Many scholars who today affirm an orthodox Christology acknowledge that any claim for Jesus' divinity cannot be defended by reference to the claims of Jesus himself and that classical Christology must be defended on other grounds.[6] But the evangelicals, like most of the sample, are unfamiliar with the results of historical criticism of the gospels and their belief that Jesus is God is based on a pre-critical reading of the text.

Evangelical Christology insists on using ontological instead of functional language, and rejects functional Christologies. 'Any interpretation of incarnation which uses the language of will, purpose, spirit, activity, presence, grace or initial aims instead of substance is regarded as heretical' (Inbody 2002: 72). The evangelical theologian Clark Pinnock asserts that 'the formula "Jesus is God" acts

---

6   John Hick cites a number of scholars who affirm an orthodox Christology, but who accept that Jesus did not claim divinity for himself. See Hick 1993: 27–8.

as the shibboleth for distinguishing orthodoxy from liberalism' and goes on to say
that:

> All such [liberal] Christologies have something in common. They seek a
> functional equivalent of Chalcedon by finding in the human life of Jesus a
> unique divine presence, a normative divine revelation, a decisive saving action.
> But none of them wishes to say that Jesus is God in the ontological sense that
> orthodoxy has demanded. They will go only as far as functional categories.
> (Pinnock and Brown 1990: 145)

Evangelical Christology, like orthodox Christology, maintains that 'Jesus was not
just radically unique but *metaphysically different* from all other human beings'
(Davis 1988: 74). Here the 'is' of identity rather than the 'is' of predication is being
used: Jesus is identical with God, one and the same as, 'of the same substance'.
Anything less than an ontological, numerical identity will not do.

All of this group have a doctrine (of sorts) of the immanent Trinity, of pre-
existence and of the incarnation of God the Son. These three doctrines are
organically related to one another and indeed presuppose one another. I shall look
first of all at what this group have to say about God as Trinity.

Tritheistic Tendencies

All of this group have a doctrine of the immanent Trinity in that they consider God
to be triune in Godself. They use the term Godhead and talk about the Godhead
being '*a three-in-one God*'. Just as the doctrine of the incarnation is abbreviated
and simplified, so is the doctrine of the Trinity. The classic summary statement
of the doctrine is 'three Persons in one God'. This doctrine is undoubtedly one of
the most puzzling aspects of Christian theology and requires careful discussion if
it is not to be misleading, but discussions of the doctrine never really progressed
beyond variations of the classic summary statement. This is hardly surprising as
expressing belief in the Trinity in words is not easy and various pitfalls await
anyone who tries. Nearly everyone in this group said that they did not understand
the doctrine of the Trinity.

Peter

'I would certainly say I believe that God was ... that Jesus was part of God from the beginning, from all time, not just from you know 2000 years ago when he was born as a man.'

'In a sense the three aspects of God, the Father, the Son and the Spirit are there even at the beginning of Genesis.'

'I wouldn't pretend that I fully understand how you get three-in-one and all the illustrations and what have you.'

Paul

'It's one God ... separated into three somehow.'

'I don't understand the dynamics of a three-in-one God. But that is where my faith kicks in, because I know that that is what it is. I know that God is a three-in-one, but ... I just have to put my trust in that ... and my faith, you know, takes over.'

'I've always struggled with there being three entities in one. I don't understand how it works. But I know, I know that's how it is. So that's it.'

Charles

'Well, as I understand it, God is composed of three parts, like ancient Gaul. God the Father, God the Son and God the Holy Ghost and they are all one. Yet there are three divisions so to speak, so Jesus Christ is God; full stop.'

Dorothy

'It's one God ... separated into three.'

'They are all different parts of the Godhead.'

The word God has two referents here: it can be used to refer to God the Father, the First Person of the Trinity, and it can be used to refer to the triune Godhead. However, listening to immanent Trinitarians speak reveals that they rarely use the word God to refer to the triune Godhead unless they are being asked a specific question about the Trinity. Like the functionalists, when they use the word God they use it to refer to God the Father. The two most important Trinitarian heresies, as we saw in the last chapter, are modalism and tritheism. The three non-evangelicals in this group tend towards modalism, talking about Jesus being '*a manifestation of God*' or '*an aspect of God*'. The six evangelicals, on the other hand, tend towards tritheism, emphasizing the distinct and separate realities of the three Persons rather than the oneness of God. Those who exhibit tritheistic tendencies all use 'person' language to talk about the triune God. They make a point of saying that they think of each of the three 'figures' as 'persons' and not just '*a nebulous sort of ... it*'. Such thinking stands in direct contrast to many of the sample, who make a point of disavowing all 'person' talk, saying that they '*do not like to think of God as a person*'. They prefer instead to think of God as '*a power*', '*a force*', '*a spirit*'. The doctrine of the Trinity is classically expressed using 'person' terminology, but this terminology is suspected today of contributing to a tritheistic perception of the Godhead. The ancient term *persona* meant something quite different from 'person' in modern English, where the word means an individual human being. Using the term 'person' today, we are inclined to think of *a* person, which leads, Lash suspects, 'to the idea that God is in some way three people. Which God, of course, is not' (Lash 1992: 31). Haight, similarly, suggests that the use of the word 'person' almost inevitably communicates to current western culture an understanding of God as three autonomous persons and thereby conveys a tritheism which is simply meaningless to their lives (Haight 2001: 171). Both Lash and Haight advocate ceasing to use the word 'person' in Trinitarian theology. The difficulties are highlighted by Peter.

> P   *I suppose ... the idea that [Jesus] is with God in heaven and it talks about him interceding for the saints and that kind of thing. And I mean it still describes him as a separate from ... separate from ... I mean there is still a distinction between Jesus as God and God as God. And I can't explain that.*
>
> A   *OK. I'm following you so far, but are you telling me that I have now got two gods in heaven?*
>
> P   *And the third one that is working in believers as well. The Spirit. To me it is the same problem as you had before. You've got three distinct aspects of God and yet as Christians we claim to be monotheistic. And so ... yeah. Good question. Good question. I don't have an answer* [laugh].

The data imply that although God is formally acknowledged as one, in practice these believers live with a picture of three autonomous persons, three gods in their imagination (cf. Borg 1999: 154). The classic doctrine enables Jesus to be declared to be God without ending up with multiple Gods, thereby preserving monotheism, but easily leads to tritheistic thinking as the data show. Whether the doctrine of the Trinity makes any difference to this group's experience and practice of faith is unclear. Moltmann complains that for most Christians, 'Whether God is one or triune evidently makes as little difference to the doctrine of faith as it does to ethics' (Moltmann 1981: 1).

Incarnational Christology

This group have a different version of the Christian story to that of the functionalists and a different conceptual scheme. Here, behind the human career of Jesus lies a divine pre-existence. All have a doctrine of Jesus personally pre-existing his earthly life as a distinct divine figure or hypostasis alongside God the Father. They all talk about Jesus being with God at the beginning of creation and of Jesus coming down to earth to live a human life. They have a three-stage, descent-ascent, incarnational Christology. Jesus is thought of as Son of God, not merely from his resurrection, or baptism or virginal conception, but from eternity.

> Peter
>
> *'I would believe that* [Jesus] *pre-existed.'*
>
> *'Um ... I mean the way that I have understood it in the past ... I mean even the first verse of the Bible talks about the Spirit of God hovering over the earth and God said ... and the way that that is a picture of ... you know there was God the Father there, there is the Spirit and there is the spoken Word which is Jesus. Um ... so you know, in a sense the three aspects of God, the Father, the Son and the Spirit are there even at the beginning of Genesis.'*
>
> *'We talk about Jesus as being the Word of God, which is an aspect of God isn't it? Um ... and so is was that particular aspect of God that became flesh.'*

Pat

*'And I mean John's gospel ... in the beginning was the Word ... so Jesus was
there at the beginning when the world was created.'*

Dorothy

'Jesus was there from the beginning of creation.'

Susan

*'Jesus made the decision to lay down his life ... before he came to earth when he
was in God's presence.'*

Several identify Jesus with the Word and talk about the Word or Jesus becoming
flesh. The functionalists do not make this connection, as these two contrasting
extracts from functionalists illustrate.

Rose

A   *[Incarnation] comes in at the carol service, at the very end. St John unfolds
     the mystery of the Incarnation. You get that reading, do you remember it,
     about the Word becoming flesh?*

R   *Yes. Yes, I do remember the thing [laugh]. Yes, you don't think ... [pause]*

A   *But you wouldn't ... you wouldn't be able to say particularly what that is
     about or ...*

R   *No. No. I think ... no. No, I don't understand.*

Suzanne

A   *So like at Christmas, at the carol service, at the end, when you have that
     reading from the beginning of John's Gospel and it is headed 'St John
     unfolds the mystery of the Incarnation', does that ring any bells? The Word
     became flesh?*

S   *Oh yes. Right. Well, I missed last year's, so it is over a year since I have
     been to that.*

A   Would you like to have a look at it? It's there ... at the beginning of John.
[hands over Bible - Suzanne reads it]

S   'The Word becoming flesh.' Crikey. So what was your original question?

Unlike the functionalists, this present group, whom I have distinguished as having an ontological Christology, have learnt to interpret the Word, in John's Prologue, as referring to a pre-existent Jesus. Pre-existence is also assumed in other passages. But, according to James Dunn, 'Only with the Fourth Gospel can we speak of a full blown conception of Christ's personal pre-existence and a clear doctrine of incarnation' (Dunn 1980: 258; cf. Kysar 1976: 29). Like other scholars, Dunn believes that the other passages in the New Testament which allegedly refer to the existence of a pre-existent divine being do not in fact do so and warns strongly against reading the later doctrines of the Church into the New Testament. He argues, for example, that the Christ-hymn in Philippians (Phil.2:6–7) does not teach the pre-existence of Jesus. He believes that the words of the Philippians' passage are only interpreted in this way because the reader brings to them the background of long-cherished popular Christian beliefs, and that the passage should be understood in a different way (Dunn 1980: 114). Several of the evangelicals interpret the Philippians passage as the story of a heavenly being who lays aside his pre-existent glory to become man. Brian Malley argues that their interpretive tradition specifies this reading. It is a tradition in which one text is interpreted in terms of another and read through selective doctrinal spectacles. The text confirms what is presupposed, namely, in this instance, Jesus' pre-existence (Malley 2004: 73).

Most of this group are insistent that the virgin birth '*really happened*' and that '*you have to believe it*'. Interestingly, in those New Testament writings where pre-existence is said to occur, the virgin birth does not, and vice versa. These two concepts are used by different writers as separate and alternative ways of expressing the significance of Jesus. Wolfhart Pannenberg goes so far as to say that the two concepts stand in 'irreconcilable contradiction' to each other. The story of the virgin birth presupposes that Jesus, God's Son, is brought into existence through Mary's conception, whereas a pre-existence Christology presupposes that the Son of God has existed from eternity (Pannenberg 1968: 143). Robinson considers Pannenberg's claim to be an exaggeration, however, arguing that the two concepts have been combined and integrated so successfully (as the miraculous insertion into history of the pre-existent Son) that most people are unaware of any contradiction (Robinson 1972: 144–5). None of this present group talk about God creating Jesus. They talk about the pre-existent Jesus becoming flesh in the womb of the virgin Mary: '*Jesus became planted in Mary's womb*', '*Jesus became flesh*'. Jesus does not become God's Son at conception/birth. Rather, for this group, the virginal conception is the point in time when the pre-existent Jesus becomes incarnate and the mystery of the incarnation takes place. There has been a successful fusing of the two concepts of pre-existence and virgin birth so that the virginal conception is now regarded as an indispensable element in the incarnation process. The suggestion that incarnation could take place without the virginal conception is completely unacceptable to all the evangelicals: '*Jesus had to come on the earth and that's the way he did*'. But for at least one of the non-evangelicals, the virgin birth is not essential, as it was not for those New Testament writers who are said to speak most of pre-existence. For Charles, the pre-existent Son of God could have become incarnate without a virginal conception. Indeed, such a notion is considered to be not only unnecessary, but biologically impossible. '*I do think when you are on this earth and reproducing you do actually need to obey the scientific rules and I really don't believe in miraculous ways of things occurring differently.*' Charles is unusual in that he has an ontological Christology: he believes '*that Jesus Christ was ... is God and came onto this earth*', but he cannot believe in either the virgin birth or a physical resurrection.

Truly Human?

The Prologue speaks of the Word pre-existing, the doctrine of the incarnation speaks of the Son of God or God the Son pre-existing, and these interviewees speak primarily of Jesus pre-existing. Are they all saying the same thing? What exactly can be said to pre-exist? A three-stage Word or Son Christology can be interpreted in various ways. By incarnation, the Word or Son becomes Jesus Christ and therefore one could say that the one who is Jesus Christ pre-existed. Yet it is clear that the human nature and bodily existence of Jesus did not pre-exist (Haight 1999: 175, n.79). Strictly speaking, what pre-exists prior to the incarnation is the

Word or Son and it is therefore a mistake to say that Jesus pre-exists. Jesus and the Word/Son are not identical. As Norman Pittenger puts it, 'It must be clear that in terms of Trinitarian theology there can be no pre-existence of the human mind, nature, self, ego of Jesus of Nazareth ... we must reject out-right any idea of a pre-existence of *Jesus* and along with this rejection an incredible amount of pious error and confusion' (Pittenger 1959: 218–9). This group, however, are not aware that they are in 'error and confusion' or that they are talking 'logical nonsense'.[7] According to John Knox, what has usually been meant by pre-existence is that 'Jesus as the particular individual he was had existed before all worlds' or that his existence as a man 'was in some self-conscious way continuous with his earlier existence as a heavenly being' (Knox 1967: 61, 106). It is along these lines that this group seem to understand pre-existence. Lampe claims that in popular piety it is the Jesus of the gospels whom the imagination of the worshipper pictures as pre-existing in heaven and descending to earth, so that Jesus becomes a kind of invader from outer space (Lampe 1977: 136).

Many academic theologians argue that the doctrine of pre-existence places an intolerable strain on the true humanity of Jesus. How can a man who is conscious of having an earlier existence as a heavenly being really be a man? Surely such a claim is not compatible with 'normal human sanity' (Robinson 1972: 151, n.17). Knox asserts that there is 'absolutely no way' of having both the pre-existence and the humanity of Jesus and he jettisons the pre-existence in favour of the humanity, arguing that pre-existence distinguishes Jesus' humanity from ours to such an extent that he cannot be thought of as 'a man like other men' and therefore he cannot be thought of as 'a man' at all (Knox 1967: 144, 63). Others, struggling with the same problem, disagree and are able to find ways of ascribing to Jesus full and genuine humanity while at the same time regarding him as a man unlike other men. The data suggest that some of this group are aware of the threat that pre-existence poses to the humanity of Jesus, but they are not unduly troubled by the issue. They do not have the same need or desire an academic theologian might have to resolve, through rational argument, the tensions or contradictions inherent within the claims being made. Peter can say, '*I would say that [Jesus] knew that*

---

[7]   Gordon D. Kaufmann accuses Barth, who says that '... the man Jesus already was even before He was', of 'logical nonsense' and 'the theological error of *docetism*'. See Kaufmann 1968: 205.

he was God, that he wasn't just a man' and, unlike Knox, he does not see this as in any way threatening Jesus' humanity. He does not conclude that Jesus could not have been a man, because he knew that he was God. The question, 'How could Jesus genuinely be a man, if "underneath", as it were, he was really God?' is not a question that these ordinary believers want to pursue or consider worth pursuing (Robinson 1972: 99). They just accept, without too much difficulty it would seem, that Jesus really was a man, but he was God as well and that his being God in no way undermined his being human. The 'absolute paradox' of the God-man is accepted by faith and the theoretical question of how one person can be both God and man, without his humanity being in any way infringed, rarely arises. This question is irrelevant to their spirituality.

The logical extreme of incarnationist Christology is docetism: Jesus becomes a god disguised in human flesh. Docetism denies the humanity of Jesus and has always been deemed by the tradition to be heretical. Jesus did not just 'appear' to be human, he really was human. But many today claim that Christological thinking throughout much of Christian history has invariably been weighted on the side of the divinity rather than the humanity of Jesus and complain of an unconscious docetism in the churches. The Gospel of John in particular has, from the beginning, been seen as 'the presentation of a celestial being walking this earth in the clothing of a humanity that is merely a disguise' and is classed by some as a docetic document (Robinson 1972: 169). Like the author of the Gospel of John, all of this group affirm the humanity of Jesus, but there is the suspicion that, as with John, docetism lurks. Dorothy asserts that Jesus was a man and then adds, *'and yet ... I must admit I find it quite hard to actually ... I think I think of him more as God than as a man'*. The humanity of Jesus is affirmed as a formal fact, but Jesus is thought of as God rather than a man. His human nature is seen through his divine nature, as illustrated by the following comment.

> *'OK, when he died on the cross, OK it would have been painful, but then he was God. He was divine, so he probably could have coped with all that.'*

Further, what counts as Jesus being God varies within this group, just as what counts as Jesus being divine varies among the functionalists. For example, some consider Jesus to possess the divine attribute of omniscience, others do not. Hick (1993: 4) reminds us that:

> our concepts of God are human constructs, and theologians are free to offer their own definitions of the essential attributes in virtue of which God is God ... Thus it is, within certain limits, up to us to decide what is to count as Jesus being God (did he, for example, have to be omniscient and omnipotent, or are these not after all essential divine attributes?), and what is to count as his being a man (did he, for example, have to be limited in knowledge and power, or could he be an omniscient and omnipotent man?). Given the relatively open character of our concept of humanity, and still more of deity, it will always be possible to adjust them in relation to each other [...].

We see this process of adjustment happening with Pat. She continues to believe, as she always has, that Jesus was both God and man, but she now thinks of Jesus as '*very, very human*', someone who '*struggled with his faith*' like the rest of us. She says, '*You often get this picture that is put across of Jesus being meek and mild and he did everything right. I don't think he was like that anymore. He was a human being*'. She no longer thinks of Jesus as perfect or sinless. Such a human being, in her judgement, is not really a human being. Many academic theologians have argued that the doctrine of the sinlessness of Jesus turns him into an unrecognizable human being. But for most of this group the sinlessness of Jesus is non-negotiable and has to be defended, primarily because they also hold a substitutionary theory of atonement and this theory requires that Jesus be without sin. They do not think of pre-existence or sinlessness as posing a serious threat, and certainly not a fatal blow, to the genuine humanity of Jesus. Neither do they find such a Jesus unattractive or irrelevant. Others in the sample obviously do.

Taking Myth Literally

Many would argue that the idea of pre-existence, the idea that Jesus had prior to his birth a conscious, personal pre-existence in 'heaven', is mythological as well as destructive of Jesus' true humanity and should be discarded because it can lead to all sorts of misunderstandings (such as those outlined above). As we saw earlier, the only pre-existence some theologians can accept, and the only kind that is seen to be compatible with Jesus' true humanity, is pre-existence in the mind and purpose of God. Any 'literal conception of pre-existence' is rejected (Macquarrie 1990: 390–1; cf. Mackey 1983: 51–65). It is now more widely accepted that the doctrine of the incarnation itself belongs to the genre of myth and that the doctrine, as expressed in the Nicene creed, is set in mythic form. (Because in common use the term myth has become synonymous with falsehood, some would prefer to use the word 'story' rather than 'myth'.) Paul Avis writes, 'In the Niceno-Constantinopolitan creed we have an extremely powerful statement of the Incarnation, a piling of metaphor upon metaphor, symbol upon symbol, culminating in the myth of the Son of God descending from heaven'. To assert the mythic character of the doctrine of the incarnation is not 'to prejudge the question of its truth and relevance … It is merely to settle the preliminary question of genre' (Avis 1999: 133, 158). Avis is insistent that a mythic understanding of incarnation is compatible with 'a full-blooded orthodox faith' and rejects any reductionist conclusions. For him, as for this group, the truth of the myth is the identity of Jesus with God (Avis 1999: 173–4). But, unlike Avis, most of this group do not have a mythic understanding of the doctrine and appear to take it literally. To take myth literally is to take it 'at face value', as though it were a statement of scientific or historical fact. Here the myth of the incarnation is taken as real, as if it were factually true, as if it really happened, and its mythic status is not recognized. Jesus, a pre-existent divine person, *'really did'* come down from heaven; it *'really happened'*, but *'how he got sucked down into a baby'* is a mystery, and the idea that it should be interpreted according to the genre of myth is an anathema.

Some theologians claim that mythological thinking at the literal level is no longer possible for people in the contemporary western world and they advocate revising the myth of the incarnation in non-mythological terms. Clearly, this is not the case here: these believers can and do take myth literally and do not need it to be revised. But some in the sample do, as we shall see in the next chapter.

Chapter 5

Sceptical Christology

Six of the sample have very serious doubts about or deny altogether the divinity of Jesus, whether this be substantively or adjectivally construed. They do not consider Jesus to be God the Son, the Second Person of the Trinity, incarnate (ontological Christology), or God's Son created by God to be God's agent or representative on earth (functional Christology). This percentage is very close to that reported by Ahern. Three out of the 30 respondents in his study doubted the divinity of Jesus.[1] Macquarrie writes, 'I do not think that, if we remain Christian, we can ever escape the fundamental paradox, that Jesus Christ is both human and divine' and he goes on to write that if the claim that Jesus is divine is denied, 'then Christianity collapses' (Macquarrie 1998: 17). But for this group, as for some academic theologians, denying the divinity of Jesus does not result in Christianity collapsing in their eyes. They can think of themselves as Christian without having to believe in a divine Jesus.

A Problem With Miracle

Scepticism and unbelief concerning miracles is, for this group, one cause of the divinity of Jesus being denied. Kathleen, for example, argues that Jesus would only be the Son of God because of the virginal conception, but she '*cannot believe in a virginal conception*'. She '*cannot take that on board at all*' and, therefore, she cannot believe that Jesus is the Son of God. She also doubts many of the other miraculous happenings, including the resurrection, and says she finds it very hard to believe that Jesus could have been divine. (She is prepared to accept some of the healing miracles.) The other five in this group all make similar comments.

---

[1]   Ahern 1987: 17. Julie Hopkins reports that 6 out of 30 women she interviewed, in a study of student ministers of the Dutch Gereformeerde Kerk, specifically denied that Christ is divine. See Hopkins 1995: 17.

John talks about people he knows '*being put off Christianity*' and '*who don't come to church*' because they cannot believe in miracles such as the virgin birth and the physical resurrection. Unlike John, these people consider their admission of unbelief in respect of these miracles to be incompatible with an acceptance of the Christian faith. They think that they have to believe in these miracles to be a believing Christian. Many of the wider sample would agree with them. They too assert that '*you have to believe in these miracles if you are a Christian*'.

But many people today do find it impossible to believe in miracles. Their worldview, sometimes called the Newtonian worldview or simply the modern worldview, sees the universe as a closed system of cause and effect, operating in accord with natural laws. The resurrection and the virgin birth would disrupt this closed system of nature and therefore '*they can't have happened*'.[2] Bultmann famously remarked that, 'It is impossible to use electric light and radio equipment and, when ill, to claim the assistance of modern medical and surgical discoveries, and at the same time believe in the New Testament world of spirits and miracles'. He argued that we should demythologize the New Testament, by translating its mythology (which includes miracles) into the language of existential (personal) decision, so that the barriers to faith are removed (Bultmann 1962: 1–44). Other scholars, however, argue that the myth is indispensable and that losing the myth would mean losing the narrative as well. So what is required to make the Christian faith credible to nonbelievers is not demythologization but deliteralization. The myth should be kept but not read literally. It should be read *as myth*, as a symbolic narrative.

It has been suggested that 'the task of apologetics, at a fairly sophisticated level, among the intelligensia, would be helped by a sensible deployment of "myth"' and at a more popular level, in view of the common association of myth with falsehood, 'its equivalents "parable" and "symbolic narrative"' should be used (Avis 1999: 166–7). One of the difficulties with this approach is that people in the contemporary western world have, it is said, lost the capacity of symbolic imagination. They cannot read myth as myth, but only read it literally (as we

---

[2]   Some might argue that these people are operating with an outdated view of science. For example, quantum science means that people can/should now believe in miracles and they need to be persuaded to do so. Keith Ward argues that problems with miracles arise from a misperception of scientific knowledge and of the personal nature of God. See Ward 1990: esp. chapters 5 and 10.

saw at the end of Chapter 4). Avis complains that 'one of the greatest stumbling blocks ... to Christian belief in the modern world is the gross literalism with which those both inside and outside the Church take the Bible and Christian doctrine' (Avis 1999: 166). Some of the sample who cannot believe in miracle effectively demythologize, saying they could '*strip away the ornament*' or '*do away with the miraculous bits*', whereas others say that the miraculous stories '*are symbolic*' and should be kept. The capacity for symbolic imagination is clearly not entirely lost, as these extracts from John's interview illustrate. He says:

> '*Once you start stripping away, you finish up with very little.*'
>
> '*I like* [Christianity] *because of its magical side. There are so many aspects that one can look at and it is not what it would be if we stripped away all the additions ... We would only be left with the bare bones of the thing which people wouldn't relate to at all. It would have no emotional impact.*'
>
> '*If you can't take the birth story or the resurrection story, don't let it put you off* [...] *if that offends you ignore it, but do try to find the truth.*'

Both demythologization and deliteralization enable the difficulties that many people have with miracle to be bypassed. Without this kind of approach, the miraculous happenings will, for many, continue to be a serious barrier to accepting Christian faith. To insist, or at least give the impression, that everyone '*has to believe in the miracles*' is, in my view, a mistake and only serves to alienate those people who might otherwise be attracted to Christianity. Haight argues that when Christian faith is equated with holding certain beliefs, 'beliefs are given the status of faith and masquerade as faith itself'. This is, he says, an all too common phenomenon. Faith then becomes 'confused with, collapsed into, and mistaken' for holding onto a set of beliefs, so that faith, which is now belief, means assenting to a set of propositions. When assent can no longer be given because a belief is no longer credible in the light of what is known through science or other forms of critical reasoning, then faith itself is threatened or even lost. Equating faith with belief in this way results in many people leaving the church (or never joining it) because they cannot give assent to the set of propositions. What is left, says Haight provocatively, 'is a community of closed, eviscerated and impoverished faith isolated from the world on the basis of archaic beliefs' (Haight 2001: 35–7).

Philip Richter's and Leslie Francis' study of church-leavers has shown that loss of faith, due in part to no longer believing in the church's teachings, is one of the main reasons for church-leaving (Richter and Francis 1998: 27–38, 136–41).

For the majority of my sample, however, miracles are integral to the substance of their faith. They appeal to the miracles, particularly the resurrection, as confirmation of the divinity of Jesus and the truth of the Christian faith, as generations before them have done. But for this present group, such an appeal would obviously be unconvincing because they do not believe that these miracles occurred (except for some healing miracles). For those who wish to promote the doctrine of the divinity of Jesus, considering it to be an indispensable element of the Christian faith, the data suggest that the doctrine must be defended on grounds other than miracles if it is to stand any chance of being accepted by the likes of people in this group. However, it is difficult to imagine any apologetic succeeding here, since none of this group need Jesus to be divine. They neither need nor want a divine redeemer who came into the world to die for the sins of the world. Their words seem to imply that they can manage perfectly well with a non-divine Jesus whose significance resides primarily in his life and teachings.

History Challenges Dogma

This group's rejection of the doctrine of the divinity of Jesus is not based solely on an inability to believe in miracles. Several of this group have also been influenced in their thinking about Jesus by books they have read on the historical Jesus and Christian origins. Four of this group have read A.N. Wilson's *Jesus*, published in 1992. One of Wilson's main claims is that the real historical Jesus has little to do with the Christ-figure of Christianity. The real historical Jesus was a simple Galilean holy man not the God-man of Christianity. Wilson considers Paul to be the real founder of Christianity. The influence of Wilson can possibly be detected in the following comments.

Ben

'I am prepared to accept that [Jesus] *got in the way of the powers that be in those days and he paid the price for it. I am very much prepared then to accept that*

Jesus Christ was martyred. I accept the rolling away of the stone from the tomb and his disappearance. I don't put any more emphasis on that, than that. I then go on over the next few years to regard someone like St Paul, as being one of the best spin-doctors of the time. I think there is no doubt about that. And I suspect that without him, and like people, I don't say Christianity would have died a death, but it would have struggled to the pre-eminence it gained, certainly in a massive area of the world then and now.'

John

'[Jesus] *was just pointing out the weak spots* [in Judaism]*and the need to open up the strict rules because they were getting in the way of faith ... so it was a small group and those who were left* [who] *formulated and wrote down stories. Paul, with his great missionary zeal, he went off and planted these seeds in other places and this is what people were looking for.'*

'I believe Paul constructed a lot of the writings ... and so I think the Trinity really comes from his Greek background.'

Wilson's view of Jesus is not dissimilar to that of H.S. Reimarus (1694–1768), the German sceptic and founder of the so-called 'Quest for the historical Jesus'. Reimarus was the first to explicitly approach the question of who Jesus was from a historical-critical perspective. He declared that if serious historical questions were asked about Jesus, then the discovery would be made that the Church's claims about Jesus were false. Jesus was not a divine figure at all: he was a Jewish revolutionary who died a failure and his resurrection was invented by his disciples to cover up the humiliation caused by his death. Not surprisingly, Wilson's portrait has been dismissed by scholars in the field. N.T. Wright, for example, argues that Wilson's portrait is a bad one, based partly on a total misreading of what first-century Judaism was actually like, and an outdated and now almost entirely discredited view of how to read Paul (Wright 1992). But these interviewees have only read Wilson, not Wright. None of them reported being disturbed or unsettled by Wilson's portrait of Jesus, and the data suggest that his book helped rather than hindered their faith because it sanctioned doubts they already had about the traditional Christological teaching, doubts brought on, in part, by difficulties with miracle. Linda said, '[A.N. Wilson's] *quite controversial, because people say that once you have read him you sort of lose your faith, but then I would say it has deepened mine'*. She talked about doubting the historicity of much of the gospel writings, '*but ... that doesn't make my faith any less, but ... I sort of question it'*.

So each member of this group allows historical research (of a certain sort) a place in Christology. They have a view of Jesus which has been influenced by Wilson/Reimarus. This view assumes a discrepancy between the historical Jesus and the Jesus of the New Testament. By contrast, most Christians, like most of the sample, assume the historical reliability of the gospels, so that the Jesus of history is indistinguishable from the Jesus of the New Testament. They assume an identity between the historical person and what the texts, and also the creeds, say about him. But this group do not. They think the Jesus of history was a Jewish religious leader, teacher and healer, not God incarnate or God's Son. However, their certainty on this matter is not absolute. Most want to leave open the possibility that Jesus might have been who the gospels and the creeds proclaim him to be. They want to keep '*an open mind*' on the issue and their denials of the divinity of Jesus are often qualified. For example, at the end of his interview Ben says, '*Jesus may have swooped down and been put on this earth. Who knows, they might be right. It might all be true'*. (This comment illustrates just how misleading the mythological language can be.)

Liberal Tendencies

Any theology that attempts to establish the grounds of authority for religious believing on some basis other than scripture and tradition (such as historical scholarship) can be classified as belonging to the liberal tradition. The liberal tradition in theology developed in response to the Enlightenment and is characterized by a willingness to subject Christian truth-claims to the authority of reason and experience and to take account of the claims of modern knowledge from either history, literary criticism, the natural sciences or, more recently, the social sciences. John Habgood characterizes the liberal theological attitude in positive terms, as representing 'an openness in the search for truth' which 'entails a positive, but again critical, approach to secular knowledge' (Habgood 1988: 2).

Stephen Sykes, on the other hand, defines theological liberalism in more negative terms, saying:

> Liberalism in theology is that mood or cast of mind which is prepared to accept that some discovery of reason may count *against* the authority of a traditional affirmation in the body of Christian theology. One is a theological liberal if one allows autonomously functioning reason to supply arguments against traditional beliefs and if one's reformulation of Christian belief provides evidence that one has ceased to believe what has been traditionally believed by Christians. (Sykes 1971: 12)

This suggests some disapproval of the attitude adopted earlier towards miracles, which Habgood would not appear to share. Liberal theology is commonly perceived to be subversive of Christian faith, serving only to erode traditional Christian beliefs (such as belief in the virgin birth and the physical resurrection). Proponents of liberal theology dispute this, of course, arguing that far from seeking to water down Christian belief, they have only sought to make it credible in post-Enlightenment contexts. From the outset liberal theology has been committed to bridging the gap between Christian faith and modern knowledge (à la Bultmann).

None of this group identify themselves as liberals, but they clearly all exhibit liberal theological tendencies. Such tendencies are not, of course, confined to this group. It is possible to be a fairly orthodox believer and exhibit liberal tendencies. Charles, for example, is one of the orthodox believers who remains fully committed to the orthodox Christological doctrines, but is unable to accept the miracles of the virgin birth and physical resurrection. Habgood describes himself as a 'conservative liberal' and such a label may be appropriate for Charles as well. Such people want to remain open to the truth-claims of Enlightenment modernism, taking account of scientific advances and historical consciousness, but at the same time want to 'treasure what is given by tradition' and are not prepared to surrender the truth-claims of the traditional orthodox Christological formulations (Habgood 1988: 2–3). By contrast, this group *are* prepared to surrender these truth-claims and are therefore best described as *radical liberals*.

Radical Liberal Christology

The dominant strand within liberal theology has *not* been to abandon the doctrine of the divinity of Jesus, but to reinterpret it. Schleiermacher, the founding father of liberal theology, offered a severe critique of Chalcedon and its doctrine of the two natures, but he attempted to reformulate the doctrine of the divinity of Jesus rather than discard it. Many present-day theologians, whose Christology is classified as liberal, give high regard, if not normative status, to the guidelines of Nicaea and Chalcedon when it comes to constructing their Christologies. They do not want to dissolve the paradox of the one person who is both fully human and fully divine and so they seek to find ways of speaking of the divinity of Jesus Christ which do not rely on out-moded metaphysics and the language of substance or being. The divinity of Jesus is something that they redefine and defend in other terms. We have already come across this type of reformulating liberal Christology in Chapter 3; functional Christologies are all of this type. Typically functional Christologies begin, using the popular terminology, 'from below', from the human side of the paradox, and then proceed to fathoming the divine side. When the move to the divine side is made, the divinity of Jesus is often maintained by claiming, in one way or another, that Jesus has in full what the rest of humanity only has in part. In other words, the divinity of Jesus is redefined in terms of Jesus possessing to the fullest extent certain qualities which humanity can hope to imitate.

However, the group being analysed in this chapter do not make any move 'to the divine side' at all. They talk about a human Jesus only and are extremely reticent about speaking of any special activity of God in Jesus, or of a distinct divine presence in him, or of his incarnating in full what the rest of humanity only incarnates in part. Two of the group are prepared to go as far as saying that Jesus '*could have been chosen by God*'. Kathleen says:

> '[Jesus] *could ... God could have ... well I think given what has happened through the centuries and since ... it could well be and I am prepared to accept that he is the man that God chose to create this religion, this set of beliefs that we now believe in, if you like. I am certainly prepared to accept that.*'

Ben talks about Jesus being '*someone who was affected and influenced by whatever was put into his mind. And let's say it was God-given*', and that he was '*something special*' and that perhaps '*from a mental standpoint, an intellectual standpoint he was different*' from everyone else. The line dividing Ben from some of the functionalists is very thin at this point, but he stops short of saying that Jesus was divine in any way. In this group the paradox of the God-man is dissolved by denying the divinity of Jesus. The divinity is neither defended nor redefined, but rejected. Let us, for argument's sake, take Ben's idea of Jesus being different from everyone else '*from a mental standpoint*' and equate it with the concept of God-consciousness, which has been at the centre of liberal Christologies since Schleiermacher. We could then say that Jesus was different from everyone else because of the quality of his God-consciousness. A theological liberal, who wants to remain loyal to Chalcedon, might then argue that because of the perfection of his God-consciousness, Jesus is fully God. D.M. Baillie, for example, does this. He uses the concept of a perfect God-consciousness in Jesus to speak about the full divinity of Jesus. He wants to make Jesus utterly unique by making the degree of his God-consciousness (understood in terms of the paradox of grace) a difference in kind and not just degree (Baillie 1961: esp. chapter 5). But none of this group would make that kind of move. They do not conclude that Jesus is different in kind and thereby fully divine, because he happens to be, in some way or other, different in degree. This kind of thinking was present among the functional group, but it is absent here.

The functionalists speak about the divinity of Jesus in the style of the liberal reformulators, that is, in terms of divine activity and presence and/or in the sense of Jesus embodying or exemplifying certain qualities. But this group do not speak about the divinity of Jesus at all. They are much closer to the radical than to the reformulating liberals. The radical liberal approach eschews Chalcedon altogether, abandoning any claims of uniqueness and divinity for Jesus. Hick (a radical), for example, criticizes Baillie (a reformulator) for claiming uniqueness for Jesus, arguing that any Christology based on the theme of God-consciousness, of humanity as responsive to God's grace, does not by itself entail that Jesus is unique. For Hick, the interaction of the divine and the human in the life of Jesus is not something that in principle is unique. It is 'a special instance' of an interaction 'which occurs in many different ways and degrees in all human openness to God's presence', and it is a mistake to single Jesus out as the supreme point of contact between God and humankind. Hick opts instead for 'a non-traditional Christianity' based upon an understanding of Jesus as someone who embodied, or incarnated, the ideal of human life lived in faithful response to God, but who was not 'the locus of final revelation and purveyor of the only salvation possible for all human beings' (Hick 1993: ix, 109–10; cf. Wiles 1986: 82–94).

Ben, similarly, does not consider that Jesus' being different from everyone else *'from a mental standpoint'* counts as Jesus being fully divine. He does not conclude that Jesus is fully divine or fully God, because he happens to be different from other human beings. He does not look for divinity in the unique quality of his life on earth. Even if it could be proved that Jesus was indeed more open to God's presence, or different 'from a mental standpoint' to everyone else (and there is no way of establishing on historical grounds that this was the case), this would only count as Jesus being fully divine or fully God because that is what had already been chosen to count as Jesus being fully divine or fully God (cf. see above, p. 75). This group do not allow anything to count as Jesus being divine. John is the most avowedly humanistic of all and his understanding of Jesus has many similarities with that of Hick. It is to a discussion of John's Christology that I now turn.

Jesus the Representative Human

John has also read other scholarly works on the historical Jesus and Christian origins over recent years and has invested considerable time and energy into thinking about the identity of Jesus of Nazareth.[3] He has reached some provisional conclusions.

> *'I think I see* [Jesus] *as an encapsulation of every man and woman if you like, in that he's faced in his life with so many situations that ... it's rarely situations that I have actually faced, except in a very watered-down strength. You read every day in the newspaper people facing situations ... standing up for what they believe or fighting administrations, governments, harsh   treatment, that*

---

3   Again the question arises, is John an ordinary theologian then?

kind of thing ... so I don't actually see Jesus as the Son of God. I see him as a son of God in that I am a son of God. That fact, I think, doesn't devalue my Christian faith, which is really in the words and the lifestyle of this man Jesus and I could, with a kind of distorted view, see myself in every situation that he finds himself in ... as with the Apostles ... people like Peter ... when you do let down friends ... it is all there. So it has really got every situation that you are likely to find yourself in and the suffering at the end ... I think we nearly all of us suffer at some stage, perhaps not to the extent that Christ had to, ... the loss of a partner, serious illnesses, things like that ... And the fact that he has gone before and you see that there are ways of handling it ... is a comfort and the great strength of Christianity.'

He later adds that '*Jesus is me and you and everybody else*' and agrees with the statement that Jesus is the *ideal*, the representative human. John places Jesus solely in the category of human being. Jesus, in his lifetime, was an exceptional human being, a rabbi, who died for his cause, which was to open up Judaism. Later, during the early development of Christianity, he was transformed into a divine figure. But, Jesus' words and lifestyle still continue to inspire and empower human living today. The emphasis here is emphatically on the man Jesus: his words, his life and his faith. '*It's really the man Christ and his words and his life which are what make me a Christian.*' It is Jesus the man, not Jesus the divine redeemer, who is at the centre of this type of Christology. John can do without miracle and dogma. It is Jesus the man that matters. Jesus is said to provide the pattern for authentic human living, showing by word and example how to live a fully human life. He is the icon of the true self; the clue to understanding what a human being is or can become.

This kind of Christology emphasizes the continuity between Jesus and other human beings. There is no 'ontological gap' between Jesus and other human beings.[4] Jesus may differ from other human beings in the extent to which he possesses certain qualities, such as his profound God-consciousness, but he is certainly not different in kind, and he is not necessarily different in degree from other significant religious figures. It is typical of liberal Christologies generally to stress the continuity between the human and the divine. All human beings have the

---

[4]   To borrow a phrase from McGrath 1994: 310.

capacity for union with the divine. As John puts it, '*God is in all of us ... we have all got God inside us. Whatever form God takes, it permeates us, rather like the sun, this is the life-force which is in all of us*'. The emphasis here is on incarnation in everyone, not just Jesus; the divinity in Jesus is the same as the divinity within every human being. But some human beings are more open and responsive to the divine presence than others and achieve a greater degree of union with God. Jesus was such a person. The quality of the divine-human interaction in Jesus was without doubt exceptional, but John makes no claims about the interaction between the divine and the human in Jesus being absolute or total or unparalleled elsewhere in creation. He says that Jesus is the channel through whom we have learnt this '*new way of living*', but we could have learnt it from another source. It was just that '*the time was perfect for that to happen in the Jewish faith*'. He goes on to say, '*So I think it was time in a sense for somebody to be highlighted. So, if it was a Ghandi-like figure, at that time, he would have become the son of God and I think that he was a son of God*'. Jesus just happened to be the right person in the right place at the right time. The followers of Jesus '*realized what a force they had here and so they interpreted it in a way that they felt was worthy of him and helpful to others*'. Jesus so embodied or incarnated the ideal of human life lived in faithful response to God that he became paradigmatic for Christians, but, in principle, someone else could have done the same job.

In this Christology, Jesus the exceptional rabbi has been transformed, not into God the Son, the Second Person of a divine Trinity come down to save the world through his atoning death, but into 'the representative human'. Several academic theologians have used this, or similar terminology, to describe Jesus. Jesus is 'the Archetypal Man' (Ritschl), 'the paradigm of humanity' (Schillebeeckx), 'the Man, the archetype of humanity', 'the representative human being' (Macquarrie), 'the proper man', 'the completely integrated self' (Robinson), to give just a few examples.[5] What does it mean to speak of Jesus in this way? Each theologian gives his own nuanced account, spelling out in some detail what is entailed in the claim that Jesus stands for or represents humanity as a whole. All recognize Jesus as the fulfilment of humanity, the representative of that authentic humanity which

---

[5]   All of the theologians listed here are reformulating liberals. They want to maintain the doctrine of the divinity of Jesus. The concept of divinity is generally adjusted to fit with what they say about Jesus' humanity.

is striving for expression in every human person. As Robinson puts it, 'We see in him what each of us could be - in his own unique way'. He is the man 'in whom we can glimpse a vision' of what is possible (Robinson 1972: 73). Linda, one of this group, sees in Jesus *'the truly spiritual person'*. She also sees this characteristic in varying degrees in the lives of other people and longs to be like this herself. She sees Jesus as embodying the ideal human-divine relationship and as someone who mediates God's presence in a particularly powerful way, just as other spiritual people do today.

Hick sees in Jesus someone 'who was exceptionally open to the divine presence and who thus incarnated to a high degree the ideal of human life lived in response to the Real'. He also calls Jesus 'the representative human' and talks about his being someone who lived in so intense and empowering an experience of the divine presence that in Jesus' presence God became a living reality to many of his hearers, and his words and life continue today to make God real to those who are inspired by him. He says, 'Jesus' life embodied a love that is a reflection of the divine love, and that the ideal of humanity living in response to God was, to a startling extent, embodied, incarnated, in his life, so that we may take him as our lord, guru, spiritual leader' (Hick 1993: 5, 152, 162). John talks about honouring Jesus and interprets worship of Jesus as *'putting-oneself-in-a-relationship with Jesus'*. Worship of Jesus is *'just relating very closely to that person and so the way I interpret it is I'm getting close to Jesus and everything that he stood for which is the whole of mankind really'*. Jesus is to be revered as the leader and founder of this new way of living founded on forgiveness and love and John's intention is to follow the same path, but so often *'the human frailty* [prevents us] *from going all the way'*.

Human not Divine

So for this group, Jesus' significance lies in his humanity not his divinity, and in his status as the representative human not the supernatural redeemer of humanity. The emphasis is on Jesus the human being who had real life experiences like ours and a sense of God like ours. The man Jesus – with his message, his conduct, and his fate – 'offers the supremely concrete criterion by which human beings can take their bearings' (Küng 1993: 47). He also points to God and encourages the Christian to be involved in a relationship with God. Jesus *'assists belief in God'*. But he does not have to be God to do all of this.

For those who want to remain loyal to Chalcedon, there has to be talk of Christology 'from above'; of God's place in it all. There has to be some way of saying that, 'All this is from God' (2 Cor. 5:18). But all such talk is virtually absent from this group. They do not use two languages to speak about Jesus, only one. Robinson argues that Jesus is the one human person of whom 'we must use two languages, man-language and God-language', because 'Jesus' words and works are not simply those of any man faithful and open to God but the self-expression of God acting in him and through him' (Robinson 1972: 113). But this group hardly talk about the God-side of Jesus at all. There is no talk about Jesus 'coming from God' or 'being sent by God', or of his 'acting for God'. It is the absence of this kind of discourse which decisively distinguishes this group from the functional group, all of whom used God-language to talk about Jesus, interpreting Jesus by reference to God. In this group the standpoint is decidedly human. Jesus is considered to be the representative human, not God's representative: the emphasis is from the bottom up and never from the top down. There is little talk about what God was doing in him and through him.

Traditionally the incarnation has always been regarded as the supreme act of God in human history. God acted in and through Jesus in a decisive and special way to redeem the world. But the emphasis in this group is on general as opposed to special revelation. We have already seen that John does not consider the Jesus-event to be a special and unrepeatable act of God. He has a very strong sense of the immanence of God and of the continuity between God and the world. The liberal approach to God's action in the world is to favour some kind of continuity between the divine and the human rather than a radical discontinuity. From this perspective, Jesus becomes a model or example of the universal pattern of God's incarnation in all things. Critics of this approach claim that such a Jesus is not special enough or divine enough to be a saviour. Pinnock complains that liberals 'see redemptive grace everywhere in the world' and that God's grace is in principle independent of Jesus. Jesus 'does not in any way cause that grace to exist. Rather, he is the symbol of it and the sacrament of it … [Liberal Christology] is really a pattern Christology, not a decisive event' (Pinnock 1990: 173).

But this group seem to manage perfectly well with a pattern Christology and a non-divine Jesus. Such a Christology is religiously adequate for them. The key question at the heart of all Christologies since the early Church has been, 'What kind of Jesus is necessary for salvation?' Inbody claims that, 'Regardless of what scripture and tradition teach, we will not let Jesus Christ be anything more or anything less than we think we need for our salvation' (Inbody 2002: 104). This group do not need Jesus to be divine to give weight or authority to his role as the representative human. But to dismiss this Christology as one that simply regards Jesus as 'just a good man' or 'a mere man' is a travesty. Such facile conclusions fail to take any account of the impact of Jesus on the religious consciousness and moral life and practice of the believer. There is no reason to suppose that Jesus has any less impact on an unorthodox, as opposed to an orthodox believer, as the following soteriological chapters will illustrate.[6]

---

[6] For a summary of the soteriological findings, see Christie and Astley 2009.

Chapter 6

Three Soteriologies

As was stated in Chapter 1, the main soteriological aim of the interview was to explore what meanings, if any, the interviewees attach to the death of Jesus and the claim that Jesus is saviour. Do they adhere to the traditional theology of the cross? Can they give an account of how the cross is salvific? In this chapter I will examine the three main theologies of the cross operating in the sample and in the next chapter I will look at some of the soteriological difficulties encountered by the sample. I will begin with exemplarist interpretations of the cross.

Exemplarist Soteriology

An Exemplarist Interpretation of the Cross

Around 12 of the sample – the six with a sceptical Christology and six with a functional Christology – articulated a clear exemplarist theology of the cross. These interviewees all considered the death of Jesus to be a martyr's death, talking about Jesus as a martyr to his cause.

Bruce
'Having got the message across, [Jesus] *has still not quite got there with everybody ... for very understandable political reasons. You can see how it all ended up like that.'*
'Jesus was a threat. There is no doubt about it. By both the Pharisees and some of the Roman rulers.'

Richard
'[Jesus] *was viewed as a subversive and yet he had the courage to stand by his beliefs right the way to the very end ... he didn't waver from his faith and his*

*calling. He had a greater sense that what he was doing was right and he had the
courage to do that ... he stood up for what was right.'*

*'[Jesus] was upsetting the status quo and people didn't like that. The more
influential people who were being disturbed from making their money, clearly, I
think, colluded with the Romans to have him caught and betrayed and eventually
put to death.'*

Kathleen

*'[Jesus] was a martyr for his cause if you like. And I think what he is saying
is ... even if it gets really difficult you shouldn't back-peddle just because it is
expedient to do so ... we should stand up and be counted.'*

Ben

'The cross is symbolic of Jesus' martyrdom.'

This group offer a purely historical account of Jesus' death, offering historical
reasons and motives for Jesus' being put to death. Jesus' death was due to his
teaching and his actions, which brought him into conflict with both the religious
and the civil authorities of his time. Jesus' death was a function of his life, of his
radical message and of his devotion to his mission or cause, which was '*to bring
people back to God*'. The cross symbolizes '*man's inhumanity to man*' and as
such it exposes the truth about the sinful condition of humanity. It 'unmasks our
fundamental condition' and 'lays bare the dark chasms of the human heart' (Inbody
2002: 158). Seen from this perspective, the cross can in itself cause repentance.
The cross is also seen as a symbol of historical evil trying to overcome good, of
self-giving love, and of commitment and obedience to a cause. Most of this group
reject outright the traditional interpretation of the death of Jesus as effecting an
atonement for human sin. They take an exemplary view of the saving work of
Jesus. Exemplarist soteriology has little room for such concepts as atonement –
in the sense of expiatory sacrifice, or substitution – of Jesus taking our place in
bearing the penalty of sin, or justification – of being counted righteous in the eyes
of God. This group do not understand the death of Jesus in these terms at all. They
interpret the phrase 'Jesus died to save us from our sins' in the following way:

Richard

'*I do believe he died to try and save us ... to take us away from that sort of sinful behaviour.*'

Kathleen

'*He wanted us to change ... he wanted us to rethink our values.*'

John

'*It isn't that he takes our sins ... I see it in a different kind of way.*'

'*When we say he died for us and took away our sins, I think I see it as ... I can't quite find the words to express it ... but it is the same as seeing other people go through a very hard time in that you are actually with them.*'

'*I think by seeing Christ on the cross ... the removal of our sins ... I don't think it wipes out anything that we have done wrong at all ... um ... putting it in the eyes of God that we have been forgiven ... is a helpful way of your feeling better about yourself ... but you still have to face up to the people that you have hurt or whatever ... it doesn't alter that at all.*'

Bruce

'[It is] *much more of a statement about dying for people.*'

'[It is about] *the ultimate sacrifice.*'

Bruce finds the analogy of people in war who sacrifice their lives for others, a helpful one for making sense of how Jesus' death can be said to save us. Jesus' death '*was a bigger version of that kind of thing*'. Bruce does not consider the cross '*to have taken sin away*'.

Ben

'*We have translated his death into that sort of phraseology. It is how we want to see it.*'

For Ben, forgiveness does not come through Jesus' death on the cross. Forgiveness is something we '*hope and pray for*'. 'Jesus died to save us from our sins' is always given an exemplarist interpretation for which the death of Jesus does not provide the basis that enables God to forgive sin. Exemplarist soteriology is illustrative not constitutive. It does not claim that salvation depends on what Jesus is said to have accomplished on the cross or that the cross achieves anything without which salvation would not be possible. It sees the significance of the cross in terms of its effect on human beings rather than on God. For this reason exemplarist theologies of the cross are also spoken of as 'subjective' theories.[1] For this group the salvific possibilities of the cross lie in its impact on human beings, and salvation, for those who are happy to use the term (and not all are), issues from the new possibilities for human existence that the ministry, life and death of Jesus open up. Jesus '*shows us how to live*' and in that way he is a saviour. Following Jesus' way results in salvation. As Richard puts it:

> '*If we conducted ourselves in the manner and the example that he did, we would be saved. We would not commit any of the sins of the nature that he is illustrating. And life and the world would be a much better place.*'
>
> [Salvation from sin is] '*salvation from a community almost eating itself or degenerating ... salvation from sort of moral or physical standards ... um ... those would seem to be the two sort of key areas that I would see.*'

The womanist theologian Delores Williams (like many others) makes the same point, insisting that Jesus came to show humans life: to show salvation through a perfect vision of right relations with God, creation, neighbour and self; and that salvation is about 'God, through the *ministerial* vision, giving humankind the ethical thought and practice upon which to build a positive, productive quality of life' (Williams 1993: 165). It follows that for Williams, and this present group, it is Jesus' whole life that brings salvation and not just his death. The cross, in itself, does not redeem humanity and only has soteriological significance in the context of Jesus' life as its climax and summation. Salvation consists in the transformation from destructive patterns of living to creative ones, inspired by Jesus' vision of right relations with God, creation, neighbour and self. This way of approaching salvation is similar to the approach of eastern Christianity, which sees salvation as the gradual transformation of human beings into the 'likeness' of God, where 'likeness' refers to 'assimilation to God through virtue'. This 'assimilation to God'

---

[1]   They are also called 'humanistic' or 'liberal' or 'moral influence' theories.

was also frequently called deification or divinization (Greek *theosis*). Deification or divinization is the goal of salvation (Ware 1963: 216–24; Lossky 1975: 97–110; Nellas 1997). This eastern understanding of salvation contrasts with the western view, which (as mentioned in Chapter 1) has primarily considered salvation to hinge upon Jesus' atoning death.

The impact of Jesus' death (and life) upon human beings cannot be fully mapped out. As the data above show, it can take the form of inspiration and encouragement to the believer to model herself upon the moral and/or religious example of Jesus. It can also take the form of inspiration and encouragement to persevere in situations of human suffering. John, who spoke of Jesus as 'the representative human', talks about the cross being symbolic of human suffering:

> '*Jesus represents humanity* [...] *He is us in that situation* [so that] *I really see myself on the cross, having stood up for something ... like possibly during the war-time or whatever'*. [Jesus' suffering] '*is something that I can share in, although I am not experiencing the full horror of it and so in a way it is relieving something out of me'*. [The cross] *is a help. A release I think of the pressure that is on you* [...] *and it is a pattern to follow'*.

Identification with Jesus lies at the heart of this soteriology. For John, identifying with Jesus on the cross is salvific, bringing release and healing. For those who suffer, the cross can be a consolation and a help in their troubles, showing them, as Nora says, that they '*aren't on their own*' in their suffering. It can empower a way of life that trusts God even in the midst of suffering and it can engender hope that life will win over death in the end. On an exemplarist understanding, the story of Jesus' death has power, in itself, to transform lives and effect salvation, and does not need to be overlaid with any kind of satisfaction atonement theory.

The data also show that the language of sacrifice, on an exemplarist reading, signifies the heroic and costly action on Jesus' part, especially in the giving up of his life, freely and willingly. The cross represents a 'sacrifice' only in that it represents Jesus giving up his life. This is how the language of sacrifice is used by this group; they do not use it to denote an expiatory sacrifice. The language of the cross as a victory is interpreted as '*Jesus having the courage to stand by his beliefs right the way to the very end*' and '*not giving up*'. This chimes in with

Tillich's approach. He interprets the victory of Christ on the cross as a victory over existential forces which threaten to deprive us of human existence. The power of the cross and resurrection lies in Jesus' triumph or victory over all the powers of negativity that can enslave us (Tillich 1957: 191–208). Paul Fiddes, in a similar vein, asserts that Jesus' victory over the power of sin in its many forms is a past event that 'creates and enables a victory in our lives in the here and now'. He writes:

> The victory of Christ actually creates victory in us ... The act of Christ is one of those moments in human history that 'open up new possibilities of existence' ... Once a new possibility has been disclosed, other people can make it their own, repeating and reliving the experience. (Fiddes 1989: 135–6; cf. 2007: 186–9; Macquarrie 1977: 324–5)

The story of Jesus has power to actually create victory or courage or perseverance or hope, and so on, in the believer. Exemplarist soteriology cannot thus be reduced to simply affirming Jesus as an example to follow; there is much more to it than that, as the data clearly indicate.

The Cross as a Demonstration of the Love of God

The type of exemplarism discussed so far has focused on the power of the influence of Jesus' ministry, life and death to transform lives and thereby effect salvation. But there is another type of exemplarism present in the sample – one that focuses on the cross as a demonstration of the love of God.

Numbers are difficult to pin down here. Several people (nearly all women) mentioned the passion and death of Jesus as revelatory of God's love, but their soteriological focus usually lay elsewhere. Like Peter Abelard, to whom the moral influence theory is usually traced, they were not pure exemplarists. Although he strongly emphasizes the subjective impact of the cross, Abelard does not reduce the meaning of the cross to a demonstration of the love of God. This is only one component of his soteriology, which includes other traditional ideas concerning Jesus' death as a sacrifice for human sin (Quinn 1993: 281–300). At least two of the women, however, both of whom hold a functional Christology, focus exclusively on the cross as a demonstration of the love of God and eschew all talk of Jesus' death as an atoning sacrifice. In both cases the cross viewed as a demonstration of God's love has had a profound impact on their lives, as these extracts illustrate.

Hilary

'I can't put into words the significance of that for me now ... that Jesus was willing to give up his life ... I find it hard to come to terms with that immense sacrifice.'

'I just feel so grateful. I just feel such gratitude. I feel so indebted ... I feel such amazing respect for somebody who could send their Son ... or see their Son be crucified in such a painful way ... Also to know that I am loved as well. I feel real comfort in that.'

Jill

'I remember when I read, and this was before I had my own children, the part where it said, "And God so loved the world that he gave his only Son", and I thought ... well it just meant so much to me to think that somebody could be willing to do that for somebody else. Not that God is a somebody, you know, but that any entity could give ... so ... for other people ... was such a huge thing and I felt ... thought ... after I had my own son, it meant even more.'

'And appreciating that Jesus, as a man on the earth at that time, was willing to give his life for other people. That was such a huge thing.'

In this kind of exemplarism, the cross primarily symbolizes the love of God for humanity. There is a shift in emphasis here as the interpretation of Jesus' death takes a theological turn. Jesus' death is not just another example of human self-giving love; God is involved. The cross as a demonstration of the love of God for humanity is a central aspect in the New Testament understanding of the meaning of the cross. It was this theme that was emphasized by Abelard, for whom the purpose and cause of the incarnation was to show how greatly God loved us, and to lead us to love God more. He writes:

His Son has taken upon himself our nature and preserved therein in teaching us by word and example even unto death – he has more fully bound us to himself by love; with the result that our hearts should be enkindled by such a gift of divine grace, and true charity should not now shrink from enduring anything for him ... everyone becomes more righteous – by which we mean a greater lover of the Lord – after the Passion of Christ than before, since a realized gift inspires greater love than one which is only hoped for. (Abelard 1956: 283–4)

Abelard highlights the subjective impact of the love of God in Christ, as do the interview extracts just cited. Hearts are 'enkindled' and inspired to love by the love of God in Christ. The story has power to create or generate love within the believer and to effect a profound change on the self. In this type of exemplarism (usually here called the moral influence theory), Jesus reconciles God and humanity by showing God's love to humanity in such a compelling way that humanity is inspired to respond in wonder, love and praise. So too for both Jill and Hilary, Jesus' death demonstrates the depth of God's love for them and evokes from them a response of love and gratitude. The story of Jesus' death and the notion of God that it embodies transforms their attitudes and lives. '*To know that I am loved by God ... It makes such a huge difference*'. Such knowledge is salvific.[2]

For these two women, salvation comes through the experience of encountering the love of God revealed supremely in the passion and death of Jesus. That God gave his Son '*knowing that it would end in a mortal death*' effects atonement. Again, the story – but this time a different aspect of it – is salvific in itself and does not require to be theologized as an atonement for human sin. Jill is '*not very comfortable*' with such theologizing. She rejects satisfaction/substitutionary theories of atonement, considering them to be '*quite a negative and punishing and retribution sort of approach that doesn't sit very easily with how much I think God loves us*'. Her salvation theory is much simpler: Jesus saves by revealing the depth of God's love. Or as Hilary puts it, '*God just loves me and that's all I need to know really. Basically, he just makes me feel, well, "I love you" . Full stop. That's the end of the story for me*'. Therein lies salvation.

---

[2]   For others in the sample the cross is anything but a symbol of the love of God. Their responses will be discussed in the next chapter.

Traditionalist Soteriology

Around one-third of the sample fall into this next category. They are mainly women, all of whom have a functional Christology. What characterizes this group is their lack of any explicit atonement theology. They cannot articulate a theology of the cross at all, questions about the cross eliciting little response beyond the repeating of set formulae. They have what I will call a traditionalist soteriology. This label is borrowed from Robert Towler, who identifies a particular type of Christian religiousness that he calls traditionalism. The very essence of traditionalism is 'unquestioning acceptance'. Traditionalists 'believe in everything conventionally included in the Christian religion', but cannot explain 'what they believe or why they believe it'. They have an attitude of 'taking for granted' and the reasons for belief are rarely examined. What is striking about this particular form of religiousness is 'the necessity of believing, rather than what is believed' and the obligatory nature of the prescribed beliefs. 'There can be no question of degrees of belief in this type of religious attitude: it is all or nothing. The tradition must be accepted *in toto*' (Towler 1984: 80–93). These characteristics appear to be typical of this group.

A Traditionalist Interpretation of the Cross

Atonement theology is carried in the language of the liturgy and hymns and this group are likely to have learned their atonement theology from there, since they rarely hear a sermon preached on the theology of the cross and they do not study the Bible. 'Jesus is the Lamb of God who takes away the sin of the world'; 'God so loved the world that he gave his only Son Jesus Christ to save us from our sins'; 'he put an end to death by dying for us and revealed the resurrection by rising to new life'; 'calling to mind his death on the cross, his perfect sacrifice made once for the sins of the whole world'; 'Lord, by your cross and resurrection you have set us free. You are the Saviour of the world.' These phrases and sentences are all taken from the service book which the sample use.[3] Such discourse is part and parcel of the church's worship and all of this group will be familiar with it, being regular churchgoers. When asked to comment on such language, however, most

---

[3] See 'Holy Communion Order One', *Common Worship* 2000: 166–205.

are at a loss and are unable to make any further theological comment, beyond repeating the set phrases given by the tradition or saying, '*I just accept that*', as if the discourse was self-explanatory. They '*just accept*' that Jesus came into the world to save sinners: '*that is what Christians believe*'.

Marion

'*Well that is what we are told in the Bible isn't it? He came to save us from our sins etcetera.*'

'*And you just accept what is there don't you in a way ... and you are brought up with it.*'

'*I suppose he did all that, didn't he, for us, because it was what God wanted him to do, wasn't it? That was the idea I suppose.*'

'*I think ... he did save us. He came here to save us really, didn't he ... through God. As I say, my faith really is quite simple. And I don't delve too much into it.*'

Rose

'*Well I do think of him as being a Saviour I suppose, but ... not too much about it. Um ... I suppose you do think of him being a Saviour.*'

'*Yes. Saves us from ... yes. I think ... I suppose so* [laugh].'

'*I suppose he saves us from our sins, from whatever ...* [voice trails off].'

Elizabeth

'*Well, as we are told, he was sent to save the world, to save us sinners ... And I think that's the crux of your faith really, isn't it? God so loved us that he sent his only, well he created his Son ... sent his only Son ... that sounds weird ... but he sent ... he had to suffer for us, so obviously ... I'm losing the thread ... tell me what did he ... ?*'

There is no explicit theology of atonement or salvation here. This group's theology is hidden and not readily available for inspection. They have great difficulty articulating their soteriological beliefs, just as they did their Christological beliefs. Regarding the soteriological significance of Jesus, two main reflex responses are given: '*he came to show us how to live*' and '*he died to save us from our sins*'. For this group, it is axiomatic that Jesus is saviour, but they cannot easily say in what way(s) Jesus is a saviour or give an account of how the cross of Jesus is salvific. Haight writes:

> Because of the fullness of the experience of salvation, and the amplitude of its existential reality, no single definition of salvation can confine its meaning. The result is that the meaning of salvation remains elusive: every intentional Christian knows what salvation is until asked to explain it. (Haight 1999: 335)

This group say that Jesus as saviour has existential meaning, but they cannot conceptualize or articulate that meaning. Whatever is 'known' by the believer is hidden from immediate self-awareness; they cannot easily give voice to the concrete experiences of saving encounters with God. They use the language of the tradition, but *'don't think about what it means'* and do not want to either. Rose, like most of this group, is not interested in *'going too deep into things'*. She *'has* [her] *beliefs'* and is content for them to remain unexamined. One of her beliefs is that Jesus died to save us from our sins. She has other beliefs too that she is equally certain about: for example that God forgives sin and everyone is going to heaven. But she is unable to make any comment on how these beliefs might be connected to the death and resurrection of Jesus. Commenting on her very certain belief that everyone will go to heaven she says, *'I must have believed that from somewhere I think ... in Sunday school days or somewhere, you know ...* [voice trails off].' Christianity is a set of beliefs that *'you just have'* and *'you just accept'*.

Others do make statements which connect the cross with forgiveness of sin and eternal life, saying, *'Jesus died so that we would all be forgiven'* and *'Jesus died so that we might have eternal life'*. But beyond these simplest of formulations, which are in effect no more than set answers, little more is generally said. This group (and others in the sample) do not present with fully worked-out theologies of salvation. Instead what we have here are a cluster of beliefs which coalesce around the death and resurrection of Jesus, but these beliefs do not form a logically coherent whole. Sociologists of religion have made the same point. For 'the average believer', says Towler, Christianity is in practice 'much more like an amalgamation of beliefs and practices held together by their common association with the church rather than by their logical relation one to another' (Towler 1974: 153). Bernice Martin and

Ronald Pluck, commenting on the construction of 'nomos' or a meaning system that will help us make sense of our world, write:

> ... it may well be that articulated intellectual *coherence* is only infrequently a feature of 'nomos' construction ... In short, *system*, if by that we mean logically coherent pattern, may be exactly the wrong word to use of the phenomenon: it is more like a patch-work quilt or much-mended net than like a system. (Martin and Pluck 1976: 47–8)

Academic theology seeks to systematize beliefs. Ordinary theology, on the whole, does not. 'Most people's practical belief is, probably, non-systematic'. It exists 'in clustered bits and pieces' (Davies 2002: 19, 21; cf. Stringer 1999: 179). Yet there is evidence of some reasoning, albeit apparently confused. Elizabeth says,

> '[Jesus] *saved us. He forgave us our sins and if Jesus hadn't come and done that how could God show, you know, that sinners were forgiven? Because I think otherwise if you had sinned ... gosh I've sinned and I'm never going to go to God ... but Jesus showed us that sinners are forgiven, so it's never too late to change. Whereas you could sin and think I'm a hopeless sinner and I'll never be saved so you would just go on sinning wouldn't you?'*

Underlying this thinking is an acceptance of the idea, fundamental to the Christian story, that sin separates humanity from God and that through Jesus the Christian receives forgiveness of sin and the promise of everlasting life. And Jesus' death was crucial in this: '*He had to suffer for us*', Elizabeth asserts. Jesus had to suffer and die in order that humanity might be forgiven. But she cannot go beyond this to give any kind of explanation as to why. '*You just take things for granted. A Christian believes these things. You just accept them.*' Diane is the only person in this group to give any hint of a causal explanation when she says '*his dying because he was so good, is the only way he could save everybody else really, because that is what God has said*'. There are hints here of the overarching Christian myth – of the Fall from paradise and of the need for a Redeemer, someone without sin who could undo the effects of the Fall and restore humanity to relationship with God – but no detailed account. What this group has is a story – an outline of the Christian myth

– which they keep in their heads *in fragments*, rather than as one overarching, coherent epic (cf. Sykes 1997: esp. xi–xiii).They can be said to have a narrative or story soteriology, albeit a fragmented one, as opposed to a systematic or analytical soteriology.

Turning to the liturgy and the New Testament we see that they are rather short on explanations too. The New Testament has been described as containing 'clusters of idea-complexes' to explain the crucifixion (sacrifice, ransom, obedience, etcetera). Stephen Sykes suggests that these idea-complexes, found in the liturgy and hymns as well, offer a variety of 'explanatory hints' as to how the event of the crucifixion plays a part in God's plan of redemption, but that these explanatory hints and suggestions are mostly undeveloped in these contexts. He argues that it is characteristic of theological communication in these contexts 'to allude to, rather than spell out' the meaning of the idea-complexes or themes. Only in atonement theories are they fully developed (Sykes 1997: 15–17). All these idea-complexes, together with the related 'sin-guilt-responsibility-freedom' nexus of ideas, will have been internalized by this group over many years of churchgoing (Sykes 1997: 42). They cannot expand on these ideas, but this does not seem to matter to them. Their theology is more imagistic and metaphorical than conceptual. It would seem that some people do not need explanations or atonement theories. They can manage perfectly well without them. Christianity 'works' for them, even though, '*I haven't really thought about it*'.

It works for them primarily at the level of affect. Primary expressions of faith, such as hymns and the liturgy, do not attempt to give a reasoned account of the truth claims that they make. The words of the liturgy and hymns provide 'a series of pegs on which to hang conscious or unconscious recollections and reflections'.[4] The familiar words of the liturgy and hymns ('Who on the same night that he was betrayed'; 'he opened wide his arms for us on the cross') become the 'carrier of rich layers of meaning and emotion and a range of implication incomprehensible in its depth and indefinite in its extent' (Sykes 1997: 13). The liturgy carries great emotional rather than cognitive weight in the faith-experience of this group and others also. Questions about the cross invariably evoked emotional rather than doctrinal (cognitive) responses, indicating that feelings, not doctrine, are primarily

---

[4]   Sykes (1997: 13) is here talking about creedal recitation, but the same principle applies to other liturgical language and hymnody.

associated with the cross. This issue will be discussed further in Chapter 8. My focus in this chapter remains on the doctrinal stances adopted by this group in respect of soteriology.

Forgiveness Without an Atoning Death

As we have seen, many in this group have learned to connect the death of Jesus with the forgiveness of human sin, but are quickly in difficulty when asked to give an account of how or why the two are connected. Without an understanding of the Jewish atonement and sacrificial rituals, the explanations are not obvious. A few of this group, however, like others in the sample, namely the exemplarists and some of those with soteriological difficulties, do not appear to connect their belief in a forgiving God with the event of the cross at all. Their belief in a forgiving God seems to bear little or no direct connection to the cross. It is to the understanding of this wider group (which includes these traditionalists) that I now turn.[5]

It is around the forgiveness of sins that the piety of many seems to revolve. As Kathleen puts it, '*we all know we are flawed*', and several comment that one of the reasons for going to church is to receive absolution, the forgiveness of sins. '*That's part of going to church. We want to be forgiven ... we want to be ... to try harder ... you know.*' '*That is why you go to church ... to say you are sorry and to try and put things right.*' There is widespread acceptance of the belief that God is a forgiving God, who freely forgives all those who truly repent. As Diane says:

> '*I think if you sort of pray about it and ask God for forgiveness then you sort of expect that he will wipe the slate clean. Whether that is too simplistic a view. But that is why you pray for forgiveness. You know what you have done isn't right and God knows it isn't right, but if you deeply believe and are sorry for what you have done then I believe that God takes that on board.*'

This belief is not dependent on the need for an atoning human death. The data suggest that many effectively bypass the traditional atonement theology surrounding the

---

[5]   Most of my groups are exclusive, but there is an overlap here between some of the traditionalists, the exemplarists and some of those with soteriological difficulties. The data quoted in this section are, however, primarily from traditionalists.

cross. Traditionally in academic theology, God's forgiving is concentrated in the central event of the atoning death of Jesus. But in much ordinary Christology, belief in God's forgiveness is largely independent of the death of Jesus. Many see Jesus as the agent of God's forgiveness and love, saying that '*Jesus taught ... that God will forgive sin*'. Jesus was God's messenger, offering God's forgiveness of sins for all those who repent. Michael Winter argues that the teaching of Jesus on this matter is 'unambiguously clear': reconciliation with God requires nothing more nor less than that forgiveness is asked for, the only prerequisite being repentance (Winter 1995: 88–9).[6] Hick holds a similar view. In the Lord's Prayer for example, we are taught, says Hick, 'to ask for forgiveness for our sins, expecting to receive this, the only condition being that we in turn forgive one another. There is no suggestion of the need for a mediator between ourselves and God or for an atoning death to enable God to forgive'. He sees this same principle at work in other places in the gospels too, such as the parable of the Prodigal Son where the father forgives his son without demanding any reparation. It can also be found outside the gospels in other New Testament writings (for example, 1 John 1:8–9) and in the Old Testament (for example, Hosea 14:2–9) (Hick 1993: 127–8; cf. Marshall 1978: 460–1, 604–13).[7]

Many in the sample operate on the same principles. There is divine forgiveness for all who truly repent. No form of satisfaction or compensation is required as a precondition of acceptance back into a loving relationship with God. All who ask for forgiveness, with penitence, are reconciled to God. Divine forgiveness for all who truly repent obviates the need for an atoning death. If we learn that God is a gracious and forgiving God from Jesus' teachings and ministerial practice, it follows that Jesus' death was not strictly necessary. As Charles puts it:

> '*I may need correcting on this, but my own belief is that it wasn't necessary for* [Jesus' death] *to happen to get God's forgiveness ... I mean, if he is a forgiving God and always has been and is eternal, I don't think it needed Jesus to do what he did in AD 30.*'

---

[6]   Forgiveness actually takes various forms in the gospels and the necessity of repentance as a prerequisite for forgiveness is disputed. See Wilmer 2000: 246; Fiddes 1989: 175–9.

[7]   For further examples of forgiveness without compensation in the gospels, see Winter 1995: 88–90.

But how can this claim be reconciled with the Christian tradition that the passion and death of Jesus were central to the whole process of salvation? Charles, like others, ends up going down the exemplarist route. The cross and resurrection reinforces '*the great story of God and God's forgiveness*'; it makes it '*more convincing*' and '*reinforces what Jesus taught and that is that God will forgive sin*'. Jesus' life, death and resurrection, was God's way of showing to humankind that he loves and forgives us. '*That was the way in which God assisted us to overcome our sinfulness and it is an example of the way in which God permanently loves us*'. The traditional language of sacrifice is '*not very helpful*', but serves to '*embellish the principle ... that God is prepared to forgive sin*'. The significance of Jesus with respect to forgiveness lies in his embodying forgiveness, as opposed to achieving forgiveness on our behalf through his death on the cross.

The data suggest that many opt (often unconsciously) for the more straightforward belief in forgiveness without the need for an atoning death, because they find such a belief easier to understand. Charles says:

> '*I just ... I don't know quite what forgiveness of sins really means. I do know that we spend our lives sinning and we shouldn't ... you get into all these terribly technical things about atonement and forgiveness. You can actually wind yourself up into the most awful ... it all becomes terribly complicated I think, unless one has done a theological degree. I haven't studied this and I can't explain all the details of this. I simply ... to me ... very simply ... God and Jesus together are prepared to forgive sins.*'

As we shall see later, some explicitly reject belief in an atoning death because they find it morally unacceptable, but the majority seem not so much to reject belief in an atoning death as to fail to understand it. Asking for forgiveness is not complicated. Understanding how the shedding of Jesus' blood effects atonement is. Skyes contends that in our contemporary world there is little natural understanding for the idea that 'without the shedding of blood there is no forgiveness' (Heb. 9:22) and wonders what people make of the complex and difficult passages in Hebrews or Romans where atonement is explained. Not a lot, he suspects; and observes that 'without considerable and repeated explanations' (which the sample are not given) congregations today are unlikely to be able to explain atonement

(Sykes 1977: 4). It would seem that people only take what they need. That God freely and graciously forgives repentant sinners is sufficient for their religious needs and it is this simpler, but no less profound theology, that is learned from scripture, the liturgy and hymnody. The more complex atonement theology that is also represented through these media is essentially ignored.

Reducing atonement to the request for forgiveness, without any need for prior satisfaction or payment, is simple, in the sense that it is not complicated; but this does not mean that it is an easy option. The request for forgiveness, when it is heartfelt, implies that the sinner has resolved to change their way of life, and the need for moral conversion is stressed by many. God is a forgiving God, but '*it mustn't stop you trying not to sin*'. '*I mean you have got to improve. Do better next time.*' Considerable emphasis is placed on the need for self-examination, sincere repentance and the need for conversion of thought and deed. This is connected to another belief that is very important for many traditionalists, and others besides, namely, belief in eternal salvation through merit.

Eternal Salvation Through Merit

Many in the sample appear to understand the word salvation primarily in next-worldly rather than this-worldly terms. Certainly life after death is really important to traditionalists (and others besides).[8] For them, '*that's what faith is all about*'. But some in the sample (around six) attach far less importance to belief in life after death ('*I'm not that bothered about it*') or else are agnostic about it ('*I'm not sure that I believe in an after-life.*')[9] Many would contend that one of the reasons why Christianity has ceased to be attractive to so many people is its after-life focus: life after death is not 'good news' for those do not need this belief or hope for their lives to have meaning (Borg 1997: 2). But for the majority of this sample eternal life is '*very important*'.

---

[8] Again, there is some overlap here with other groups.

[9] One survey shows that 78 per cent of churchgoers of various denominations believe in life after death. See Francis 2000: 181. A more recent survey of *Church Times* readers shows that 88 per cent of committed Anglicans believe that there is life after death. See Francis, Robbins and Astley (eds) 2005: 31.

Elizabeth

'[My faith] *makes a purpose in life. I mean, if you hadn't a faith, all be it a simple faith, what, where are you going? At least you are living for something in the future ... there is a point in living ... I think it is only that hope that keeps you going at times.'*

Tom

'I'm convinced that there is an after-life ... I don't see any point in being on the earth if there isn't an after-life.'

It is not just Christians who believe in life after death, but for the Christian the grounds for hope of eternal life lie in the death and resurrection of Jesus.[10] Life after death or eternal salvation is made available and possible through Jesus. As the liturgy (and New Testament) puts it, 'God so loved the world that he gave his only Son Jesus Christ to save us from our sins, to be our advocate in heaven, and to bring us to eternal life' (*Common Worship* 2000: 168 – based on John 3:16). Jesus was raised, Paul claims, as the 'first fruits' or guarantee that believers will also be raised (1 Corinthians 15:20, 23) with an immortal, 'spiritual body' (15:44) and it is Jesus' resurrection that is traditionally emphasized as the ground of hope for the Christian's own resurrection. However, the data suggest that many have never considered the grounds for their belief in life after death and they do not connect this belief in any specific way with the death and resurrection of Jesus. Life after death is '*inbuilt in Christianity*', but as to the grounds for this belief, '*Do you know, I honestly don't know. I just accept that it is part of Christianity.*' There appears to be very little therefore that is specifically Christian about this belief. It is '*just something that I believe*'. Here is yet more evidence in support of the claim that much ordinary theology is unsystematic and disconnected.

The irrelevance of Jesus' death and resurrection to eternal salvation is confirmed by the evidence of Pelagian tendencies throughout the sample, evangelicals excluded. Many talk about eternal salvation being dependent, not on belief in

---

[10]   Another survey shows that churchgoers are more likely to believe in a life after death than non-churchgoers (78 per cent compared with 53 per cent). See Buckler and Astley 1992: 399.

Jesus and/or in what Jesus has done, but on how this life is lived. They can be said to have a 'Parable of the Sheep and the Goats theology' (Matthew 25:31–46).

Tom

'*I do actually try now to put things in the plus pan of the scales.*'

'*I ... think what would God think when it comes to judgement day.*'

Valerie

'*I think that only good people will be saved.*'

Kathleen

'*When we are lined up* [laugh] *and we are being judged, the fact that we went to church every Sunday ... is not actually going to weigh up as to whether we were morally a good person. To my mind that would be much more important than how often you went to church.*'

'*If there is life after death ... then only the morally upright will get it ... that's what is being preached at us. That you had to deserve it.*'

'*That is certainly the impression that comes across to the lay person who hasn't done a lot of study about it.*'

'*If you have got to be so deserving, then I probably wouldn't get there anyway* [laugh] *... so as far as I'm concerned it is not worth worrying about or thinking about.*'

Sheila

'[Salvation] *is not automatic. I've heard vicars say coming to church is not an automatic salvation. There is more to it. You should live ... the life ... but that doesn't mean to say you can't be forgiven a few times. It doesn't mean you will go to heaven just because you have been to church. It depends how sincere your prayer is and how you live your life.*'

Jan

'*Sometimes I think* [the idea of salvation] *is all a load of cobblers and sometimes I get really worried and think I ought to do the right thing because I have my immortal soul to consider.*'

Richard

*'I personally do think that if you conduct yourself in a manner akin to Jesus
Christ and the way that he behaved and you listen to God and what God is
telling you, that you will have ... there is another life.*

There are obvious similarities with Pelagian thinking shown by many in the
sample, who both emphasize the importance of personal moral responsibility and
play down the role of Jesus' death in achieving salvation. Over half of the sample
consider Jesus' role as exemplar to be of prime soteriological significance.[11]
However, unlike Pelagius, they also recognize that human beings fail and
constantly require God's help and assistance (grace) to live a life pleasing to God.
They do not have a religion of works alone. Their thinking, 'like much Christian
thought, is in tension, glorifying the amazing grace of divine forgiveness while
being cautious lest justice, virtue, and order are undermined by too much of it'
(Wilmer 2000: 246). They pray for forgiveness in the present and hope for it in the
future at the final judgement where *'you will have to answer for whatever you have
done on this earthly life'*. In such a scheme, an atoning death has little part to play.
But for some in the sample Jesus' atoning death is absolutely crucial to salvation.
It is to their theology that I now turn.

Evangelical Soteriology

Substitutionary Atonement

The substitutionary theory of atonement is a widely accepted hallmark of
evangelicalism and all the evangelicals in the sample subscribe to a version of this
theory. What is surprising is that nobody else does. No other person in the sample
speaks about the cross in the same way as the evangelicals. Admittedly, certain
aspects of the theory are present in the theology of some of the traditionalists, but
it is always inchoate – a full-blown theory never emerges. The traditionalists never
offer an explanation as to how the death of Jesus on the cross effects atonement and

---

[11]   See below, pp. 144–7.

the forgiveness of sin; the evangelicals all do so, using a characteristic phraseology and theology which is illustrated in the following extracts.

Dorothy

'Jesus paid the price for me on that cross. He was sent by God and even if I was the only one, that's what God would have done ... because I feel ... well that's the way I have been taught I suppose, but that is the way I've felt as well ... and just realizing the cost that Jesus paid, the price he paid for me.'

'... it was God's plan. It had to be, because that was the only way ... because God, sorry Jesus, is perfect, God's Son ... and there had to be a perfect sacrifice for the sin of ... um ... me ... of the world ... Jesus was the only person ... figure ... God ... um ... you know ... God's Son was ... um ... the only thing that could actually wipe the slate clean.'

'Because I mean we have all fallen short of what God planned. God planned a good creation that he had made and for people to live in harmony and because of sin everybody wants their own wishes and they, including me ... um ... do their own thing and ... that way there is a separation between ... there cannot be communion between God and me because of the sin that I have done. Jesus is the way that that bridge can be ... um ... that gulf can be bridged between God and me and um ... so I mean I see him as a bridge to God and um ... a sacrifice that was given for me.'

Paul

'Jesus died to pay the ultimate price for everyone's sins. Once and for all.'
'Jesus paid the penalty for all those things I had done wrong.'
'[Jesus] died for the sins; to set us free from the chains of bondage.'
'I think a penalty had to be paid because of the grand scale of sin.'
'The reason that he was on the cross was that he could pay the debt for people that have done wrong things in their lives.'
'The reason that he died on the cross is me ... I have contributed somewhat to all the pain and suffering that he went through ... the pain and the suffering he has gone through is because of people like me.'

Peter

'Our sin separates us, separates me from God. And this idea that God is holy
and perfect and there has to be some way of dealing with the things that separate
me from God ... the fact that [sin] *creates a barrier, a separation between us*
and God and that in order to deal with that barrier, to make the bridge if you
like, Christ had to die on the cross to pay for our sins or to meet the demands of
justice for our sins.'

'God through Christ paid that penalty. God pronounced what the penalty was,
but at the same time he actually paid the penalty himself in order that we could
actually ... that there wouldn't be a barrier between man and God. So that is why
the cross is so central, from my perspective, because without the cross the barrier
would remain.'

The length of these extracts indicates that the evangelicals, in contrast to the majority of the sample, all had a lot to say about the cross. This is because substitutionary atonement is the cornerstone of their theology. The extracts are peppered with the set phrases of substitutionary atonement theory. Paul Zahl, an evangelical theologian, asserts that 'the content of theology is the substitutionary atonement of Christ'. It is 'the fulcrum for all theology' (Zahl 2000: 58, 52).[12] Substitutionary atonement has its roots in Anselmian satisfaction theory. It can employ a variety of categories (for example, penal, victory, sacrifice – as the extracts above show), but at its heart is Jesus as our substitute. Jesus pays the price for sin 'in our place': he does for us what we cannot do for ourselves.

Substitutionary atonement is constitutive (or 'objective') and not illustrative (or 'subjective'). Unlike exemplary atonement, it *does* claim that salvation depends on what Jesus has accomplished on the cross and that Jesus achieves something for humanity – something without which salvation would not be possible. So concepts which were absent from exemplary atonement – such as expiatory sacrifice, substitution and justification – are all present here.

It would appear that the evangelicals have explicitly learned substitutionary atonement theology during the process of socialization into evangelical Christianity.

---

[12]   In recent years the diversity of evangelical thinking on atonement has been recognized, see Jones 2010: 44. On the recent heated debates within British evangelicalism regarding substitutionary atonement, see Holmes 2007: 125–30.

They have not just implicitly learned it from the liturgy or hymns. As the data from the rest of the sample show, this just does not happen. Rather, they have been specifically taught it. Although evangelicals have a theology of the cross, however, they do not engage in systematic theological reflection any more than anyone else. Like many of the traditionalists, they too *'just accept'* the theology they have been given and are quickly in difficulty when pressed for further clarification. Paul, for example, after reciting the scheme he had been taught, then said, '*I've never actually thought about why Jesus had to die on the cross for our sins ... an analytical mind might want to know. I just accept it.*' Or as Peter says,

> '*You look at the mechanics of ... you can explain in a sort of transaction way what happened on the cross, but you know, that still leaves so many unanswered questions. You know, about why God should do it and how he did do it. And I suppose I don't dwell on those things.*'

No one ever expressed any objection to the interpretation of the cross which they have been given. Indeed, they all considered substitutionary atonement to be the required theory for every true Christian. A Christian was *'someone who has accepted that Jesus paid the price for their sins on the cross'*. But the satisfaction and substitutionary theories of atonement, as mentioned earlier, face considerable pressure in academic theology today.[13] J. Denny Weaver for example, a pacifist theologian, argues that satisfaction atonement allows 'accommodation of the violence of the sword' and rejects satisfaction atonement in favour of a nonviolent account of atonement. In the course of his argument he states that 'satisfaction atonement, which assumes that God's justice requires compensatory punishment for evil deeds committed, can seem self-evident in the context of contemporary understandings of retributive justice in the North American as well as worldwide system of criminal justice' (Weaver 2011: 3). But my data suggest otherwise. Many of the sample have heard a recitation of satisfaction atonement and tacitly reject it. Something about it offends. They are *'not very comfortable'* with it. They do not buy into its schema of retributive justice. There is avoidance of any model of God as the author or agent of the death of Jesus and of any suggestion that the cross of Jesus was a necessary part of God's plan or will. The image of God which

---

[13] Various critiques will be mentioned in the next chapter in dialogue with the data.

such models embody is clearly unacceptable to many. As Jill says of substitutionary atonement, '*it strikes me as quite a negative and punishing and retributive sort of approach*'. Many in the sample seem to opt for a different kind of justice, one that is satisfied by repentance and a turning to God as did the Prodigal (cf. pp. 106–9 above).

When objections were raised in the interviews against substitutionary atonement with a couple of the evangelicals, the force of this argument was generally acknowledged, but there was a reluctance to engage in discussion, since to do so '*would be threatening*' to faith. Substitutionary atonement and the doctrine that Jesus is God are both essential elements of this version of Christianity, so it is not surprising that any challenge to their veracity will almost inevitably provoke a defensive response. Substitutionary atonement will always appeal to some, especially, says the feminist theologian Julie Hopkins, where feelings of guilt, insecurity and inadequacy are running high: 'To be told the "good news" that Jesus' death takes away guilt and eternal damnation need not be feared because Jesus' blood has paid the price for sin, can bring enormous relief' (Hopkins 1995: 48). But substitutionary atonement is not the whole of evangelical soteriology.

A Personal Relationship with Jesus

Mention must be made, albeit very briefly, of another key feature of evangelical soteriology, namely, that Jesus is an experienced reality in the life of the believer.[14] All of the evangelicals, bar one, talked at length about Jesus as a present reality with whom they have a personal relationship. Much is made of the need for personal conversion in evangelicalism and of '*letting Jesus into your life as Lord and Saviour*'. Being a Christian '*means accepting what Jesus has done for you on the cross and ... letting him into your life*'. Personal conversion involves coming to know Jesus in a direct, immediate and personal way as '*the Lord of your life*'. It involves 'a particular kind of experience of encounter and appropriation of Christ within one's inner life, viz., to be "born again" in an immediate and direct experience of God or Christ or Jesus as a loving and present companion in one's

---

[14]   The experience of Jesus as a present reality with whom one maintains a personal relationship is not actually exclusive to the evangelicals. The piety of at least three of the functionalists (all women) is also of this type.

inner life' (Inbody 2002: 79–80). All the evangelicals in the sample talked about their conversion experiences and of '*coming to know Jesus*'.

Evangelical piety, which has its roots in pietism, places considerable emphasis on the religion of the heart. Jesus must be known personally, directly and intimately in one's heart rather than in one's head. As such, some would argue that evangelical piety is a distinctive form of mysticism. Inbody, for example, argues that evangelicalism offers, through its soteriology, a distinctively modern version of the mystical tradition:

> The tradition of direct, immediate knowledge of God or Christ or Jesus has a distinctly modern Protestant form, viz., North American evangelical Christianity. Salvation by faith alone is thought of not so much in terms of justification and imputed righteousness through divine grace (as in the Protestant Reformers), but rather in terms of a direct, immediate awareness of God as a loving and forgiving God (assurance) and Christ or Jesus as an immediate and constant companion in one's heart or by one's side. Saving faith is mystical knowledge of immediate union and continuing companionship with Jesus in one's heart. The person who has 'been saved' knows that God or Christ or Jesus loves her or him with a direct, intuitive awareness that goes beyond the bonds of any kind of 'normal' knowledge, including the 'normal' religious knowledge in the means of grace provided by the church, such as reading Scripture, reciting creeds, participating in the liturgy, or any other kind of ecclesial mediation. (Inbody 2002: 76)[15]

At the centre of evangelical soteriology, then, is a mystical experience of Jesus as a loving and present companion in one's inner life. And this companion is '*everything*'. He is everything because he is the friend who is always to be relied upon, the constant companion who is always near, the healer and restorer who brings new life. The following extracts illustrate the phenomenon:

Susan

'[Jesus] *has been a constant companion to me. There is never a moment that I am not aware of his presence beside me. It is just the most wonderful glorious relationship.*'

---

[15]   English evangelicalism, we might argue, adopts a similar position.

'Oh I love him. I just love him. He has just become everything to me ... He has filled every gap that there was in my life, every need that there was and there were many and he has just led me through and completed areas of my life that were empty and barren.'

'Whatever happens to us, whatever difficulties there are in this life ... he will bring us through and show us the way.'

Hannah[16]

'[Jesus] is my dearest friend. I ... I mean ... you know ... um ... he is a person who is always with me. I talk to him. Constantly apologize to him. I know that I don't live up to his ... desires are for me. But, equally, I know that he would never let me down. And ... I'm trying to think ... there is great comfort in the spirit of him.'

Dorothy

'[Jesus] is the most dependable friend that you could ever have. Somebody that is completely supportive in the sense of, yes, you have made a mistake, but I love you still ... in spite of the error of your ways and ... yeah ... I think really it is the best friend that you can have.'

Pat

'[Jesus] has completely revolutionized my life.'

'It was as though I was in a very, very deep pit, covered with sticky spiders' webs. And I was struggling to get out. And I was being helped out by Jesus.'

Paul

'In a nutshell, Jesus is my everything. That says it all. He is what my family are to me, but more. And nothing is more precious to me on this earth than them. Put what value I have on them and multiply it a hundredfold and you have got Jesus.'

Around seven women and one man talk about Jesus in this way – as an invisible, spiritual presence in their hearts. The Jesus who resides in their hearts is the risen

---

[16]   Hannah is not one of the evangelicals. She has a functional Christology and an exemplary view of atonement.

Christ '*who has gone to heaven and then comes back to your heart ... a spirit*'. But listening to these people speak, some will just as easily talk about God being with them as Jesus. God and Jesus are often used interchangeably, suggesting that 'Jesus' is a label or name for a felt experience. What really matters is the *experience* – the experience of love, acceptance, assurance, healing, intimacy and companionship. But which Jesus do believers have in mind when they say that Jesus is with them as their constant friend and companion? According to Harold Bloom, the Jesus who stands at the centre of American evangelical piety is a very solitary and personal American Jesus. Furthermore, he is the resurrected Jesus rather than the crucified Jesus or the Jesus who has ascended to the Father. 'When they speak, sing, pray about walking with Jesus, they mean neither the man on the road to eventual crucifixion nor the ascended God, but rather the Jesus who walked and lived with his Disciples again for forty days and forty nights' (Bloom 1992: 32). Or as Inbody puts it, 'Jesus is the resurrected friend, walking and talking to me along the side of the road or "beside the Syrian sea" or "in the garden" in moments of private luminosity with the repentant sinner. "He walks with me, and he talks with me, and he tells me I am his own"' (Inbody 2002: 87).

There is no direct evidence from the data to suggest that the Jesus people inwardly converse with is Jesus, the resurrected friend, and more empirical work needs to be done in this area. Quite what connections there are between the Jesus of the heart and the Jesus of the gospels remains unclear. Kuitert claims that the Jesus of the heart is certainly not a first-century social prophet; he is more like a teddy bear! 'Jesus has to be there for comfort, just as a child has to take its teddy bear to sleep peacefully.' In the type of 'Jesus-mysticism' outlined above, Jesus becomes the vehicle 'by which people can express their religious longings, their need for acceptance, for comfort' and its emotional value cannot be overestimated (Kuitert 1999: 198–9). The data clearly show that Jesus as a constant companion in one's heart or by one's side brings much reassurance, security and comfort. Knowing Jesus in this way is reported to be transformative, that is, salvific. So, for the evangelicals in the sample, Jesus saves in two main ways: he saves through his atoning death and he saves by being a constant companion.

To summarize the soteriological findings so far: the evangelicals and the exemplarists, who together make up just over one-third of the sample, both have their own distinctive, if antithetical, theologies of the cross. The traditionalists have what can only be described as a passive theology of the cross; leaving just under a third of the sample unaccounted for. This last group are united in finding the cross '*very difficult to understand*' and can perhaps be said to have a confused theology of the cross. The next chapter seeks to address some of their difficulties or '*muddles*'.[17]

---

[17]   Some of these difficulties are experienced by the exemplarists and traditionalists as well. Those with a 'confused' theology of the cross nearly all have a functional Christology.

Chapter 7

Soteriological Difficulties

Saved From What?

For those who have a confused theology of the cross, the key technical terms – atonement, redemption, salvation – all '*do not have much meaning*'. Such vocabulary is 'dead capital'. It has no 'legal tender'.[1] The term salvation is virtually meaningless for many as they have no sense of having been (or being) saved. The idea does not seem to relate to their own religious experience at all. '*Saved from what?*' they ask. This coheres with Wiles' observation that, 'For people today the language of "salvation", the whole idea that men and women need to be "saved", has far less resonance than it did in the past' (Wiles 1999: 75). Words like salvation and its associates 'saviour' and 'save', fail to 'touch down' in people's experience (Sherry 2003: 2). The data show that it is not just these words which fail to communicate meaningfully. Much of the traditional soteriological language fails to touch down also. Unlike the traditionalists, those with a confused theology of the cross admit to be puzzled by many of the traditional soteriological affirmations and openly acknowledge their lack of understanding. The phrase 'Jesus died to save us from our sins' typically elicits this kind of response. Sheila, a life-long churchgoer, says:

> '*I don't understand what "he saved us from our sins" really means. I think that is a difficult one.*'
> '*I don't quite understand redemption. Yes. I know what is said and I listen to it, but I'm not quite sure ... what saving from our sin means ... or ... well, that's it. I could have a lesson or two on that* [laugh]. *Could you describe what you understand by redemption?*'

---

[1] To borrow phrases from Keck 1972: 158.

It has been said that 'Christ Jesus died for our sins according to the Scriptures' (1 Corinthians 15:3) is the single most frequently used lens through which Christians in the New Testament came to understand Jesus (Zahl 2000: 52). The data suggest that many today have difficulty understanding Jesus through this lens. They cannot make sense of the language. They do not know what conclusions to draw from it. The traditional ways of theologizing the death of Jesus, using ideas of forgiveness, salvation, sacrifice, penalty, remission of sins, substitution, justification – to name just a few – do not seem to connect with many in my sample. They find such theologizing of Jesus' death '*very difficult to understand*'. It follows from this that they are not attaching the same theological significance to Jesus' death as the tradition does. Haight highlights the difficulties when he writes, 'The language of Jesus suffering for us, of being a sacrifice to God, of absorbing punishment for sin in our place, of being required to die to render satisfaction to God, hardly communicates meaningfully to our age. These concepts do not intersect at all with present consciousness' (Haight 1999: 241). And in a similar vein, Monica Furlong says:

> If the Christian churches are to survive their present crisis then they need to find, as the early Christians did, new language and fresh thinking. Slapping down the old money – unity, salvation, hope, the Son of God, forgiveness – as if it is still legal tender, will not work. We bite the coin and find it counterfeit.[2]

The reasons people gave for their puzzlements with the traditional soteriological language are many and various. Those most frequently cited are mentioned below. (It must be said that not every soteriological difficulty is felt by all.)

Where is the Evidence?

Several find it hard to make sense of the claim that Jesus came to save the world from sin, because of the lack of any empirical evidence to substantiate such a

---

[2]   Cited in Sherry 2003: 2. The original citation comes from a review by Monica Furlong of Pope John Paul II's book *Crossing the Threshold of Hope* in the *Independent* in 1994. Cf. Wakeman 2003.

claim. If Jesus has saved the world from sin why isn't there more evidence of it? In view of the persistence of sin and evil in the world, the claim that Jesus has saved the world from sin can seem presumptuous if not offensive, especially to those who are particularly sensitive to the problems of human suffering.

Edward

'I don't understand the concept that Jesus came to save us from sin. I don't understand ... I mean that almost implies that BC there was this massive amount of sin. Jesus comes along and saves us all and then you know, somehow AD, it is all different. I don't understand that.'

Suzanne

'To say that Jesus died for our sins ... I have trouble relating to that because we are still sinning now, but he died all those years ago and I can't relate the two things together.'

Sin, evil and suffering, the perennial foci of the human condition, have not been 'made well' through Jesus' death on the cross. '*Sin did not cease to be once Jesus had come*'. Evil continues to ravage the world. Therefore how can sin and evil be said to have been dealt with? The same problem is raised by the Japanese novelist Shusaku Endo in his novel *The Samurai*. The samurai is looking at a crucifix and is puzzled:

'I ... I have no desire to worship you,' he murmured almost apologetically. 'I can't even understand why the foreigners respect you. They say you died bearing the sins of mankind, but I can't see that our lives have become any easier as a result. I know what wretched lives the peasants lead in the marshland. Nothing has changed just because you died.' (Endo 1982: 173; cf. Sherry 2003: 23)

The samurai had been told that Jesus would save all mankind, but he could not understand what that salvation meant. Jews too are puzzled by the problem of how Christians can believe that the world has indeed been saved. Martin Buber has said that 'to the Jew the Christian is the incomprehensibly daring man, who affirms in an unredeemed world that its redemption has been accomplished' (Buber 1963:

40). In view of the lack of apparent evidence that the world has indeed been saved or redeemed, how can the death of Jesus 2,000 years ago be said to have made such a difference? The world does not look redeemed and these Christians do not feel redeemed.

Colin Gunton is aware that the power and persistence of sin and evil in the world makes the constitutive (or 'objective') view of atonement vulnerable to attack. He raises the question of whether 'the real evil of the real world is faced and healed *ontologically* in the life, death and resurrection of Jesus', and argues that there must be some sense in which this is true. If not, he fears a slide back into exemplarist (or 'subjective') understandings of salvation which deny that salvation for the whole world depends on what happened on Good Friday (Gunton 1988: 165). But why is there not more empirical evidence to demonstrate that the particular event of Jesus' death has effected such a change? Gunton accounts for the limited empirical effects of the Christ event by insisting that the ontological healing of real evil in the real world has to be 'realized' (in the sense of 'made real') in time and space by and through human responses (Gunton 1988: 170). He also finds resources for defending the constitutive claim in eschatology. The response to the empirical embarrassment of failing to show clear evidence in support of the constitutive claim is often defended by stressing the eschatological dimension of Christ's saving work. As Vernon White argues, 'Because the full effects of reconciliation are "kept in heaven" then we should not expect to see it all empirically realized in this world, either within or beyond Christendom'. So, to the extent that the main effects of Christ's victory are conceived as taking effect in the eternal realm rather than in earthly history, the constitutive claim can be asserted 'without fear or favour from historical evidence (or lack of it)' (White 1991: 17). But this defensive strategy is unlikely to convince those, like Edward, for whom life after death is '*not something that is particularly important*'. He is more concerned about life before death. What use is it for him to know that real evil in the real world has supposedly been healed ontologically in some other world? What help is that in the midst of this-worldly struggles against historical evil? When what matters is salvation from sin and evil in this world, Edward finds his exemplarist account of atonement sufficient; and besides, it is the only one that helps him.

Why Did Jesus Have to Die?

As mentioned above, the mythic language and mythic symbolism of atonement theology (cf. incarnation theology) is considered by many to be unintelligible in a postmodern culture. It is certainly unintelligible to some of the life-long churchgoers in my sample. Eleanor has attended an Emmaus course (as have several of this group) and had substitutionary atonement explained to her by her evangelical housegroup leaders, but she still says:

> *'What I have raised a query about, is why did Jesus have to die? I'm still ... I don't understand why Jesus had to die for the sins.'*
> *'I find* [the cross] *all a bit complicated* [laugh]. *I think I will forget about that one ... what I don't understand is why he had to die for our sins.'*

Every 'explanation' of the cross which she has been given has failed to convince. She just cannot understand why a death was necessary for God to forgive sin. As Mary says, it was *'totally unnecessary'*. As we saw in the last chapter, others also have difficulty with any claim about the necessity of an atoning death, indicating that there is a widespread problem with this idea. If atonement, understood as the forgiveness of sins through the death of Jesus, is indeed the very heart of the faith, as many contend it is, then the fact that this idea is problematic for so many must surely be a cause for concern. But the difficulties for this sample are obviously not that grave – after all they are all still regular churchgoers. That the problems with such a key concept can so readily be laid aside, suggests that atonement is not the very heart of faith for them; they do not place as much emphasis on Jesus' death as academic theologians (or the evangelicals) do. It may be said that they tend to circumvent atonement. They can do this because they have no need for a redeemer or mediator, substitute or representative to 'do something' about sin. It does not follow from this that they have a weak or inadequate understanding of sin – the charge usually levelled against non-constitutive theories of atonement. Rather, the data suggest that it is precisely because they take the power and persistence of sin and evil in the world so seriously that they cannot accept that somehow it has all been 'dealt with' on the cross.

Puzzlement arises from the fundamental soteriological claim that the cross reconciles God and estranged humanity. The most oft-repeated query was, '*Why did Jesus have to die?*' One of the basic problems is that people cannot see why a specific act is required in order for reconciliation to occur. The fact that the specific act is a '*hellish violent*' and '*gruesome*' crucifixion only exacerbates the problem. This response may be even stronger now for those who have seen Mel Gibson's film *The Passion of the Christ*. Many in the sample have never felt that their being 'a sinner' has prevented them from entering into a relationship with God. Because they experience God as always willing to enter into a relationship with them, they cannot understand why Jesus' death was necessary for God to be able to accept sinners. If God is loving and forgiving now and always has been, then why was Jesus' death necessary for God to accept sinners? Such puzzlements make the constitutive claim that the death of Jesus achieves forgiveness of sin for the whole human race difficult to accept, and help explain why the majority of the sample opt for a theology based on God's free forgiveness for penitent sinners.

Puzzlement also arises from the how question concerning the causality of Jesus' saving work, as well as the why question. How can the shedding of one man's blood actually effect forgiveness for the sins of the world? There is a consensus among many modern writers that the New Testament is silent about the causality linking Jesus' death to the forgiveness of sins. The writers of the New Testament certainly make no attempt to offer a causal explanation as to how the death of Jesus effects atonement. The workings of sacrifice, for example, are never explained and no proper theory is ever given as to how the act of sacrifice could remove sin and guilt from individuals or communities.[3] Michael Winter complains that many modern authors also fail to solve the question of causality convincingly. But reasonable explanations are, he claims, what today's enquirer, be she agnostic or believer, so urgently needs. He writes:

> The modern reader, who finds the death of Jesus so repugnant ... desperately
> needs to be given a positive and cogent account of how humanity was liberated
> from sin, in order to make sense of an apparently senseless crucifixion. The

---

[3] Michael Winter gathers together a number of modern writers who all agree that the New Testament offers no explanation as to how the atonement was effected. See the references cited in Winter 1995: 30–7. See also 11–27.

intrinsic efficacy of sacrifices no longer convinces the modern mind, and contemporary enquirers are entitled to something satisfactory with which to replace the ancient convictions about blood offerings. (Winter 1995: 30)

Winter offers his own explanation to the question of causality: Jesus secured reconciliation for the human race by intercession, by asking for our reconciliation with God (Winter 1995: 87–114). I have my doubts whether the believers studied here would find his solution any more compelling than any other. As Valerie says:

'Occasionally when it is discussed on the radio I do listen on purpose. But I suppose I have given up because every explanation that they try to give, or I have heard given, is unsatisfactory. I find it unsatisfactory ... But I have a sneaking suspicion that I will never feel at ease with it, no matter what explanation is given to me.'

Unlike Winter, none of this group feels the need to defend a constitutive view of atonement. They therefore do not need explanations in the same way that constitutivists do. For many, Jesus' death *is* a senseless crucifixion: '*Why couldn't he have lived a lot longer?*' They find it very hard to see how a positive evaluation can ever be put on such a '*heart-breaking*', '*violent*', '*horrendous*' and '*cruel*' event. Haight asserts that 'the strange and tortuous explanations' that are generally given of how the cross could have been positive and salvific cannot begin to make any sense to a postmodern imagination (Haight 1999: 345). These data suggest that he is right.

A Sadistic God?

There is evidence that the primary reason why some people prefer '*not to think too much about* [the cross]' and its meaning is not because they have no need for an atoning death, although this certainly seems to be the case, but because they have an innate aversion to '*all that suffering*' and to the notion that something as '*awful*' and '*horrendous*' as the killing of Jesus could possibly accommodate a positive interpretation. How can the suffering and death of Jesus be anything but evil?

What can possibly be good about Good Friday? Atonement is 'territory strewn with images and assumptions of violence' and some of the women in particular (around five) are put off by this (Weaver 2011: 2). Atonement theology can be said to start with violence – with the killing of Jesus – and the data suggest a deep repugnance to this violence, which may account for low attendance at Good Friday services. As Jan says:

> *'I am very squeamish about physical pain. I'm someone who hates going to the dentist. So I don't like to think too much about* [the cross]. *And then the Methodist hymns that I learnt as a child. Man of sorrows and things. Why am I singing about this? Um ... so that is all muddled.'*

That this violent death was in any way necessary or required for the salvation of sinful humanity is something they *'just don't understand'*. *'Such a violent death. And then the spear in the side. It's all ... oh I think it is heart-breaking'*. There is considerable antipathy towards turning the crucifixion of Jesus – the killing of an innocent victim – into something good. Traditionally the cross has been celebrated as something good because it resulted in the salvation of sinful humankind. Without atonement what is there to celebrate about the cross? Only atonement for human sin puts the good into Good Friday and, as we have seen, for many in the sample (not just these five women) this is missing.

Inevitably, there is also some resistance to the idea that Jesus' death and suffering was in any way required by God to make salvation effective, for what kind of God would require it? A God who expects or demands the death of his only Son is *'a cruel Father figure'*, or as Julie Hopkins puts it, 'not a God of love but a sadist and a despot' (Hopkins 1995: 50). Valerie says:

> *'When Jesus cries from the cross, "My God, my God, why have you forsaken me?", I always think that that is the most sympathetic thing that he ever says. Because you do, you think, where the hell were you and why did you let him go through that? And I have always thought that they are very powerful words. And sometimes I feel a little bit alienated from God in some of those ... particularly when it comes to the Easter time, because it was ... perhaps it comes down to one of the television programmes I saw at a very young age ... it is an horrific*

story. It comes down to, how could God put Jesus through that? And you always think, whenever you watch it or hear it, perhaps something will happen and he will get let off and he never has to be crucified. But maybe there is that masterful thing ... it all comes back to Milton doesn't it ... all that masterful thing about God being a bad person and a cruel Father-figure to actually put him through that [...] So God as a sort of omnipotent big bully ... that's never really left me.'

It is the contention of many pacifist, black, feminist and womanist theologians that not only the traditional sacrificial view of atonement, but also the satisfaction and substitutionary models, have promoted a punitive view of God. What kind of God can require his own dearly beloved Son to suffer on a cross? Is this not a picture of God as a sadist, a monster, a tyrant, a '*big bully*'? Certainly, for those such as Valerie, the cross does not function as a symbol of God's love, as it does for others in the sample (see above, pp. 98–100). She cannot see it that way: a God of love would never have allowed Jesus to go through the crucifixion. Rather than demonstrating the love of God, the cross reveals God to be '*a cruel Father figure*'. For Valerie, the difficulties with traditional atonement doctrine stem from the interpretation of the death of Jesus as a sacrifice. She says:

'I don't believe in sacrifice in that sense anyway. You read those awful things. About that torso that was found in the Thames. I mean it has all those resonances about it. As soon as people mention sacrifices and first-borns being slain, I just don't understand it.'

'Every year when we come around to Easter and this sacrifice ... the issue of sacrifice and the lamb to be slaughtered to save us from our sins ... how, you know, Jesus being crucified on the cross helps me be saved from my sins. I don't understand.'

Because the ancient practice of sacrifice and belief in the powerful religious efficacy of shed blood is completely alien to the modern mind, it is not surprising that most people today find the idea of human or animal sacrifice, as expiatory or propitiatory, abhorrent. Sacrifice, certainly in this sense, has become a dead metaphor. But some theologians whilst recognizing this, still want to carry on using it because 'the notion of sacrifice, tired and misused as it often is, remains a matchless conceptual expression of the theological significance of all that Jesus began and continued among us' (Gunton 1988: 127; cf. Fiddes 2007: 183–5). However, for people like Valerie, the language of sacrifice only has negative connotations and remains an unhelpful, dead metaphor, which has no currency, serving only to promote a negative view of God. Not only can the idea of Jesus' death as a sacrifice suggest placating an angry God, it can also suggest that God in some way demands the blood of the innocent victim before he will enter into relation with his people. This raises moral questions, and can also appear sado-masochistic. Because the metaphor of sacrifice can so easily be misunderstood, many other theologians have advocated abandonment of the metaphor altogether. Feminist theologians, in particular, have been strident in their criticisms. They were the first to use the image of divine child abuse (now commonplace in atonement discussions) to portray the suffering of Jesus at the hands of the Father, provocatively claiming that, 'Divine child abuse is paraded as salvific and the child who suffers "without even raising a voice" is lauded as the hope of the world' (Brown and Parker 1989: 2). Some would say that to conceive Jesus as the victim of divine child abuse is to commit the sin of reading metaphorical language literally, but the feminist critique is (in part) levelled against the language of metaphor being treated literally. In the feminist critique, 'Father', 'Son' and 'sacrifice' are all models (systematic and relatively permanent metaphors) that have 'gone astray' by being treated literally and used exclusively (McFague 1982: esp. 145–94). When the language is taken literally (as it is by Valerie) it is not surprising that the image of abuse in traditional models of atonement offends. Many feminist critics then go on to make the point that the image of divinely sanctioned abuse, which appears in the traditional theories of atonement, functions to justify and reinforce the suffering and acceptance of abuse by Christians, and especially by women. In Joan Carlson Brown and Rebecca Parker's view, the central image of Christ on the cross as the saviour of the world who 'died for our sins' communicates the message that suffering in general is redemptive. It is claimed that the image of divinely sanctioned, innocent suffering has contributed to the victimization of women both in churches and society, because Jesus, by functioning as *the* model of innocent and passive submission to abuse, encourages women to also submit passively to abuse and reinforces their role as victim. This kind of atonement theology is thus said to encourage 'martyrdom and victimization'. It is even claimed that, 'The image of God the Father demanding and carrying out the suffering and death of his own son has sustained a culture of abuse and led to the abandonment of victims of abuse and oppression'. Because it sanctions a sacralization of suffering and abuse, traditional atonement theology is considered to be 'an abusive theology that glorifies suffering', and should be done away with (Brown and Parker 1989: esp. 2, 3, 9, 26). Some feminist critiques also voice specific concerns about the effects of atonement theories upon women's psychological, spiritual and physical well-being. They argue, for example, that instead of 'saving' women, the death of Jesus only deepens their guilt, for if woman had not caused sin in the first place (by tempting Adam with that apple) then Jesus would never have had to suffer to save humanity from sin. Jesus' suffering cannot therefore be salvific as it only serves to reinforce feelings of guilt and unworthiness in women who already feel guilt at having caused the sin that made the suffering necessary (Ruether 1989: 31–41; 1998: 95–107).

It is unclear to what extent the feminist critique can be applied to the women in the sample. The data show that at least one woman rejects the traditional sacrificial view of atonement because it suggests both a sadistic God and divine child abuse, and others are clearly troubled by it. But the full impact of the traditional atonement theology on the behaviour and attitudes of those who imbibe it through worship is difficult to assess as the interviews were not designed to explore this. My instinct is that those who question the traditional atonement theology are far less likely to be negatively influenced by it than those who passively accept it, as the evangelicals and the traditionalists tend to do. But this can be little more than a guess. What the data do suggest is that many of the women in the sample are far more discriminating than many feminist theologians presume. They do not internalize the supposed 'theology of abuse' implicit in the liturgy and hymnody, but resist it. Valerie, for example, says, '*I hate the business that it is Eve that tempts Adam*' and dismisses the story of the Fall (along with much of the teaching of St Paul, whom she considers to be a misogynist) as '*not very helpful to us*'. There is no passive acceptance of blame or guilt evidenced here. Hopkins asserts that 'When theologians, missionaries, and preachers blame on a subjugated people or an inferiorized sex the sins that lead to the death of Christ and demand penitential self-denial, the result is not redemptive'. When women are blamed for the sins that lead to the death of Jesus they are 'loaded with a sense of interiorized guilt and self-hatred'. Atonement theology is thus 'a recipe for depression and self-hatred' (Hopkins 1995: 50–4). Brown and Parker make the same point, saying that atonement theology, because it reinforces the victim role for women, 'can lead to destruction of the human spirit through the death of a person's sense of power, worth, dignity, or creativity' (Brown and Parker 1989: 7). There are hints in the data that this could be happening with some, but equally there is strong evidence of resistance to the scapegoat and victim role in others. Suzanne says, '*I suppose I don't like to think of him being put to death because of my sins*', and Pat remarks:

> '*I've always found Jesus' death rather difficult* […] *When I went to church, not long after I had become a Christian* […] *in the communion service there is a bit where it says something like, Jesus died for you, he laid down his life for you. There are a lot of "for yous" in it. And I found myself becoming very, very uncomfortable and feeling acutely guilty. And what I wanted to stand up in church and shout was, "I didn't bloomin' well ask you to die for me. What are you talking about? I didn't ask you to do that"* […] *So I have always had a bit of a hang-up about the cross. I have never really got deeply into it. I tried … I did try desperately hard to get into it.*'

Both Suzanne and Pat go on to report an increased sense of self-worth and value since '*going back to church*' or '*becoming a Christian*', indicating that whatever their difficulties with traditional atonement theology might be, they do not prevent them from experiencing Christian salvation: a salvation that is most likely to be mediated via Jesus, but which has little to do with his cross, certainly as the cross is traditionally interpreted. This leads on to the question of how Jesus does save, if he does not save by atoning for human sin.

How Does Jesus Save?

As we have seen, the data quite clearly show that much traditional atonement theology and language is a stumbling block to many. Some find it offensive; most are simply puzzled by it. Either way, it is beyond dispute that the traditional ways of interpreting the cross do not communicate meaningfully to a number of the sample. The data show that those who find the traditional atonement theology difficult or puzzling, or even offensive, simply circumvent it. They *'put it on one side'* or *'park it'*, saying *'there is too much else that is important to let that get in the way'*. They do not allow the difficulties it presents to get in the way of their spirituality. One wonders, of course, how many others have not been able to do this. For how many is traditional atonement theology a barrier which they cannot circumvent, a barrier which prevents them, not necessarily from appreciating Jesus Christ, but from participating in organized religion? Only further empirical work among non-churchgoers can answer *that* question.

Some academic theologians (such as Gunton) argue that the language of traditional atonement theology is still usable and continues to contain rich treasures of meaning for Christian thinking about the cross. Many others, however, insist that it functions only as an obstacle to faith and should be removed from contemporary liturgies and Christian teaching about redemption. Ruether argues that 'feminist liberation critiques of the classical theology of the cross should force Christian theologians and liturgists to tell the Jesus story in a different way, a way that [she believes] is more authentic to its historical reality'. Jesus did not come 'to suffer and die' or to offer his life as the necessary means of redemption, but to bring 'good news to the poor, the liberation of the captive'. Redemption occurs 'through resistance to the sway of evil, and in the experiences of conversion and healing by which communities of well-being are created' and the symbol of the cross should be re-clothed in this theology (Ruether 1998: 104–5). Although many people do not get as far as re-clothing the cross in any articulate theology (there are hints that if they could they would follow in the same general direction as Ruether), they do effectively undress the cross of its traditional theological clothing. They do not view the cross through the theological trappings of traditional atonement theory at all. By questioning the need for the crucifixion, even considering it to be *'totally unnecessary'*, they are implicitly rejecting the traditional atonement theology. They do not consider the cross to be the pivotal point in time when God reconciled the human race to himself, nor do they perceive the cross to be a necessary condition for the forgiveness of sin. For this group of churchgoers, Christianity without atonement may be said to be their dominant theological position. The death of Jesus remains, for many, an appalling tragedy which they do not theologize into something good.

Several comment that Jesus' death had to be a very public death so that he would be '*marked out*' as the link to God. Such comments confirm that they are not interpreting the cross in terms of traditional atonement theology at all. Edward says:

> '*I suppose his whole death and his resurrection had to be done in a way that people would notice because otherwise his purpose on earth would somehow have been missed.*'

And Jesus' purpose, according to Edward, was not to suffer and die as an atonement for human sin, but to be the link to God. '*The reason Jesus came was to establish and provide a link to God ... Jesus has provided the link ... by his legacy of life on earth.*' Most people in this group point to the life of Jesus as the primary source of salvific potential. Jesus' death remains a potent symbol, as the death of any innocent victim does (especially one designated Son of God), but they do not claim salvation by it. Rather they claim salvation (if they claim it at all) through the whole Jesus event. Here the death of Jesus does not carry the same theological weight it does in academic (or evangelical) theology. Jesus died. Attaching the theological phrase 'to save us from our sins' seems to add little, but most say that they are happy to '*go along with what is given*', for '*it is part of the tradition*'. Unlike the revisionist academic theologians they do not plead for the language to be changed. These ordinary churchgoers are not theological radicals; they do not champion construction of a new set of theological metaphors, but make do with the old, even though they do not find them particularly helpful or comprehensible. This perhaps suggests that when they use the traditional atonement language in worship they may be using it expressively or non-cognitively. This interpretation will be discussed further in Chapter 8.

It does not follow that when traditional atonement theology is disregarded or is not understood, Jesus' death on the cross ceases to have redemptive possibilities. Exemplarist soteriology has shown that the cross *can* be separated from the traditional interpretations without loss of redemptive possibility or power. Revisionist theologians have similarly shown how the cross can be reinterpreted as redemptive in ways which avoid the problems of the traditional models. But as far as most ordinary believers go, these redemptive potentialities of the cross are largely unfulfilled, since they prefer to keep the cross at arm's length as '*a mystery*', something which they '*don't want to think too much about*'. Academic theology seeks to understand how the cross can be an answer to the problem of sin and suffering. Much ordinary theology would not think of looking to the cross in this way. The cross is '*an ordeal that Jesus went through*'; it is a compelling narrative, which evokes emotional rather than reasoned/articulated theological responses. Ordinary believers do not analyse theologically the narrative of the cross or look to it to provide answers to the perennial human problems of evil, sin and suffering. Rather they see it as a part of a *story*: Jesus' death is the event that climaxed his life. It is something that happened to him; they do not think through or develop the story into doctrine. They do not stake out a theological position on the cross or agonize about how it should be understood.

It has been said that Protestants unlike Catholics require a correct doctrine of atonement to guarantee access to God's grace (Weaver 2011: 2). But it would seem that many in this sample do not. For these Christians, God's grace and saving presence is not dependent on right doctrine, but is freely available to all. Churchgoing helps because it nurtures right relationship with God, but it is by no means essential. Such an egalitarian and democratic approach to encounter with God renders atonement doctrine (amongst other things) superfluous. From this perspective, salvation is no more and no less than God's self-gift or presence to a person. Jesus plays his part in this, not by atoning for human sin, but through being God's representative on earth. As such he reveals and mediates God's saving presence to humanity. In short, Jesus saves because Christians encounter God in and through him, as he bears God's love, forgiveness and friendship to humanity. For many, it is Jesus' life, as much as his death or resurrection, which mediates God's saving presence. Like the exemplarists, it is Jesus' life and public ministry that many people turn to as the focal point of his salvific activity, a life which '*opens up new possibilities for us*' and which they can more readily engage with. As Julia puts it:

> *I know the cross is pivotal ... and it is a vital part of the whole picture, but I am not hung up on it. To me the story of the life of Jesus and the things that happened when he was living are just as important as how he died and even why he died and also the things that happened after his death ... you know ... the way*

the gospel was spread, the early church, the relationship with Paul and all of those things that we can learn from there mean as much to me.

Many contemporary theologies also stress that the whole of Jesus life is important for soteriology. They emphasize the redemptive significance of Jesus' public ministry and do not 'isolate his death from his life-praxis and posit it alone as redemptive in itself' (Schüssler Fiorenza 1975: 101–2). For Delores Williams (who was mentioned earlier in relation to exemplarist soteriology) it is not Jesus' death which redeems us but his life: 'Humankind is, then, redeemed through Jesus' *ministerial* vision of life and not through his death' (Williams 1993: 167). It follows from this that it is the gospels, more than Paul's letters, that provide resources for constructing a Christian understanding of salvation that speaks meaningfully to people today. Much of the ordinary soteriology of this sample is narrative rather than conceptually-based and seems to be little influenced by the complex atonement theology of Paul. It also refuses to tie the concept of salvation too closely to the death of Jesus. As we have seen, many find it hard to understand how the death of Jesus can be said to save us and are much more comfortable with the idea that salvation comes through Jesus' life and teaching. Those who do focus on the death of Jesus as the means of salvation, that is, those who hold a substitutionary view of atonement, tend to give the impression that the life of Jesus is of secondary importance, since what really matters is that a blood price was paid. Their accounts of how Jesus saves tend to ignore both the historical circumstances which brought about his death and the redemptive significance of his life. For them, salvation comes through the cross alone. However, as the transcripts show, the life of Jesus does play a large part in their present experience of salvation and cannot be said to be of secondary importance. It is ironic that those who eschew reference to the salvific potential of Jesus' life in their theoretical accounts of salvation are the very ones who in practice are most likely to experience salvation through it, since they are the ones who engage in spiritual practices that foster salvific engagement with the life of Jesus.

Emphasizing the life of Jesus as salvific, rather than his death, brings this ordinary soteriology, like the exemplarist soteriology discussed earlier, closer to the eastern rather than western approach to thinking about Christian salvation. As we saw in the last chapter, on the western view, to be saved is to be relieved of guilt by Jesus' atoning death, whereas on the eastern view salvation is conceived of as deification. In the eastern understanding of salvation there is a strong link with the doctrine of the incarnation, since it is through the incarnation that the possibility of deification is made possible. An emphasis on the whole of Jesus' life as salvific inevitably shifts the focus of attention in soteriology onto the incarnation. One could say that these ordinary believers are redeemed by the incarnation (albeit understood functionally), rather than by the cross. Inbody would encourage such a view. He writes, 'We are redeemed by the incarnation, not the cross. It is through the power of the God who is incarnate in the life, preachings, teachings, healings, passion, death, resurrection, and promised consummation of Jesus Christ we are redeemed. Grace, grace, all is grace' (Inbody 2002: 163). The modern liberal view of salvation, initiated by Schleiermacher, is not dissimilar to the eastern understanding of salvation. One could say, therefore, that much ordinary soteriology is effectively *liberal*, as is much ordinary Christology (cf. Chapters 3 and 5). Liberal soteriologies, because they are exemplarist and therefore illustrative, do not claim that Jesus' saving work effects salvation for everyone, irrespective of whether or not they have heard about Jesus or whether they consider themselves to be Christian. This leads to a *pluralist approach* to religious truth which is what we find here. The data show that the majority of the sample are effectively pluralists with respect to religion and it is to a brief survey of this theme that I now turn.

Salvation through Jesus Alone?

Three broad approaches to the Christian understanding of the relation between Christianity and other religious traditions are usually identified, namely exclusivism, inclusivism and pluralism. In a nutshell, exclusivism holds that Christianity is the one true religion and that 'outside the Church there is no salvation'. This approach has been the teaching of the Church throughout most of its history, but today exclusivism is a minority position, usually identified with Protestant fundamentalists and conservative evangelical Christians. My data confirm this picture. It was only the evangelicals who strongly asserted that salvation was through Jesus alone and that only Christians would be saved, that is, receive eternal life:

Paul

'Without accepting that Jesus died on the cross for your sins, without accepting
that he was the Son of God, then there is no eternal life for you. Like it or not,
that's it ... when your life is over, that's it. It's over.'
'That's as cut and dried as it is. I mean, that is what it says in the Bible. The only
way to get to heaven is through Jesus.'
'I know that somewhere in the Bible it says that the only way to the Father is
through the Son.'
'People who have different faiths ... they won't go to heaven.'

Susan

'I don't agree and I never will agree that there are many ways to God, as I have
heard people say. There are many ways to Jesus, but only one way to God and
that is through Jesus.'

Dorothy

'All Christians will be going to be with Jesus ... But for those who have not
chosen to follow Jesus in this life [Jesus' second coming] will be terrible and
terrifying.'

Exclusivism, as the data show, takes an extremely negative attitude towards other
religions. Christianity is uniquely superior; it alone is the one true religion. The
exclusivist position was usually defended on the grounds that *'that's what is says*
in the Bible'. Certain texts are appealed to and read pre-critically; an exclusivist
interpretation being assumed in them.[4] A corollary of exclusivism would appear
to be missionary obligation. Since only Christians will be saved, converting
non-Christians to the Christian faith becomes imperative. Evangelism is indeed
another hall-mark of evangelicalism. It follows that on the exclusivist view only
a minority of human beings will actually be saved, since only around a third of
the world's population are said to be Christian. Exclusivism, in its extreme form,
would also exclude many Christians from eternal salvation, since *'they haven't*
accepted Jesus into their lives as Lord'. *'They know of Jesus ... but they haven't*

---

[4]   The key texts here are John 14:6, Mark 16:15–16, Acts 4:10, 12, John 3:16, 18 and
Romans 10:9–15.

yet come to that personal awareness, relationship.' A couple of the evangelicals in the sample do classify other church members as '*churchgoers not Christians*', because they have not had a 'born again' conversion experience. On this view, the exclusivist claim is not just that Jesus Christ alone constitutes salvation, through being the only 'God-man' and therefore the only person who could make a full atonement for the sins of the world, but also that knowledge of this only saviour is necessary for salvation. One must acknowledge Jesus explicitly before one can be saved. This harsh view is frequently toned down with some such rider as '*it is up to God to know what is going to happen to them ... It is God's decision*', or '*at the end of the day, my belief is that God is just and that he will do the right thing*'. This is effectively a way of dissipating any cognitive dissonance that is set up between the claim that God is all-loving and wills the salvation of all, and the exclusivist conclusion that most will in fact be lost. '*It's God's problem not mine.*' All such let-out phrases are easy ways of avoiding the serious theological problems that the exclusivist position poses.

Inclusivism is an attractive option for those Christians who want to distance themselves from the exclusivist claim that only Christians will be saved, but who want to maintain the traditional claim that the particularity of the Jesus event is constitutive of universal salvation. Inclusivism holds that salvation is available through other religions *and* that Jesus is the constitutive cause of this salvation. What truth there is in other religions is constituted by God's work in Jesus Christ. Karl Rahner is usually cited as the most significant proponent of this model. It was Rahner who coined the phrase 'anonymous Christians' to refer to those who have experienced divine grace through Christ without necessarily knowing it. No one in the sample comes close to holding the kind of Christocentric inclusivism advocated by Rahner. This, I venture to suggest, is because Christocentric inclusivism is a theological position constructed by an academic theologian for other academic theologians, that is, those people seeking an *intellectually satisfying* answer to the problem of retaining the Christian claims to finality while including all of humanity into the work of Christ.[5] Most ordinary Christians are not theologians

---

5   Rahner's view depends on a sophisticated metaphysics of the Trinity. According to Haight, 'Only by means of a theoretical or speculative, metaphysical construction can one attempt to understand how Jesus Christ had a causal influence on the salvation of those who have never come in contact with him historically, or who existed before the appearance

in this sense and besides, they have no constitutive claim to defend. They are effectively pluralists in their approach to other religious traditions.[6]

The widespread assumption throughout the sample (evangelicals excepted) that all religions are different ways to the same God is evidence of this pluralist approach.[7] Most people admitted that they '*couldn't go into it deeply*', but their view was that people of other religions '*are praying to a greater being who in their view is to them what God in the Christian faith is to us*'. On this view, Christianity is one religion among many religions leading to God. Very few saw any theological problem with adopting this approach. This is because there is no problem when one holds a functional or sceptical Christology, coupled with a non-traditional understanding of atonement for such a theology allows for a pluralist understanding of religious truth. On this view there is no theological reason for claiming that Christianity is the only one true religion or that all salvation is constituted by Jesus. The majority do not have, and never have had, a theology that would lead them to conclude that only in Jesus can true salvation be found or that Jesus caused or causes the salvation of all. In their theology, God can and does save in other ways which are not dependent on or caused by the Jesus event. They have never assumed or learned that the Bible or the Church teaches that Jesus is the only way of salvation. Therefore several expressed surprise when this suggestion was put to them. This shows that the 'traditional' view is no longer the received doctrine.[8]

This theology is consistent with the pluralist approach as advocated by Hick, one of the most significant exponents of a pluralist approach to religious traditions. He argues that Christianity is 'one among a number of human responses to the ultimate transcendent reality we call God'. The different religions are, 'so far as we can tell, equally authentic spheres of salvation/liberation, through which the

---

of Jesus'. See Haight 1999: 349. Most ordinary believers eschew such metaphysical speculation. See below, pp. 150–9.

[6]   In one survey, only 44 per cent of churchgoers hold the view that Christianity is the only true religion (Francis 2000: 181). In the recent survey of *Church Times* readers, 46 per cent of committed Anglicans believe that Christianity is the only true religion (Francis, Robbins and Astley 2005: 32).

[7]   A few people were unsure about what perspective to adopt towards the non-Christian religions and no data were available for four interviewees.

[8]   A few people were aware of the teaching that outside the church, or outside Christianity, there is no salvation, but expressed disquiet about it.

universal presence of the Real, the Ultimate, the Divine is mediated to human beings' (Hick 1993: 140–9; 1995: 27–59, 128). The pluralist position is that there are several ways to the one Ultimate Reality (which Christians call God), and that people of different religious traditions are all worshipping the same Ultimate Reality. Time and time again interviewees would say '*we are all praying to the same God*'. Marion's responses are typical. She says:

> '*God's God, isn't he ... whether he is the Christian one or the Muslim one or whatever.*'
> '[A Muslim's] *God is probably the same as ours, but just ... they see it in a slightly different way.*'
> '*It is all one God.*'

This popular attitude, that all religions are essentially different paths up the same mountain, assumes that all religions share a common object of devotion and/or a common religious experience. The apparent differences between the religions are 'merely accidental, culturally conditioned elements of time and place' (Inbody 2002: 191). As Ben says, '*if you strip away the ornament,* [other religions'] *perception of God is probably very similar or the same to one's own*'. The viewpoint that the devout in all religions are really worshipping the same God is based on a theocentric view of reality, which presupposes that there is one God at the centre of the 'universe of faiths'. The centre is not Christianity or the Church or Jesus Christ, but God. Hick argued for this kind of approach in his *God and the Universe of Faiths*, declaring that it was time to move away from the traditional view that outside the Church, or outside Christianity, there is no salvation toward the view that Christianity is but one way among many leading to God. Describing this change as a 'Copernican Revolution', he argued against 'the dogma that Christianity is at the centre', advocating rather that 'it is *God* who is at the centre, and that all religions of mankind, including our own, serve and revolve around him' (Hick 1973: 131, 120–32). The shift required here is from a Christ-centred to a God-centred approach. In his later writing, Hick recognized the problem of using the term God, a distinctly theistic concept, and reformulated his theocentric view of the other religions by referring to the Ultimate Reality or the Real.

Like Hick, those who hold a pluralist perspective in this sample speak from a particular Christian, or at least monotheistic viewpoint. Their belief that other religions are equally authentic ways of salvation is not a neutral judgement, but one founded on particular Christian views about Ultimate Reality/God, namely that God is all-loving and wills the salvation of all. Non-Christians are saved because the God whom Jesus Christ has clearly revealed God to be – a loving, gracious and forgiving God – is merciful toward all God's children and desires all humankind to be saved. Such a God would not save only a minority of human beings. Their pluralist outlook is therefore a consequence of their belief in one God, maker and sovereign Lord of all, who is a God of love and who wills the salvation of all people. They reject the exclusivist claim because it is incompatible with this belief.

Marion

'God is a God of love ... and Jesus loves us ... are they really going to condemn all these other people just because they haven't become Christians?'

Tom

'I don't believe that the benevolent God that we have would say, "tough", to everybody else ... "you are all out".'

Bruce

'I couldn't go along with [Christianity as the only way of salvation] because it actually goes against some of the things that Jesus taught in his own life. Because at the end of the day, if we are talking about a forgiving God, an understanding God ... I just don't see how that squares with ... this is the only way to do it argument and attitudes. It just doesn't gel together properly.'

Schubert Ogden similarly argues against exclusivism on the grounds that it runs counter to the core of Jesus' preaching of a God bent on human salvation. He adds that, in terms of our experience today, the experience of being saved through Jesus provides no grounds for saying that God cannot save in some other way, or that only Christians are saved (Ogden 1992: 27–52). God has no special, favoured way in which to achieve salvation; the different world religions each serve as one of God's means of salvation. The primary mediation of God's presence and salvation for Christians is the person of Jesus of Nazareth, but in other religions the fundamental mediating focus of God's salvific presence is someone/something else. Jesus is not the only norm (Haight 1999: 405–10).

There are other non-theological reasons that people give for rejecting the view that Christianity is the one true religion. Several of the sample have been influenced in their thinking about other religions through their contact with adherents of other faiths, through work, travel or their social life. At least six of the interviewees have friends and family who are practising members of another religion and they do not find them to be any less sincere or devout than they are. They recognize that Christianity is to them what Islam is to the devout Muslim or Judaism to the practising Jew. To hold that Christianity is the only way of salvation is '*arrogant*' and '*wrong*'. '*We have no right to judge*'. The exclusivist claim offends postmodern relativistic sensibilities, where each religion is seen as partial, incomplete, limited, one particular way of looking at things. Historical consciousness, one of the most recognized features of the postmodern world, has deeply influenced people's attitude towards the non-Christian religions, in that people now recognize pluralism as part of the historical conditions of human existence and are generally more open to other religions than they were in the past (Haight 1999: 395–8). It is evident that the religion to which one adheres normally depends upon the accident of one's birth. As Tom says, '*I believe in God because I was born English. If I had been born in Indonesia, you know, what would have happened?*' He goes on to say, '[If Christianity is] *right, that means that about three-quarters of the world has got it wrong. And I have difficulty with that ... How can so many others be wrong?*' Historical consciousness promotes acceptance of other religions as true (but not necessarily equally true) paths to God.[9]

Alongside acceptance of religious pluralism, there was a widespread unease within the sample, if not an outright opposition, towards missionaries and proselytising. It is worth noting that if this attitude extends towards evangelism in

---

[9]   Pluralism does not imply that all religions are equally true, and I cannot say how many of my sample hold the view that all religions are equally true, because I did not ask this specific question. One survey in an Anglican parish shows 50 per cent of churchgoers and 46 per cent of non-churchgoers affirming that all religions are equally true (Buckler and Astley 1992: 399). By contrast, in the *Church Times* survey only 11 per cent of committed Anglicans say that all religions are of equal value (Francis, Robbins and Astley 2005: 32).

general, and the data suggest that it might, then evangelistic initiatives are unlikely to receive enthusiastic support. One of the concerns expressed about a pluralist approach to other religions is that it undermines or destroys missionary outreach. Certainly it must change it, for faith in Jesus Christ can no longer be commended on the grounds that salvation is constituted by Jesus alone. For most of this sample, Christianity is '*one way of getting to God*' and there is no Christological or soteriological reason for thinking otherwise.

Before moving on to discuss more general issues to do with ordinary Christology I want to conclude this chapter with some brief reflections on the dominant soteriology in the sample – Jesus as exemplar.

The Default Soteriology: Jesus as Exemplar

In view of the fact that so many people have difficulty understanding how the death of Jesus can be said to save us, it is perhaps not surprising, although it was initially quite unexpected, that Jesus as exemplar is *the* dominant soteriological theme in the sample; the default position. For well over half of the sample, Jesus is saviour because '*he shows us how to live*'. When asked about Jesus' function and significance, they would reply by saying:

'[Jesus] *purpose was to show us what it is to follow God and how to be a good person.*'

'[Jesus was] *God's way of getting through to us humans how we should conduct ourselves.*'

'*He set out by his example the way we should all live.*'

'[Jesus was] *sent from God to teach us how to live.*'

'[Jesus] *gives us the rules for living.*'

'*He came to get us all back on track.*'

It is not just those who hold a sceptical (or low) Christology who emphasize Jesus' role as exemplar. Many of the functionalists do too, as does Charles, who holds an ontological (or high) Christology. Charles may have an ontological Christology, but soteriologically he has no need of it: Jesus does not *have* to be God ontologically in order to function as exemplar. So exemplarists can be found across the whole Christological spectrum. Robert Towler's sociological study of conventional religion makes the same point. He identifies 'exemplarism' as a type of religiousness that sees in Jesus' teaching, life and death an example for all to follow, and he offers examples of exemplarism from a wide range of traditions within the church as well as from 'the great company of the unchurched' (Towler 1984: 19–37). When people say that Jesus shows us how to live, they could be casting Jesus in the role of moral, spiritual, and perhaps even theological, exemplar. But it is Jesus' role as a moral exemplar that seems to be uppermost in many of our exemplarists' minds. Towler characterizes exemplarism as 'a moral type of religiousness' (Towler 1984: 22).

The interviews were not designed to investigate people's moral life and it was only after the data was analysed that Jesus as moral exemplar became an issue of importance. I had not anticipated Jesus as exemplar playing such a prominent role in soteriology, since in academic theology it is always the cross and atonement that dominate soteriological discussion. Only after the interviews had been conducted and analysed did it become apparent that many ordinary believers have different soteriological priorities to those adopted by professional theologians. It is not at all clear, therefore, to what extent Jesus does shape the moral life of the interviewees and further empirical work would need to be carried out to investigate the extent to which persons do allow their thinking and conduct to be shaped by the model provided by Jesus. But I do want to offer a few observations here that have some bearing on the discussion to follow in Chapter 9.

The (admittedly limited) data suggest that following Jesus' example means *'helping others'*, *'doing good acts'*, *'being nice'*, *'not doing bad and wrong things through your life'*, *'following the code of conduct'*, *'being public-spirited'*. In sum, it means *'being a good person'*. A good person is someone who follows certain lines of conduct (they do not *'do bad and wrong things'*) and who is characterized by certain virtues (they are *'kind and good'*). In Richard Hoggart's study of working-class culture in the 1950s, he reports on the working-class identifying

Christianity with morals. Doing your best to be an 'ordinary decent' person is what Christianity really means (Hoggart 1957: 87–94). This corresponds closely with Edward Bailey's more recent studies of the folk religion of English people, where '"Christianity" ... is a way of life that is readily (if anachronistically) summarized as "the Ten Commandments", or "the golden rule" or (now, only occasionally) as "the Sermon on the Mount", or by the oft-repeated paradigm of "helping a little old lady across the road"' (Bailey 1989: 155).[10] It has been suggested that this identification of Christianity with 'a rather undemanding type of kindness' may be a particularly English form of Christianity (Astley 1997: 101; cf. Towler 1984: 22). Identifying Christianity with morality in this way also means that '*you can be a Christian without going to church*', since 'being Christian' means 'being good'. Anecdotal evidence suggests that there are many in the parishes who consider themselves to be Christian but do not go to church, and my data show that some churchgoers do not consider churchgoing to be an essential part of being a Christian either.[11] '*It is how you live your life is being a Christian*'. What matters is '*being morally a good person ... that is much more important than how often you go to church*'. '*Going to church is nothing*'.

Priority is given to praxis in this type of exemplarism, but it is praxis of a certain kind. The emphasis is on personal as opposed to any form of socio-political morality. Most consider Jesus to have given a code of conduct for personal morality and little stress seems to be laid on the public or political dimensions of morality. Moral priorities are seen to rest with the local community and 'doing good' there. 'Doing good' does not seem to involve the believer in social or political radicalism and the four churches with which we are concerned here are not preoccupied with a concern for social justice. People will give money (more or less willingly) to Christian Aid or other good causes, and many are involved in various kinds of charity and voluntary work. Such praxis is challenged by liberation theologians, however, who advocate that the poverty of the poor demands a new praxis involving, not acts of generosity to alleviate their plight, but 'a compelling obligation to fashion an entirely different social order' (Gutierrez 1980: 8). These findings chime in with

---

[10]   Bailey is best known for defending the concept of 'implicit religion' – a concept that shares some similarities with folk religion. See Bailey 1998: 32–3.

[11]   The statistics from Richter and Francis' study show that well over two-thirds of their respondents believed that churchgoing was unnecessary for Christians. See Richter and Francis 1998: 12.

Nancy Ammerman's characterization of American Christians as 'Activist', 'Golden Rule' or 'Evangelical'. Activists define the Christian life in terms of social action and working for justice; Golden Rule Christians in terms of doing good and caring for others; and Evangelical Christians in terms of being saved (Ammerman 1997: 196–216). Her study of American congregations suggests that Golden Rule Christianity may be the dominant form of religiosity among middle-class suburban Americans. It appears to be the dominant form of religiosity among these rural Anglicans too.

It is also worth noting here that *if* Jesus is to be a norm for moral life, then there must be some serious engagement with the story of Jesus as portrayed in the gospels for Jesus cannot be the authorizer of the moral life 'if externally he is a stranger or a casual acquaintance about whom one knows a few stories and sayings' (Keck 2000: 167). A commitment to certain spiritual practices (such as meditative Bible study) is therefore desirable, if not essential. However, for the majority of our exemplarists, personal or group study of the scriptures is not part of their spiritual practice. They listen (perhaps) to two Bible readings when they come to church on a Sunday. One of the interviewees admits that when the scriptures are read that is the time when she '*switches off most*'. This raises the question of whether Jesus really is functioning as exemplar, and is an issue to which we will return in Chapter 9.

There is also some evidence to suggest that the morality of some in the sample is motivated and shaped by beliefs concerning the character and activity of God, rather than through any striving to be like Jesus (which is acknowledged to be impossible). These beliefs include 'we are all made in the image of God', 'all things come from God' and 'God is the God of peace'. They all have implications for how we should behave. They all 'entail practical commitments' (Volf 2002: 253). So for some exemplarists, 'doing good' may be motivated more by a desire to love and serve the Creator-Father God, than through any self-conscious attempt to follow Jesus. Exemplarists' faith is usually theocentric, and (as I shall show in Chapter 9) Jesus may not be that important for some believers. Certainly, we should not be misled by the set soteriological answer 'Jesus shows us how to live', for although it implies that Jesus plays a large part in moral life in practice he may not. Also, exemplarists talk about Jesus as '*the conduit*', '*the bridge*', '*the link*' to God, and of Jesus '*showing us what God is like*', '*acting as God*' and '*assisting belief in God*' – all of which suggest that Jesus may be more important as a *revealer of God* than he is as an exemplar of human existence.

Chapter 8

Some Formal Characteristics
of Ordinary Christology[1]

In the course of the analysis of the Christological and soteriological data in Chapters 3 to 7, various formal characteristics of ordinary Christology have come to light. In this chapter I seek to address some of these.

Ordinary Christology is Story-Shaped

The importance of story or narrative in ordinary Christology has been hinted at already. Several times in the preceding chapters I have talked about people having a story about Jesus. Chapters 3 to 7 can be thought of as explications of the various Christological and soteriological stories operating within the sample. A few people tell the story of the pre-existent Son becoming incarnate to save us by his atoning death; many more people tell the story of God creating Jesus, his Son, to show us how to live. It is always a story that is told; ordinary Christology is *story-shaped*, narrative is its preferred mode of discourse. This should not surprise since narrative is central in both religion and in human life and experience (see Crites 1989: 65–88; cf. Tilley 1985: 23–6; Cook 1997: 39–49). The conceptual language of doctrine and theology is secondary discourse that arises out of the primary language of religion.[2] McFague, for example, describes how doctrines are 'funded' by metaphors, and Terrence Tilley asserts that 'The key concepts of Christian faith – creation, fall,

---

[1]   The term 'ordinary Christology', as used here and throughout Chapters 8 and 9, is shorthand for 'the ordinary Christology of this sample'. I make no claims about the extent to which my findings can be generalized. In qualitative research the reader or user (not the researcher) determines the extent to which findings from a study can be applied to other situations. See Merriam 2002: 28–9.

[2]   On the primary language of religion and the secondary language of doctrine, see Avis 1999: 68–77 and Nichols 1997: chapters 1–3, as well as the references cited below in n.4.

incarnation, atonement, church, eternal life, trinity – are all metaphors at rest, metaphors which have become Christian doctrines' (McFague 1982: 50, 22–9; Tilley 1985: 3).[3] Cook argues that, whilst theoretical models and paradigms play an important and necessary role in religion, they should not lead to the priority of system over story. 'All human attempts at systematic conceptualization and formulation have their originating ground in stories that have metaphoric impact and must constantly return to these stories as the only adequate context for meaning' (Cook 1997: 39). There has been a turn to narrative in much recent theology. Hans Frei, for example, a leading narrativist theologian, argues that the identity of Jesus is given in the biblical narratives in an irreducible way. The Christological question 'Who is Jesus?' has to be answered by the scriptural story which is the telling of his identity. Jesus is what he did, what he said and what happened to him; and all that can never be fully explained, only described. 'One can, up to a point – and only up to a point – render a description, but not a metaphysics, of such interactive unity ... Jesus *is* his story' (Frei 1993: 35, 42).

Ordinary Christology can also be thought of as a type of narrative theology in that it too emphasizes the story of Jesus. It gives priority to narrative discourse. Gerard Loughlin asserts that any theology that remembers the story is in part narrative or narrativist in character (Loughlin 1996: x). Ordinary Christology speaks in narrative mode as it remembers the story of Jesus' birth, life, death and resurrection. Indeed it hardly thinks of Jesus in abstract terms or philosophical categories at all, but as a person whose identity and significance is given by the story. Sometimes the story may be seen through doctrinal spectacles, but as we have seen, quite often it is not. The stress on narrative can be clearly seen in the responses that were given to questions about the passion and crucifixion, for people invariably responded by telling a story. They have a story about Jesus' passion, not a doctrine. They talk about what Jesus went through – his betrayal and arrest, the carrying of the cross, his cry of dereliction and intense suffering. The doctrinal content of the story – Jesus dying to save the world from sin – is often bracketed out. Similarly, they have a story of the annunciation, not a doctrine of the incarnation.

Story is the 'first voice' of ordinary Christology.[4] And in ordinary Christology the first voice of story is usually its last word. It does not develop into conceptual

---

[3]   On the relationship between narrative and doctrine, see also McGrath 1997: 52–66.

[4]   This phrase is borrowed from William Bausch, who writes, 'Theology is a secondhand reflection of ... an event; story is the unspeakable event's first voice.' See

discourse as happens in academic Christology, where 'the narratives function within a larger, intellectually-disciplined, investigation ... so that theology cannot be reduced to storytelling' (Kreig 1988: 164). Ordinary Christology, by contrast, is largely content with storytelling and does not attempt to move into abstract, conceptual discourse. Stories suffice, I would argue, because they meet the religious and spiritual needs of most of the sample. Believers have no need or reason to abstract from them. Hence ordinary Christology is more metaphorical and imagistic than conceptual, preferring concrete images and concrete ways of thinking rather than their conceptual language and thought forms. As Bruce put it, *'You can't use abstracts with 95 per cent of the population. It doesn't work. They need something that they can visualize or hang onto'*. Ordinary Christology thus tends to eschew metaphysical speculation. It is not interested in pursuing theoretical questions, such as how Jesus relates to God or how one person can be both human and divine at the same time. It is in good company. According to Frances Young, the theoretical issue of how Christians could 'proclaim one God and one Lord ... without ending up with two gods' never seems to have troubled St Paul (Young 1991: 34). And Jesus too 'did not analyse; he addressed' (Keck 2000: 157).[5] Academic Christology on the other hand frequently specializes in metaphysical speculation and usually insists that theological reflection about the person of Jesus requires it. Macquarrie, for example, writes, 'Although the New Testament itself is almost devoid of philosophical terms, we cannot reflect theologically on its claims for Jesus Christ without getting involved in ontology' (Macquarrie 1990: 7). The affirmations that people use, from the simplest, such as 'Son of God' or 'agent of God', to more complex expressions, such as 'Jesus is slightly less than God' or 'Jesus becomes God', all have ontological implications. Academic Christology seeks to make these explicit; it is always pressing towards conceptual clarification and ontological explication. Ordinary Christology, by contrast, is not concerned with metaphysical conceptualization and speculation; it is content with the story and is untroubled by these metaphysical issues.

Bausch 1984: 28.

[5] According to Keck, Jesus' teachings 'contain no disciplined reflection on the nature and ground of the good or the just or their opposites ... he did not explain how his various admonitions and imperatives are related to each other or how they flow from a root principle' (Keck 2000: 157).

There are always exceptions, of course. Some ordinary believers will be interested in Christological speculation, as is Charles:

> *'What fascinates me is, if the Creator's Son came to this speck of dust to see*
> *us humans, what about all the rest of creation? Is he now, for example, visiting*
> *the rest of creation? Or are there very many Jesuses? Can God have very many*
> *Sons? Are there many Jesus Christs? I don't know. You don't.*

The question of multiple incarnations is still a live issue within some parts of academic theology (see Hebblethwaite 2001: 323–34). But equally there are other academics who want to bring the practice of theology back from its metaphysical to what they regard as a proper, ordinary use (see Holmer 1978; cf. Phillips 1988: 235–7). The contextual Christologies mentioned in Chapter 1 also tend to steer clear of metaphysical issues. According to Macquarrie, this shift away from metaphysical questions is 'part of a wider tendency to understand Christianity in primarily practical terms and to avoid the more strictly intellectual and theological issues'. But, he insists, 'It would be dangerously irresponsible to commend faith in Jesus Christ without having thought as deeply as possible on the grounds for such faith', and he warns against anti-intellectualism (Macquarrie 1990: 7–8). But is 'intellectualism' really necessary for faith?

Don Browning distinguishes between different sorts of reason. Practical reason 'answers the questions, What should we do? and How should we live?' He continues:

> The tradition of practical reason or practical wisdom has its origins in Aristotle's
> concept of *phronesis*. Jesus used the word *phronesis* in the Sermon on the Mount
> (Matt. 7:24) to refer to the 'wise' persons who listen to the message of Jesus and
> build their lives upon it. Reason as *phronesis* can be distinguished from *theoria* or
> theoretical reason, which is often thought to ask the more dispassionate, objective,
> or scientific question of What is the case? or What is the nature of things? It is also
> distinguished from technical reason or *techne*, which asks the question, What are
> the most effective means to a given end? (Browning 1991: 10)

Practical thinking is said to lie at the centre of human thinking; both theoretical and technical thinking are abstractions from practical thinking. As we have seen, academic Christology tends to concentrate on *theoria* or theoretical thinking whereas ordinary Christology prefers *phronesis* or practical thinking. Being a 'wise' person, one who listens to the message of Jesus and builds her life upon it, is not dependent on *theoria* or intellectual skill. In other words, spiritual depth is independent of intellectual depth. Macquarrie himself acknowledges that 'it is possible to have an existential or "saving" faith in Jesus Christ without assenting to or even understanding something like *anhypostasia*, or without having an opinion as to whether he actually stilled a storm on the Sea of Galilee' (Macquarrie 1990: 21). Faith in Jesus is not dependent on either right doctrine or cognitive skill; being a disciple hangs on neither. Academic theology is a specialist activity that a few Christians engage in. Theorizing may be a help, if not a need, for some people: intellectualism, as Macquarrie calls it, may be necessary for their faith. But for most peoples' faith, it is not. They can do without it; it does not help them in the living of the Christian life. It is not salvific for them. Does this mean that ordinary believers do not engage in doing Christology?

Do Ordinary Believers 'Do Christology'?

Every believer has a Christology, but do they *do* Christology? The majority of the interviewees had clearly not given any serious thought to Christological questions prior to the interview. (The data show that more thought had been given to soteriological questions.) Unlike the author, these believers were not on a Christological quest; they were not seeking answers to the questions regarding the nature and significance of Jesus Christ for Christian faith. The existential question, 'Who is Jesus Christ for us today?' was not their question. Many openly admitted that they were not interested in exploring their beliefs about Jesus or about God, and they did not want to subject their religious beliefs to scrutiny or enquire too closely into the grounds for believing.

> Eleanor
> *'I don't really think. My faith is just there.'*
> *'I know what I believe and I don't want to ...* [voice trails off]. *'*

Percy

'I don't really want to analyse it.'

Mary

'I haven't really thought about it too much. I've always said I didn't want to go too deeply into it, because ... um ... I think people would soon lose ... um ... you know ... if you looked into it too much.'

'I don't want to know. I'd rather just believe in what I believe in and ... [voice trails off]*.'*

Elizabeth

'I sometimes think it's better not thinking [laugh] *because it is harder to believe.'*

'I don't feel that I need to know.'

Lesley

'Oh dear, it's awful to think that you accept so much without questioning things and without really, really being absolutely sure about why you think what you think or why you believe what you believe.'

The phenomenon of reluctance to engage in critical enquiry (understood as *theoria*) is widespread amongst believing Christians. Hornsby-Smith reports that most practising Catholics 'were completely unconcerned' about theology (Hornsby-Smith 1991: 31). Theological educators frequently report being appalled at 'the vacuity' of students' Christological statements and complain of them arriving at theological college with 'an unformulated, even uninformed, set of beliefs' (Inbody 2002: 13). Unquestioning and uncritical faith is heavily criticized by many who argue that in the life of faith 'no one is excused the task of asking questions or the more difficult one of providing and assessing answers' (Barth 1961: 498). It is every believer's responsibility to seek understanding. 'Mindless fideism' is not an option (O'Collins 1983: 1). Daniel Migliore is powerfully persuasive about the need for every Christian to engage in serious theological reflection, describing theology as 'faith asking questions' and the task of theology as 'a continuing search for the fullness of the truth of God made known in Jesus Christ'. As an enquiry, theology can never merely repeat traditional doctrines, but 'continually calls in question unexamined assumptions about God, ourselves and our world'. Christian faith must be a thinking faith. He writes:

> If we believe in God, we must expect that our old ways of thinking and living
> will be continually shaken to the foundations. If we believe in God, we will have
> to become seekers, pilgrims, pioneers with no permanent residence. We will
> no longer be satisfied with unexamined beliefs and practices of our everyday
> personal and social world. If we believe in God, we will necessarily question
> the gods of power, wealth, nationality, and race that clamour for our allegiance.
> (Migliore 1991: 4–5)

Migliore recognizes that theology has not and does not always serve faith. It can become divorced from Christian life and practice and lose itself in 'pointless and endless talk', for there is such a thing as 'unfruitful, abstract theology that gets lost in a labyrinth of academic trivialities'. Theology such as this deserves to come under criticism. By contrast, the understanding that faith seeks should always bring 'wisdom that illumines life and practice'. Yet he argues that commitment to Christ can never be a matter of the heart only, but must involve the whole person, including the mind. Thinking faith does not replace trust in God or in Christ, but deepens it, whereas unquestioning faith 'soon slips into ideology, superstition, fanaticism, self-indulgence and idolatry' (Migliore 1991: 1–9).

All this is well said, but many ordinary believers remain to be convinced of the value of serious theological reflection, which they equate with alien academic study. There is a strong suspicion that studying theology, certainly in the academy, is more likely to destroy faith. There is a genuine fear that asking questions would *'take away rather than build up'* faith. There is also a widespread perception that academic theology *'has nothing much to do with the everyday person who goes to church'* and therefore *'is not something that the everyday person really needs'*. Academic theology is considered to be *'an intellectual exercise'* for an elite minority, and one that has little or no relevance to the faith and life of the ordinary believer.[6]

---

[6] Cf. Paul Holmer who writes, 'The popular view is that theology is painfully abstract, that it is a specialist's domain, that it is impractical, that it is of no use to the laity, and that it is about matters that do not and cannot concern those who are nonacademic' (Holmer 1978: 1).

It turns out on closer inspection that everyone has come up against intellectual challenges to their faith (of course, everyone does), but these challenges are seldom taken up *intellectually*. Faith does raise questions, but rarely seeks understanding. This is perhaps hardly surprising. After all, many of the questions are extremely difficult. Searching for answers, assuming they are to be had, is an 'arduous', 'strenuous' and 'risky' business (Migliore 1991: 1–9). In addition, there is the problem, highlighted by ordinary believers themselves, that the 'answers' (about which the experts, in any case, disagree) may not be that helpful to faith. Some academic theologians agree. George Lindbeck complains that most contemporary academic theology is 'useless for spiritual formation', and Browning contends that although academic theology may be less rationalistic than it used to be, it is still 'largely unrelated to the average person' (Lindbeck 1996: 293; Browning 1991: 5).

We saw earlier that soteriology raised most questions. But those with soteriological difficulties also talked about not having the time, the inclination or the will to pursue their soteriological (or other) queries. As one respondent put it, '*I don't really have the time to think about it, so let's just move on*'; or as another said, '*I really can't be bothered to find out about it*'. The need to resolve queries is rarely acute. Most of the sample are not concerned about providing themselves with theories or explanations. They can '*put to one side*' their difficulties. Becoming clear is not an issue for them.[7] This attitude may be roundly condemned, but the rational, analytic or systematic kind of thinking required for tackling the cognitive challenges of religious belief is very demanding, and not everyone is a *theoria* thinker. As Lindbeck puts it, 'Relatively few people have much aptitude or interest in second-order reflective activity. They … have no talent for thinking theologically themselves' (that is, for *theoria* thinking) (Lindbeck 1996: 295).

So do ordinary believers *do* Christology? If Christology (as a subdiscipline of theology) is defined as the deliberate, critical and systematic reflection (that is, *theoria* thinking) on the person, being and doing of Jesus Christ, then the answer would have to be 'no, they do not'. However, Christology, like theology, can be more broadly defined. If it is defined as 'talk about Jesus Christ' then the answer to the question is no longer clear-cut. All of the sample managed to do some talking about Jesus during the interview. Does this count? In the eyes of the ordinary believers themselves, it

---

[7]   This does not apply to all the sample. At least four of the interviewees were clearly troubled by their soteriological (and other) difficulties.

would not. They clearly consider theology to be an academic, scholarly, specialized discipline, and certainly do not think of themselves as theologians. Theology is something that other people (clerics, academics, students) do; it is not for them. This commonly accepted but narrow view of theology, as a scholarly discipline or activity, has been challenged by many. Edward Farley, for example, has drawn attention to an older understanding of theology (he prefers the term *theologia*) that has been largely lost. He argues that for most of Christian history, theology had a broader meaning than that of a scholarly discipline or inquiry. It was used as a term 'for an actual, individual cognition of God and things related to God, a cognition which in most treatments attends faith'. In this sense theology is 'a habit (*habitus*) of the human soul' whose end is personal knowledge of God. This form of theology was not abstracted from its concrete setting, but was concerned with and developed with 'the believer's ways of existing in the world before God'. It was 'a *practical*, not theoretical, habit having the primary character of wisdom'. This kind of knowledge – the sapiential and personal knowledge that attends faith – is a part of every Christian's existence. On this account, theology is not just for the scholar, but is the wisdom proper to the life of every believer (Farley 1983: 31, 35–7; cf. Schreiter 1985: 85–7; Astley 2002: 54–5). Theology as a habitus of the soul has to do with learning how to live before God and is firmly rooted in the religious and spiritual life of the believer. It does not require an academic context.

Broader definitions of theology, such as that proposed by Farley, allow for theology to be understood more generically as 'reflection about God' or 'discourse about God'. But should *all* thinking about God or talk about God count as theology? For Macquarrie it does not. Whilst he equates theology with 'God-talk' – 'a form of discourse professing to speak about God' – he immediately qualifies this by saying, 'Not all God-talk would qualify as theology, for we reserve this name for the most sophisticated and reflective ways of talking about God' (Macquarrie 1967: 11). Astley notes that George Pattison, similarly, has been reluctant to extend the use of the term theology to include the God-talk of every Christian, preferring instead to 'distinguish sharply between the way in which "ordinary" believers use religious language, symbols and practices and what professional theologians do'.[8] But in later writings, Pattison modifies this view, applying the term theology to those

---

[8]   From an unpublished paper by George Pattison given at Artists and Theologians Colloquium, University College, Durham, 5 September, 1995, cited in Astley 2002: 123.

outside the academy: 'The language of even the simplest, most unlettered believer is always going to involve some element of reflection, judgement and interpretation and is, thus far, "theological"' (Pattison 1998: 105). Astley's own view is that ordinary believers (that is, those who have not studied theology formally at all) 'are inevitably involved in doing their own theology if and when they speak and think about God, or at all events when they do so with any seriousness' (Astley 2002: 56).

So do the interviewees do Christology? Merely repeating set phrases from the tradition hardly seems to count as 'serious' speaking and thinking about Jesus. Farley stresses that 'existence in the world before God requires a wisdom that is not merely spontaneous but self-consciously interpretive' (Farley 1988: 90). Serious reflection must also surely involve a critical element. Others are willing to identify a critical element to all theology, including ordinary theology.[9] However, my data suggest that a few of the sample are highly resistant to any kind of critical reflection and evaluation of their faith. It must be said again that theological reflection and criticism, when this is understood in intellectualist terms, is difficult, even at a fairly basic level, for those who have little cognitive skill. Some may never develop any measure of competence in this area simply 'because there is no significant critical element in their natures to be developed. They will never be "critical thinkers"; but feelers, and doers, or believers' (Astley 1994: 113–4).

But a closer look at the data reveals that there is a lot more 'doing Christology' around than one might as first think. Explicit and implicit rejection of traditional doctrines (and there is a lot of that about) must involve some measure of serious or critical reflection. Here people have thought for themselves, and found the doctrines wanting. I believe that, in so doing, they have been involved in doing Christology. Also, if the notion of 'reflection' is broadened out to include 'consideration of' or 'meditation on' or 'contemplation of', then the range of what is allowed to count as theology may be vastly expanded. Whenever a believer is involved in any serious reflection, in this broad sense, on the story of Jesus then they can be said to be doing Christology. Now doing Christology this way, in a more 'ordinary' way, is going to be a very practical, personal and spiritual activity. Here we encounter a theology that is practical and devotional rather than theoretical and philosophical. In the interview situation an ordinary believer engaged in ordinary theology may be able to do little

---

[9]   For a full discussion of this theme, see Astley 2002: 140–5.

more than repeat set phrases from the tradition. They may practice meditative or contemplative reflection on the gospels (that is, they may do ordinary Christology), but have 'only the most meagre ability to articulate and describe their patterns of belief and practice' (Lindbeck 1996: 292–3). For them, doing ordinary Christology involves turning to the story of Jesus to see, as Julia puts it, '*if there is anything that I can find in Jesus' life that is useful to me, that will help me to look at this differently or help me resolve this issue*' or '*that will help me in living the Christian life*'. This sort of ordinary Christology might be said to challenge academic Christology to do the same, and so 'produce answers of the kind individual persons are looking for in order to find direction for their lives', rather than to produce 'academic results which clearly are not on eye-level with people's lives' (Schweitzer 2001: 178).[10]

Ordinary Christology and Affective Christology

Stories address themselves to the whole person – to the imagination, the will and the emotions as well as the intellect. In academic Christology, response to the story usually takes a cognitive turn as it seeks to understand, clarify and explain via 'hardheaded, critical and cognitive reflection' (Astley 2002: 143). Ordinary Christology, on the other hand, responds to story primarily in an affective mode. The interviewees (particularly women) invariably react to questions about the cross, for example, by giving an emotional (affective) response rather than a doctrinal (cognitive) one, talking about feelings not conceptual theology. The cross is affect-laden rather than theory-laden in much ordinary Christology. To give just two examples: Sheila says, '*I don't understand what "he saved us from our sins" really means*', and then goes on to say:

> '*Last year when we were on pilgrimage* […] *When we had all gathered* [near the Church of the Holy Sepulchre in Jerusalem] *we sang "When I survey the wondrous cross". And* [starts crying] *it just killed me … it was so emotional … so perfect for the occasion … it was just lovely … and for me I find that* [voice

---

10   Some theologians do advocate a more concrete, practice-orientated approach to certain theological problems as opposed to an abstract, theoretical one. Kenneth Surin, for example, favours a practical rather than a theoretical approach to theodicy. See Surin 1986.

falters again] *a beautiful hymn and for me a perfect expression of the crucifixion. Um … I find it difficult to sing it now … For me … [falters again] … especially the last verse … sums up, you know, my feelings … [falters] … whether I can live up to it or not, but that's the way I would like to be. Does that say enough?'*

Rose responded to a question about the cross by saying:

'*… at Easter you sort of, the services there, like Good Friday and things, you do feel … there is something inside that you feel about that cross isn't there? Well, I feel there is. Um … [long pause] … it's almost like losing someone yourself isn't it? It is a sad … um … I know I come away feeling differently after that … about this cross … um … well the death I suppose. I don't know. I just feel … [voice trails off].'*

'*It's not the same sort of feeling … um … like Maundy Thursday and things like that … there are feelings that … yes … there is something. And then you come to Sunday and I mean it is a completely different thing isn't it … the feeling about it.'*

'*There is a feeling of … I suppose it is like grief isn't it, in a way. But there is a sadness, isn't there? Um … I can't explain it, but you do get these sort of feelings. As I say it is not perhaps the same every year. It can be different […] I suppose it is how you are feeling at the time though as well sometimes, isn't it. You know, other things as well […] I think [Jesus' death] is something that you can relate to isn't it? […] I think you almost tend to go through it don't you, day by day.'*

The multidimensional character of Christology was mentioned in Chapter 1, a little more detail may be added here. A believer's Christology, like the rest of their religion, involves cognitive, affective and conative dimensions of the human person. These different dimensions are interrelated and interacting. They can only be distinguished from each other by treating them 'as *conceptual abstractions* from the concrete whole that is a thinking-feeling-experiencing-acting person' (Astley 1994: 113). The Christian educationalist, James Michael Lee recognizes this in arguing for a position he calls 'holistic functionalism'. Holistic functionalism recognizes that human cognitive and affective activities are contrasting but also interrelated and interdependent functions of the same person: cognition refers to intellectual functioning, whereas affect has to do with the feeling and emotional aspects of human activity. He writes:

> The holistic concept of *homo integer* suggests that no human function or activity exists independently of other key aspects of the person ... there is no intellectual activity without some sort of concomitant affect, and there are no affective functions taking place without cognitions being somehow involved ... Cognitive activity is never un-affected. In short, every human behaviour has its cognitive component, its affective component, its psychomotor component, and so forth. What makes one activity cognitive and another affective is the basic mode and axial thrust of the particular human behavior or set of behaviours. (Lee 1985: 130–1)

John Bernsten also recognizes that all human acts are cognitive-affective and that solely cognitive or solely affective acts do not exist. 'Consequently we should not contrast emotion and thought, reason and passion or, ultimately, religious experience and doctrine. They are not opposed but entail each other.' Emotions accompany beliefs and beliefs accompany emotions. Hence religious teachings can 'be held in the mode of the emotions'. He describes Christian religious education as primarily a matter of 'the shaping of religious emotions and affections in the context of teaching doctrine' (Bernsten 1996: 229–33). Lee and others also espouse an holistic understanding of Christian religious education 'in which the different elements (cognitive, affective, lifestyle behaviour) are all present in dynamic integration, so that the whole person is addressed' (Astley 1994: 120).

Academic Christology is rarely holistic in this way. It is primarily a cognitive affair, addressing the cognitive function of the human person and tending to abstract out the more affective and volitional aspects. Much ordinary Christology, by contrast, is affect and action centred. It tends to abstract out the cognitive dimension of Christology, as evidenced by the lack of interest in doctrine and the emphasis on feelings and behaviour. Many would argue that in religion, affections and/or behaviour are the more important elements. William James is reported as saying almost a century ago, 'I do believe that feeling is the deeper source of religion, and that philosophic and theological formulas are secondary products, like translations of a text into another tongue' (cited in Bausch 1984: 10). Astley, similarly, argues that affectivity is the most important element in religion and also that religious learning is primarily a matter of learning feelings. 'No one can be fully and properly Christian who does not feel appropriately' (Astley 1994: 135; cf. 111–56). Affect is said to be more distinctively human, and stronger, than cognition, so it should not surprise that ordinary Christology, to use a slogan, 'feels' rather than 'thinks' (see Lee 1985: 199, 205–6). For this, in highlighting the affective dimension of Christology, ordinary Christology reminds academic Christology that there is more to Christology than factual beliefs. Christological feelings, emotions, attitudes and values are important too. In particular, learning pro-attitudes towards Jesus, such as trust and loyalty, and learning to value him, such that there is a deep affective bond between the believer and Jesus, is arguably the greater part of Christology. To *believe in* Jesus is to give one's heart to him and to be moved by him (cf. Sheila above). For this, affect is indispensable. Right doctrine is not. A believer may have very limited or unorthodox beliefs about Jesus (as both Sheila and Rose do), yet be passionately committed to Jesus and his cause. Doctrinal orthodoxy is no measure of this belief-in Jesus.

The importance of affect in Christology will come up again later on in this chapter and in the next. I want to say here, however, that the feelings and emotions generated by the story of Jesus may *not* develop into attitudes and values. Feelings and (most) emotions are usually treated as transitory occurrences, attitudes and values as enduring dispositions that lead to corresponding actions. The feelings and emotions evoked by reading the gospels, or watching Franco Zeffirelli's film *Jesus of Nazareth*, or by singing, 'When I survey the wondrous cross', or participating in Holy Week services, may or may not develop into longer lasting and more stable states. Affective responses that do not lead to volitional action, or to transformation of the person in any other way, perhaps deserve to come under criticism. Affective Christology that only entertains warm feelings is superficial. Many argue that the regular pedagogy of religious practices can help train the religious affections and evoke stable dispositions. The practice of giving thanks to God, for example, can create a disposition to be grateful to God and other people, just as the practice of telling the truth can deepen into the disposition to be honest. The disposition of gratitude 'notices and appreciates the generosity of others. In this way, it engenders a character-based readiness to act generously towards others. It makes no sense to appreciate a quality without wanting to embody it ourselves'.

These dispositions, Spohn insists, 'carry over into ways of action that are consonant with the disposition' (Spohn 2003: 37, 41–2). In other words, affectivity *motivates* behaviour, as the extract from Sheila's interview demonstrates. However, data from other respondents suggest that sometimes there is little movement beyond feelings and emotions. The passion and death of Jesus can move the believer to feel a short-lived pity and/or compassion and/or sympathy for Jesus, but not lead to a commitment to him or his 'cause'.

On Not Learning Christological Dogma

As we have seen, another characteristic of ordinary Christology is that it is resistant to learning Christological (or other) doctrines. Nearly every week functionalists recite the Nicene creed. How are they reading it? According to McGrath, the Nicene creed is a brief summary of the main points of Christian belief 'which every Christian ought to be able to accept and be bound by' (McGrath 1994: 17). Functionalists, especially those of the traditionalist kind, typically respond to the creed by saying, '*It sums up what I believe*'. '*It's putting it in a nutshell really*'. '*I can agree with it all. This is what I believe.*' And then they can say little else. As Marion puts it, the creed '*is something I just say parrot fashion ... You say these things because you have always said it. Habit*'. Or as Eleanor says, '*Well yes. Yes. Well I just do believe it ... But I have never really thought about it, you see.*' People say that they '*totally and utterly*' believe in the creed, but what they actually believe in is not Nicene orthodoxy.

The creed of the Council of Nicaea, on which the Nicene creed is based, was intended to define orthodox teaching. It bristles with anti-Arian clauses which were somewhat awkwardly inserted into an existing baptismal creed, with the explicit intention of excluding Arianism (Kelly 1972: 255–6). But as we saw in Chapter 3, Arianism persists. Functional Christology is effectively Arian. One might suppose that one of the key faith-images of Jesus to have had a paradigmatic impact on the Christian consciousness would be the image of the pre-existent Son in the Nicene creed (cf. Cook 1997: 7, 109–46). But the data from the functionalists suggest otherwise. The doctrine of the pre-existent Son represents 'an epoch-making paradigm shift'. It effectively separates conceptually the eternal relation of Jesus to the Father from his concrete existence in history, so that 'between scripture and Nicaea, the same message of Jesus as Son of God appears in a completely different "thought system" or interpretative system' (Küschel 1992: 503). But the functionalists have not learned this doctrine of pre-existence and so do not make this shift into a different conceptual framework. They do not transpose Jesus as Son of God into an eternal relation with God the Father. Rather, for them, Jesus as Son of God appears to be anchored in the historical life of the human Jesus (and/ or perhaps the risen, ascended Jesus).

There are some clues in the data as to how the Nicene language referring to the eternal relation of Jesus to the Father is being understood. Thus the anti-Arian phrase 'begotten not made' is commonly understood as referring to the special creation of Jesus.

Diane

'Well I think, "begotten", well that is obviously an antiquated word, but he obviously wasn't conceived in the way that normal people are, so I suppose "begotten" would be the word you would use to describe Mary coming with child.'

Lesley

'"Begotten" ... what does that mean?'

'I guess "not made" refers to [laugh] *that he wasn't made in the conventional way.'*

Edward

E   *I suppose 'begotten not made' ... I suppose I would regard that as making a differentiation in terms of the process of creation of Jesus.*

A   *So the word 'begotten' would be to do with the virgin birth?*

E   *Conception. Yes.*

To take another example, the phrases 'God from God, Light from Light, true God from true God' are typically passed over with no comment, or else the following kind of comment is made.

Suzanne

'These words mean nothing to me. And it is not really something that I have looked at or thought about.'

'So to actually look at the meaning of the words, that's not ... [voice trails off].'

'I mean the first [prayer] that we say in the service, "Almighty God, to whom all hearts are open", that means a lot to me and I can understand all the words. But I think the [creed], I think I just tend to roll it off without thinking about the words.'

'I mean, "We believe in one God", you can say that with all your heart because that is what you believe, but the other paragraph further down ... I suppose really, some of it ... To me it is very theoretical. It is way above my head ... Until you get to this bit here, "For our sake".'

Diane

'I don't know that I ever think about that. It is sort of sad to say that you say these things, but you don't always sort of, every time you say them, think, well what does that mean?'

'You know, you do it every Sunday because it is laid down in the forms of worship. It is easy to carry on saying it and your mind can often be somewhere else ... you sort of switch off.'

Harvey Whitehouse has explored the problems of habituation and the difficulties of learning and remembering complex theological concepts. He asserts, 'When people end up performing rituals largely as a matter of automated habit, they become far less likely to reflect explicitly upon the possible symbolic meanings of these rituals ... Audiences can obviously become habituated to doctrinal repetition and can simply switch off'. He also argues that complex 'hard-to-acquire' theological concepts are invariably 'vulnerable to reformulation in cognitively simpler terms' (Whitehouse 2004: 5, 129). The conceptual framework in which the creed is cast is clearly difficult for most ordinary believers to grasp. They do not adopt its metaphysic; they have a simpler monist and absolutist metaphysic, more akin to Arius. The key anti-Arian clause, the *homoousion* (translated as 'of one Being' in Common Worship), is interpreted in the following way: Jesus and God are 'of one Being' because *'you can't separate them.'* As Edward puts it:

> *'"Of One Being with the Father". I suppose what I would take from that is*
> *that you can't separate the two. You know, all one Being. Somehow they are so*
> *strongly connected that whilst as I say I wouldn't say Jesus was God, they are ...*
> *you know ... connected.'*

'Of one Being' is thus taken to signify a relational not an ontological identity between Jesus and God. It patently does not carry the doctrinal meaning intended for it; it is not read as an ontological statement or as philosophical, conceptual language, but as figurative, poetic language describing Jesus of Nazareth's relationship with the God he called Father. Similarly, 'Son of God', in functional Christology, remains firmly metaphorical or analogical in character and is not turned into an ontological term. Son of God has undoubtedly been a key, if not *the* key faith-image of Jesus that has had a paradigmatic impact on the Christian consciousness, but for functionalists 'Son of God' does not appear to be shaped by Nicene orthodoxy. Instead, 'Son of God' takes its meaning from the story of Jesus' life (from the birth stories primarily and from other stories, such as the story of Jesus' baptism where he is declared to be 'the Beloved Son') as well as from the 'vast network of commonplaces associated with paternal and filial behaviour that we all have' (McFague 1982: 113).[11] The word Son seems to be firmly associated with the concrete historical figure of Jesus of Nazareth, not the Second Person of the Godhead.

The modernization of the term *homoousion*, from 'being of one substance with the Father' to 'of one Being with the Father', has been criticized for introducing new heretical meanings. The reaction of the panel responsible for the revision 'seems to have been: "Well, they'll know what we *mean*"' (Frost 1973: 10). The data show just how naive this response is. Martin Stringer, a liturgist trained in anthropology, provides a helpful perspective on this issue. In his article on 'Situating Meaning in the Liturgical Text' he explores the nature of meaning in liturgy (Stringer 1991: 181–95). The problem of meaning, says Stringer, is a hermeneutical one: is the meaning of the liturgy to be found entirely within the texts of the liturgy or is the 'meaning' of the rite to be found primarily in the minds of those who attend

---

[11]   For further discussion of creedal language, see McFague 1982: 111–17.

it and thus be subject to individual variations?[12] Stringer describes how from the fourth century through to the revisions of the 1960s, apart from a brief interlude during the Reformation, liturgical language has always been accepted as 'archaic'. Church members were not expected to understand its 'meaning'. When liturgical revision came, in both the Roman Catholic Church and the Anglican Church in the 1960s and 1970s, the express purpose was to make the language of the liturgy more understandable. But, says Stringer, it became increasingly apparent 'that most of the ordinary members of the congregation still did not understand what much of the text actually "meant". This is simply because most ordinary people did not really understand the meaning ... of many of the technical theological terms that were constantly being used'. As a result, the pressure has continued to build for a language which people can understand, a language that is 'concrete and tangible rather than abstract and theoretical', a language that makes the liturgy more approachable 'for the vast majority of people who cannot handle the jargon of academic theology'. Locating meaning exclusively in the text, argues Stringer, leads to liturgical language having to be as understandable as possible in order for it to bear the full weight of responsibility for meaning. This in turn leads to meaning being *imposed* on the rite and raises further questions of power and authority. Furthermore, the imposed meanings are still 'theological meanings, meanings that were, to all intents and purposes, irrelevant to the majority of people who actually used the rite'. Liturgists, says Stringer, should accept 'that religious language will never be fully "understandable of the people" and never should be' (Stringer 1991: 183–5, 188, 193). He turns to other sociologists of religion for support. David Martin, in his critique of Anglican liturgical revisions, has argued that liturgical language has a 'meaning' which goes beyond the particular dictionary definition of the words that are being used. He suggests that the words themselves are not words with meanings as such, but religious texts almost devoid of any real meaning that have some kind of power or mystery in their own right. Martin writes, 'Religion is less a rule book than a set of spells by which people are bound in a certain direction. A community is held spell bound by an image,

---

[12]   Stringer's dichotomy between meaning as a function of the text *or* of the worshipper is, quite rightly, criticized by Bridget Nichols. Following Gadamer, Nichols argues that 'meaning *happens* in liturgy' in the fusion of horizons between text and worshipper. See Nichols 1996: 18–40.

transfixed by a verbal incantation' (Martin 1980: 82).[13] Martin's main argument is that texts, as items in themselves, often relate people to their own past and must be retained as whole texts because of their personal associations or wider symbolic values. Stringer also emphasizes the symbolic nature of religious language and its capacity to accumulate a depth and range of meaning, some of which will be entirely personal and individual. The hankering after understandability is viewed by these writers as mistaken. It misses the whole purpose of liturgical language, which is to be 'evocative and ambiguous' rather than 'understandable' (Stringer 1991: 184).

The data confirm Stringer's thesis that ordinary believers do not understand the technical meaning of certain theological terms used in the liturgy (how could they, without proper instruction in their use?), and that liturgical language has primarily an expressive and emotive function. A professional theologian will be attuned to the technical/doctrinal meaning of the creed, ordinary theologians are not. Clearly, technical phrases, such as the *homoousion*, can and do take on new meaning and significance when they are released from their moorings in academic theology and let loose in the world of ordinary religion. As Martin and Pluck write, 'The meaning which inheres in any set of words may be far from self-evident and may rest less in its apparent intellectual content than in its context: the verbal formula may convey a range of different meanings depending on custom and context' (Martin and Pluck 1976: 8). So Graeme Smith reports from his experience of talking to people inside the churches, that although they use the words and phrases of the liturgy, when the meaning of these words are explored in greater depth the meaning attached to the words is rarely that of 'the orthodoxy of the Churches' official statements' (Smith 2002: 15).

Another approach to the meaning of the *homoousion* is provided by George Lindbeck. Influenced by Wittgenstein, he suggests that religions can be compared to languages, with religious doctrines functioning as rules for religious language. As such, doctrines should not be understood as propositions making ontological truth claims, but as a way of regulating language. Doctrines have a second-order grammar. Thus, the *homoousion* should not be understood as making an ontological reference, but as regulating language concerning both Jesus and God.

---

[13]   Cf. Mary Douglas 1970: 59–76. Douglas highlights the tendency for symbols to take on cultural and social significance over and above their original religious function.

Whatever is said of the Father must be said of the Son, except that the Son is not the Father. Whatever we say of Jesus, we must not suggest that he was only a man or only God, nor that he was some sort of hybrid God-man (Lindbeck 1984: 94).[14] In functional (and sceptical) Christology, however, the *homoousion* does not function either as a first-order proposition making an ontological claim *or* as a grammatical rule. Functionalists simply have not learned the grammar of orthodox Christological discourse. They do not say of the Son what they say of the Father. Yet they are following rules, but other rules. As Lindbeck acknowledges, beneath the ancient creedal *homoousion* rule lie three other, deeper rules, which 'have been abidingly important from the beginning in forming mainstream Christian identity'. These three rules are: first, there is only one God; second, Jesus was a real human being; third, that every possible importance should be ascribed to Jesus which is not inconsistent with the first two rules (Lindbeck 1984: 94–5). It is these three simpler, uncontroversial rules (which are compatible with subordinationism and Arianism) that our functionalists follow, rather than the more complex *homoousion* rule. For functionalists, the *homoousion* rule would appear to be a grammatical mistake, not correct grammar.

Lindbeck claims that one acquires an understanding of religious language through performance (Lindbeck 1984: 34). Paul Holmer similarly claims that a religious concept 'is learned by mastering the way the word is used' in the tradition. To learn how the word 'God' is used is to learn theology. When we learn that God is 'the Father, the Almighty, maker of heaven and earth' we are learning theology. 'Theology is a name, then, for the ruled way, the correct way, of speaking about and worshipping God' (Holmer 1978: 133, 199–204). Understanding the concepts of faith is thus a matter of learning the grammar and vocabulary of the tradition. The data suggest that Holmer, like Lindbeck and other postliberals, presents an idealized and idealistic account of ordinary theology. He describes what he thinks should happen. A study such as the present one shows what actually happens and

---

[14]   Lindbeck's setting aside of the ontological reference of the *homoousion* has come under criticism. McGrath demonstrates that the regulative function of the *homoousion* in the patristic period was based on its substantive content. He writes, 'Given the ontological relation of Father and Son, the grammatical regulation of language concerning them follows as a matter of course'. In other words, the rule must be kept because Jesus *is* God (McGrath 1997: 29). Avis concurs: 'Doctrines do indeed have a cultural-linguistic function, but they only have that because they have a primary and determinative cognitive function' (Avis 1999: 168).

suggests that most ordinary believers do not come to understand key concepts such as 'incarnation' or 'atonement' or 'salvation' through performance. However, more detailed empirical work still needs to be done in this area. What would count as having learned and understood these concepts? Clearly most of the sample do not have (or cannot articulate) a cognitive/intellectual/technical understanding of these terms, but they may have acquired an affective/non-cognitive/non-technical 'understanding'. It is the non-cognitive dimension of ordinary Christology that I want to address in the next section.

Is Ordinary Christology Essentially Non-Cognitive?

Many would claim that the primary function of liturgical language is not to convey information but to act as a vehicle for Christian religious affections (see Avis 1999: 85–9; cf. Stringer 1991). Its purpose is to lift the hearts and minds of believers to God in worship and to act as a vehicle for the controlled expression of religious emotion and feeling. As Avis puts it, 'Liturgy exerts a profound effect on the worshipper by expressing Christian religious affections in a restrained and disciplined form that protects the worshipper from being overwhelmed by an experience of the numinous ... Thoughts that defy expression, emotions that are too strong for human nature to bear, are constrained, contained and made manageable' by the traditional liturgical forms (Avis 1999: 88). Astley, drawing on Ninian Smart's definition, contends that 'worship is an activity which *expresses* certain religious attitudes, affections and experiences and tends to *evoke* them. In their worship, Christians express Christian attitudes and emotions' (Astley 1996: 245). On these accounts, the language of worship primarily performs non-cognitive rather than cognitive functions. It is the non-cognitive aspect of religious language that I want to focus on here.

Some clarification of terms is required first. Cognitive statements are statements that are either true or false (that is, 'factual' or 'truth-claiming'). Non-cognitive expressions, on the other hand, are neither true nor false. They include commands, exclamations, expressions of feelings and attitudes. Unlike cognitive language, non-cognitive language does not directly assert facts or provide descriptions. A non-cognitive approach to religious beliefs therefore 'treats them as expressions of feelings, emotions or attitudes to life or of commitments to a certain way of behaving. On this view, rather than imparting information, religious language arouses and deepens attitudes and emotions and stirs people to moral and religious action' (Astley 2004: 71). Logical positivists famously argued that statements only have meaning if they can be empirically verified or are tautological. Since the propositions of religion (as well as those of aesthetics, ethics and metaphysics) clearly were neither, they were regarded as cognitively meaningless. Religious and ethical statements could therefore only be regarded as expressing attitudes or feelings towards life, not as statements of fact. They do not make cognitive claims, at best they are expressions of emotion and feeling possessing what was sometimes described as 'emotive meaning' (Kerr 2000: 608–10). Similarly, the empiricist philosopher, Richard Braithwaite, argued that religious beliefs do not, properly understood, make cognitive claims at all, but they still have a *use* despite the fact that they are not empirically verifiable or falsifiable. He held that religious beliefs shape our attitudes and the way we live mainly by expressing our commitments. Christianity and other religions provide a treasure chest of stories – stories which need not be true – that express attitudes and inspire people to live a certain moral way of life (Braithwaite 1971: 72–91).[15] More recently, thinkers such as Don Cupitt have also adopted a wholly non-cognitive approach to religious belief. For Cupitt, no religious truth is descriptive or factual, all are practical and necessarily subjective. For him, a corollary of non-cognitivism is non-realism. Christian non-realism, as espoused by Cupitt, asserts that, 'Belief in the God of Christian faith is an expression of allegiance to a particular set of values, and experience of the God of Christian faith is experience of the impact of those values in one's life' (Cupitt 1980: 69). This non-realist viewpoint interprets religious language, not as referring to a transcendent reality, but as expressive of our emotions, our basic moral insights and intentions, or our way of seeing the world, or as referring to our moral and spiritual ideals.

Whilst acknowledging the important non-cognitive dimensions of religious language, however, most scholars have continued to insist that religious language does additionally refer to a transcendent reality, and that it does make cognitive claims either directly or by implication. Ian Ramsey, for example, held that religious

---

[15] For further examples of religious language treated as wholly non-cognitive in form, see Dan R. Stiver 1996: 67–72.

language serves to evoke religious experience and 'disclosure situations', but it does also indicate – admittedly in indirect and approximate ways – something of the content of the disclosure. In other words, religious language represents as well as evokes the divine. It is not completely non-cognitive (Ramsey 1957). Many others defend a realist position, whilst acknowledging the emotional power of religious language. Frederick Ferré is another example of a realist who asserts that religious language first and foremost evokes feelings and forms attitudes, shaping our ways of seeing, feeling and behaving 'more than we may know'. Religion has a 'kind of power over our emotions and our legitimate aspirations,' he writes (Ferré 1968: 331, 338).

Speech-act theory has also highlighted the non-cognitive dimensions of religious language. John Austin showed that much of our ordinary language is rarely limited to straightforward cognitive statements. Speech-act analysis reveals that language can perform many different functions. In every act of saying something (the locutionary act), we also do something (the illocutionary act or acts). Austin identified a number of different kinds of illocution, including commands, requests, promises, warnings, expressions of attitude and so on. In addition, he also distinguished between these illocutions (what is done *in* saying something) and what is done *by* saying something. He called these actual effects of the request, command, promise, expression, and so on, the perlocutionary act. Despite an early distinction between 'performatives' and statements, Austin finally concluded that descriptive statements, or 'constatives' as he called them, are also a form of illocutionary act. Constatives are the only type of illocution that can be judged true or false; that is, that are cognitive. All other types of illocution are non-cognitive (Austin 1962).

Speech-act analysis can be fruitfully applied to the language of religious worship. Such an analysis shows that very many illocutions of worship language are non-cognitive. Expressive illocutions, for example, express what the believer thinks or feels. Utterances such as 'Holy, holy, holy, Lord God of hosts; heaven and earth are full of your glory' or 'My soul thirsts for God' contain or 'carry' an expressive. Expressives can be expressions of attitudes or feelings (such as trust, longing, joy, guilt, awe, praise) or expressions of convictions, beliefs or intentions, as in the utterance, 'In all things God works together for good with those who love God.' (This illocution also has constative force, that is, it is not *just* expressive.) The language of worship may contain a variety of other illocutionary acts, including prayerful requests and commitment to an action or way of behaving, all of which are non-cognitive.

Speech-act theory highlights the complexity of religious language and shows how rarely it consists simply of descriptive statements. Much of the language of worship consists of non-cognitive expressives (and/or commissives and prescriptives). Sometimes it might not be directly asserting facts at all, although non-cognitive illocutions are usually considered to *imply* or *presuppose* a constative, that is, a cognitive illocution. Thus Brümmer argues that we cannot express our own trust in or thanksgiving to God 'without presupposing that this God exists in fact' (Brümmer 1981: 268). Consider the affirmation, 'The Lord is my shepherd' from Psalm 23. This is more an expression of an attitude and an intention than a statement of fact, but it presupposes that there is a Lord and that the Lord acts kindly towards his people and would 'misfire' if there were no 'Lord' (Stiver 1996: 84). For non-realists like Cupitt, however, non-cognitive illocutions do *not* imply any constative or cognitive claim about the real existence of God. For them, God is only an idea or ideal. All of the sample we are analysing here, however, have a realist understanding of God. They would not agree that 'there is no other God other than the God we have made' or that 'religion is, *without remainder*, a human creation' (Crowder 1997: 3–4). All are realists and at the heart of realist faith is the belief that God (albeit variously conceived) exists in reality and not solely in the mind, or in culture or language.[16] So when this sample make non-cognitive illocutions, as they do during worship, a constative is usually implied or presupposed.

However, it may be that much ordinary Christology is *primarily* (but not wholly) non-cognitive, in that its *focus* is on the expression and evocation of certain feelings, emotions and attitudes towards Jesus, and not on the declaration of facts about him. It is clear from the data that for most of the sample the Christological language of worship functions primarily as a carrier of affection rather than of cognition, and is therefore primarily emotionally not cognitively significant. As we have seen, most of the sample do not have a doctrinally rich spirituality. They use liturgical language, but '*do not understand what the words mean*', which

---

[16]   It may be the case, of course, that a highly transcendent realism or apophaticism is in practice indistinguishable from non-realism.

suggests that they are using it primarily non-cognitively. Clearly, the words of scripture, liturgy and hymnody (cf. a painting or a piece of music or a poem) do not have to be cognitively/intellectually/technically understood in order to have an effect. Patrick Sherry reports how the words of Isaiah on the Suffering Servant, 'He was despised and rejected of men, a man of sorrows, and acquainted with grief … surely he hath borne our griefs, and carried our sorrows … with his stripes we are healed' (Isaiah 53:3–5) move him. They are words that appeal to his 'heart and imagination' rather than his intellect (Sherry 2003: 1–3). Similarly, several of the interviewees report being profoundly moved by certain words or phrases or hymns, whilst having little cognitive understanding. Pat says that the words 'our sins have been washed away by the blood of Christ' mean a lot to her, even though, as she put it, '*I don't understand the cross*'. We might say that the words have affective/non-cognitive meaning, rather than cognitive/intellectual meaning. As we noted above, the hymn 'When I survey the wondrous cross' is for Sheila a powerful vehicle for her to express religious affections – of penitence, trust, adoration, commitment, and so on. This hymn also contains a certain theology, but the data suggest that it functions *primarily* as a vehicle for religious affections rather than as a carrier of explicit theology. That this is so is confirmed by other comments Sheila makes, such as, '*I like singing Charles Wesley's hymns … they mean a lot to me*', but '*I don't understand redemption*'. It is as if the explicit theology is neither here nor there. It is enough to know that Jesus' death is an act of love that somehow benefits believers, without having to understand why or how this might be so. Only 'oblique, aesthetic assent to the realities presupposed or celebrated in the hymn' seems to be necessary (Sherry 2003: 69).

If, for Sheila, the hymn 'When I survey the wondrous cross' functions primarily as performative (non-cognitive) discourse rather than doctrinal (cognitive) discourse, then it may be said to do something rather than state something. It expresses and evokes pro-attitudes towards Jesus and makes the believer feel differently about herself. Similarly, singing the words 'My chains fell off, my heart was free; I rose went forth and followed thee. No condemnation now I dread; Jesus, and all in him, is mine!' has a (perlocutionary) cathartic, therapeutic, salvific effect on the believer, without her ever having to understand particular theories or doctrines of atonement. It is Avis' contention that liturgy has aesthetic power rather than rational power, that its meaning is grasped by the imagination rather than the intellect, and that it functions as evocative poetry rather than fact-asserting prose (Avis 1999: 85–9). In other words, the liturgy primarily structures feeling and generates emotive/affective meaning rather than intellectual/cognitive meaning. It functions as a container for spirituality.[17]

Sheila also sings 'Died he for me who caused his pain', but the rest of the data from her interview show that she does not have a substitutionary theory of atonement. The words do *imply* a doctrine of substitutionary atonement, but she does not appear to make these implications. This suggests that she is using the language primarily non-cognitively. However, because she does not explicitly deny the implications, we cannot adopt a wholly non-cognitive analysis of her discourse. What is clear from the data is that the constative or cognitive claim that is explicitly implied or presupposed by many in this sample is rarely that of orthodoxy. When functionalists confess 'Jesus is Lord', for example, they are not making a cognitive claim about how Jesus exists in the hierarchy of being. They are making a different cognitive claim, namely, that he is '*a pre-eminent person*'. It thus seems that many use what appears to be cognitive language in order to make only the vaguest cognitive claims. The analytic chapters have shown that the cognitive content of many people's faith is '*very vague*'. They may accept the saving efficacy of Jesus' death, for example, but for them the content of the concept of atonement is amorphous and ill-defined. All this suggests a primarily non-cognitive theology.

The analytic chapters have also shown that the majority of the sample are effectively liberal in both their Christology and their soteriology. Liberals are said to be, to a greater or lesser extent, non-cognitivists in their understanding of some aspects of Christian doctrine (See Badham 1993: 183–4). Wiles and Hick, for example, both contend that incarnation language is essentially expressive (that is, non-cognitive) rather than fact-asserting. For Wiles, incarnational language is a very effective way of expressing the significance of Jesus and should not be understood 'in a strict metaphysical way' (Wiles 1979: 24). For Hick, 'the real point and value of the incarnational doctrine is not indicative but expressive, not to assert a metaphysical fact but to express a valuation and evoke an attitude'. The traditional liturgical language which speaks of Jesus as God the Son, God

---

[17]   On the relationship between liturgy and feeling, see Nichols 1997: 72–95. See also Davies 2002: 86–90.

incarnate, God from God, is considered by him to be the language of devotion and 'the hyperbole of the heart' (Hick 1977: 178, 183).

Lindbeck observes that the Nicene creed itself 'has acquired liturgical and expressive functions that are in some respects more important than its doctrinal use for large parts of Christendom. The act of reciting it is for millions a mighty symbol of the church's unity in time and space'. The chanting of the Nicene creed 'can be an immensely powerful symbolization of the totality of the faith even for those who do not understand its discursive propositional or regulative meanings' (Lindbeck 1984: 95, 19). For some Christians the creed is undoubtedly of great doctrinal importance and they do use it *doctrinally*, one might say, rather than expressively. But this is not the case for the majority of the sample being analysed here. John, who has a sceptical Christology and cannot give intellectual assent to the creedal Christological dogmas, is unusual in that he *knows* he is not using the creed doctrinally, yet he continues to recite it because '*it is important to go along with what is given*'. He views the creed as an important marker of Christian identity: by reciting it he is identifying himself with the Christian community both past and present. The functionalists, however, may *think* they are using the creed doctrinally, but it would appear that they are (at least primarily) using it expressively. My conclusion, therefore, is that it would seem that much ordinary Christology is primarily non-cognitive (that is, it uses Christological language to express attitudes, rather than make fact-asserting statements), with cognitive implications of only the vaguest kind. More detailed empirical work would help confirm or deny this analysis.

Chapter 9

Living Christology

Engaging With the Story of Jesus

As we have seen, all of the sample, irrespective of the doctrinal positions they hold, engage to a greater or lesser extent with the story (or more accurately stories) of Jesus, and identify with the figure of Jesus, and it is this complex hermeneutical process that lies at the heart of ordinary Christology. It is said that the story of Jesus is, or should be, the dominant story by which Christians live their lives. But is it? To what extent does Jesus story find its way into our story? Just how significant a story is it? It is, of course, impossible to tell from one interview the extent to which the story of Jesus penetrates an interviewee's life or shapes their identity, but there are enough hints in the data to suggest some reasons why Jesus' story does not easily find its way into our story and I want to begin this final chapter by mentioning some of them.

Difficulties of Engagement

For the majority of this sample, church services are the primary means by which they engage with the story of Jesus. The liturgy, prayers, readings, sermon and hymns are the 'text' with which they hold a hermeneutical conversation.[1] I cannot hope to give any detail about the hermeneutical strategies employed by my sample as this was not the aim of the research. Suffice it for now to say that most Christian educationalists argue that for Jesus' story to become in any way our story there must be a critical conversation between our story and the story of Jesus. In other words there must be 'an engaged reading' in which the believer brings her own questions and concerns into 'the world of the text', interrogating it from new angles, and at the same time she must let the text interrogate her, allowing it to

---

[1] It is ordinary believers' interpretation of the biblical text, rather than the liturgical text or any other 'text', that I am primarily concerned with here.

challenge her own ideas and assumptions (cf. Spohn 2003: 16; Gadamer 1982; Chapter 2 above). An engaged reading presupposes that believers actually want to 'learn to "sacrifice" themselves, over and over again, to the community's narrative texts' and that they consent 'to be interrogated by these texts in such a way that they learn, slowly, laboriously and sometimes painfully, to live the way of Jesus' (Surin 1989: 217). But, clearly, not everyone does. As was mentioned earlier, the majority of this sample do not have the habit of reading the Bible. They hear the Bible read in church, but they do not read or study it for themselves. They are familiar with many of its stories, and fond of them too, but they see no need to pay further attention to them and do not seem interested in doing so.

> Eleanor
>
> *'I don't particularly want to know the Bible terribly, because I know what I believe and I don't want to ... I don't particularly want to know what has gone on beforehand because it has got no relevance really. I don't feel I need to know.'*

> Margaret
>
> *'I have read the Bible, some years ago now. But I wouldn't say that I sort of think about the stories and parables a great deal.'*

Here the Bible is not self-consciously used to nourish or inform personal spirituality and in practice is given little intentional authority. One of the reasons why believers do not pay much attention to the text is that they already think they know what the Bible teaches and what pattern of life Jesus commends: they already know what 'the rules' are and what is involved in 'doing good' and behaving Christianly. But an engaged reading of scripture would not presume to know what Jesus' message is or what he was about. Neither would it presume, as some in the sample do, that Jesus' values are largely identical with *'the Christian ethos'* or *'the British way of life'*. Such presumptions tend to produce a culturally accommodated version of Christianity. Allowing oneself to be interrogated by the text means being open to the possibility that certain, already existing values and patterns of behaviour deemed to be 'Christian' may have to be deconstructed rather than upheld (Surin 1989: 217). It is at this point that awareness of one's own pre-understandings becomes important for without such awareness there is the constant danger of unconsciously projecting our own pre-understandings onto the story of Jesus. Jesus then becomes who we want him to be and we mould him to fit into the moral (or other) life we already have (perhaps, the British way of life and mores). An engaged reading, by contrast, tries to maintain the otherness of Jesus, because 'only the Jesus who is other, different, intriguing, frustrating, fascinating can change what one already is. A Jesus who is like the self only reinforces what is already in place' (Keck 2000: 162). Some would say that historical study of Jesus is also necessary for an engaged reading, but most of the believers here do not come to the text having pursued a critical quest and the results of historical scholarship are not widely used in sermons. The data show that neither biblical scholarship nor awareness of one's own pre-judgements are essential for a transformative encounter with the text, but without these things we are more likely to keep Jesus in our own image.

Another factor that mitigates against an engaged reading is the problem of routinization. This sets in when believers no longer listen to the familiar stories expecting fresh meaning to be generated. It is said that parables, for example, 'can shatter worlds', disturb and unseat conventional understanding and generate new possibilities for those 'who have eyes to see and ears to hear' (Cook 1997: 50–2). But familiarity breeds, in this instance, complacency and in a complacent reading the parables no longer generate surprise or shock. They lose their impact, becoming stale, familiar and routine. No longer do they disarm the listener or generate dis-ease. The tension of the tale gets lost and its point is missed (Thiselton 1980: 14–15; cf. Astley 2004: 45–6). Similarly, with Jesus' own story: we know he dies on a cross and simply cannot get worked up about it. We have become desensitized to it. Harvey Whitehouse observes that 'One effect of hearing the same parables and teachings over and over again can undoubtedly be varying degrees of boredom'. This can lead to what he describes as 'the tedium effect – a state of low morale arising from over familiarity with religious formulae and routine' (Whitehouse 2004: 98). There is evidence to suggest that some believers do indeed switch off when the scriptures are read (as perhaps they do when the sermon is preached?). The familiar stories wash over them and they do not look to make connections between their own story and that of Jesus. As one respondent commented, '*Sometimes, rarely probably, can you apply what you read to your own circumstances ... many times you can't apply it at all because it is something*

that ... um ... hasn't affected you or is irrelevant'. A 'classic' text is said to have
perennial human relevance because it communicates effectively in a variety
of historical and cultural circumstances. But for some, the text often seems to
be irrelevant, with nothing much to say to their lives. It does not communicate
effectively and they do not easily connect with it. Others *'have a suspicion of texts'*
and consider aspects of the text to be alienating rather than transforming. *'They are
not very helpful to us.'* Feminist hermeneutics has convincingly shown that not all
of scripture is helpful. What to do with texts of terror or offensive soteriological
discourse or stories that do not easily communicate in our postmodern world is an
issue that Christian communicators cannot ignore.

As hinted at earlier, another reason why believers resist an engaged reading
is that they do not want their identities to be reshaped or their present ways of
behaving challenged. An engaged reading might well lead to the overturning of
some of our most important values, including the values of 'self and security, and
especially the values of worldly status, authority and power' (Astley 2000: 117).
So it is any wonder that engaged readings are resisted? Spiritual practices (such
as participating in the Eucharist) all have moral dimensions inherent in them,
but these often remain hidden and 'any attempt to bring them to the fore will be
resisted by those who want to keep their piety safe and comforting' (Spohn 2003:
14). It is noteworthy that time and again people talked about how comforting their
religion was, not about how *challenging* they found it.[2]

But even when there is an earnest desire to inhabit the story of Jesus, forging
links between Jesus' story and our story is not easy. Take the event that climaxes
the story of Jesus, his passion and death. How does this event link with our
own lives? The story of Jesus' passion and death, unlike some of the stories and
parables in the gospels, is a story that believers can easily relate to and identity
with in so far as it generates an emotional response, in much the same way as
any other story of the tragic death of an innocent victim would. But Jesus' death
is not just a story like other stories, it is the story which is to shape Christian
discipleship. The Christian must consciously appropriate the work of Christ on
her own behalf and take up the cross. However, following the story of the passion
and death of Jesus is one thing, figuring out its application for life today quite

---

[2]   See John Hull 1991: esp. 141–3, where he describes 'the spirituality of passivity'
that avoids the challenges of 'the dreaded belief system'.

another. What does it mean in the life of a believer or a community of believers to take up the cross? For Macquarrie, to take up the cross as one's own involves 'a turning away with Christ from the temptations of the world, the temptations of power, wealth, sensual indulgence and so on, to the things of the kingdom of God'. It is a life of self-sacrifice, understood as the offering of the self to God. Being joined to Jesus means 'joining in the self-offering of his sacrifice, and so living to God and for God rather than for any merely selfish or worldly ends' (Macquarrie 1990: 403). Not surprisingly there is little evidence in the data of any deliberate or intentional hermeneutical reflection on what it means to accept Christ's cross as one's own. The implications of the story for life today are not self-consciously drawn out. However, there is evidence of implicit learning. Through continual re-entry into the story of Jesus believers do learn, often unconsciously, *something* of what it means to take up the cross. I guess most would say they intended 'living to God and for God rather than for any merely selfish or worldly ends'. But without further empirical work it is difficult to know how the story of Jesus does impact on ordinary believers' attitudes, values and behaviour. Perhaps all we can say here, is that those who do engage in the spiritual practice of Bible study and/or meditative Bible reading (around one third of the sample) are more likely to be shaped by the story of Jesus, than those who do not, since they are actively seeking to make connections between their own story and the story of Jesus. Regular meditation or devotional reading can help make the images and stories of the gospels 'the background music of life', so that they become 'affective paradigms for moral dispositions', an 'internalized norm' that we bring to bear on our relationships and decisions (Spohn 2003: 120, 141). But it would seem that the majority of the sample do not deliberately seek to enter into a conversation with the story of Jesus. When conscious correlations or resonances between Jesus' story and their story do occur they are largely unsought. They occur *en passant*, as when the preacher's sermon suddenly strikes home or a Bible passage heard several times before suddenly comes alive.

The Story and Salvation

Having said all this, what the data do show is the intimate connection between the story of Jesus and salvation. As we have seen, it is as believers engage with the story of Jesus that salvation can occur. Or putting it another way, the story of Jesus is salvific as it grasps people or impacts upon them in ways that bring healing, wholeness or new life. Several examples of the salvific power of the story have already been given (see esp. Chapter 6). Ordinary Christology thus highlights the centrality of narrative for soteriology as well as for Christology. It shows that the story of Jesus is indispensable to soteriology and that salvation can never be thought of in purely abstract terms that can be separated from the story of Jesus. Ordinary soteriology shows that salvation is rooted in the actual connections that exist between the story of Jesus and the story of the believer. Ordinary soteriology may therefore challenge academic soteriology to produce soteriological explanations that are grounded in the concrete soteriological patterns, 'the web of storied connections', that actually exist between the believer's story and the story of Jesus (cf. Root 1989: 274). Michael Root argues that soteriology must construct 'augmented, expanded forms of the story of Jesus, viz., narrative redescriptions of the story of Jesus that include the ongoing experience of the believer/community', so that our stories are included in the story of Jesus. He notes that 'while the patterns in the text may be able to place limits on soteriological construction, they are not sufficiently specific to dictate a particular soteriology and thus eliminate the need for contemporary soteriological construction'. So the story must be recast, and 'it is precisely in this creation of a new version of the story that the soteriological task is carried out' (Root 1989: 275–6). Terrence Tilley, similarly, sees one of the main tasks of narrative theology to be the recasting of the narratives of the tradition to bring them into the context of our own stories. This will mean finding new ways to tell the story of creation, for example, as well as the story of redemption (Tilley 1985: 14). New ways of telling the story of how Jesus' death is redemptive are clearly needed for some in the sample. As we saw in Chapter 7, telling the story of Jesus' death as an atonement for human sin fails to connect with many believers' lives. Storied connections cannot be made.

When it is recognized that salvation comes through engagement with the story, it also becomes clear that Jesus' whole life is decisive for salvation and not just his death. And this salvation will always be particular and personal, arising out of the various connections that are made between the believer's story and the story of Jesus. What 'saves' one, will not 'save' all. A particular Bible verse or story, for example, may have a profound (or superficial) salvific effect on some, yet leave others completely cold. Salvific encounters are always 'diffuse and far-ranging in the experience of individual persons' and can never be fully explained in terms of theoretical generalizations (Haight 1999: 408; cf. Root 1989: 274). The generation of salvific connections between the story of Jesus and the story of the believer is clearly not dependent on a network of doctrines, hence Jesus can and does save irrespective of whether one holds the right doctrine about him.

When we 'look and see' what people's experiences of salvation actually are we also discover that salvation does not come through Jesus' story alone, but through other stories as well, most notably those of the Hebrew (Old Testament) scriptures. God saves through Jesus, but he also saves in other ways too. In much ordinary soteriology the concept of salvation is not in fact tied so closely to the life, death and resurrection of Jesus and there is no bifurcation between God's general salvific and creative action, on the one hand, and the particular story of God's saving action in Jesus, on the other. This chimes in with the theological principle that wherever there is wholeness, wherever there is healing, whenever things go right, then '*God is at work*' and salvation occurs. This fundamental claim is well expressed by Ruether, who writes:

> Redemption happens whenever we resist and reject collaboration with injustice and begin to taste the joys of true well-being in mutual service and shared life. When life is lived in solidarity with others in mutual well-being, every act of sustaining life becomes a sacrament of God's presence, whether this is bread broken and shared, sexual pleasure between lovers, tilling the ground, making a useful product or giving birth to a baby. God calls us into abundance of life here on earth. (Ruether 1998: 103)

Living within the all-embracing power and love of God is salvific. So, some seem to say, why bother paying attention to the story of Jesus?

Is Jesus Really That Important?

It has to be admitted that the story of Jesus may not be that significant a story for every Christian. There are enough hints in the data to suggest that some people do not actually pay that much attention to it. Of far more importance is their '*belief in God*' or their '*spirituality*'. Jesus just does not seem to be that important. Traditionally, Jesus is said to be important for Christian faith because he mediates God's salvation and the Christian understanding of God, insofar as it is specifically Christian, must lead back to Jesus as its source, origin and foundation. This means that for the Christian, God should be 'Christologically specified' (McGrath 1997: 174–5). Or as John V. Taylor and others put it, 'God is Christlike' (Taylor 1992: 5).[3] Such an approach places a heavy emphasis on revealed religion. It goes without saying that all the interviewees, to a greater or lesser extent, have been shaped in their thinking about God by the Christian scriptures and the story of Jesus. It could not be otherwise. What is less clear is whether Jesus is their *primary* source for understanding God or for encountering God. Many in the sample place a heavy emphasis on natural religion, as opposed to revealed religion, laying considerable stress on creation (nature) as a source for understanding and encountering God. There are obvious links to be made here with the type of religiousness Towler describes as 'theism'.[4] Theism, according to Towler, is the foundation of all western styles of religion. It focuses on God and God's creation and is grounded in a sense of wonder and awe in the face of the beauty and order of nature. The creator God of theism is a benevolent God whose presence can be discerned in and through the natural world. With such a strong sense of the presence and power of God in and through creation, theism accords to Jesus a place of only secondary importance. It does not accept that Jesus is God and rejects the doctrine of the Trinity as an account of God. Theism is firmly monotheistic and the doctrine of the divinity of Jesus is 'a gratuitous extra' that only detracts from a proper attitude to God and human nature. Nor is human nature essentially bad and in need of a redeemer. Why would another redeemer be needed to save the world, when the world has a perfectly good Creator-Saviour God already present? Theism is typically unchurched, not because theists do not need to express and celebrate in ritual form the sense of the sacred, but because the church fails to provide the appropriate means for doing so. Theists who do

---

[3]   This phrase of Taylor's is inspired by Archbishop Michael Ramsey's famous remark, 'God is Christlike and in him is no un-Christlikeness at all', in Ramsey 1969: 98.

[4]   What follows is a summary of theism using Towler's own words. See Towler 1984: 55–67.

attend church survive by ignoring doctrine and by imposing their own meanings and interpretations on the services.

It hardly needs to be said that attitudes such as these are not uncommon among the sample. Theism (as described above) highlights the enduring importance of natural religion. It may be recalled that it was the sense of a universal human experience of the sacred and belief in a common 'object' of worship that accounted for over two-thirds of the sample adopting a pluralist approach to other religions. Traditional Christianity has generally downplayed natural religion, viewing it as a prolegomenon to revealed religion. But the results from this study suggest that natural religion, rather than revealed religion, may be the main story by which at least some people live their everyday lives. The data indicate that churchgoing theism, like much popular spirituality today, pays little attention to the doctrines of the tradition. Like popular spirituality, it says, '*I am more of a spiritual person than a religious person*', and like popular spirituality it feels close to God '*in the garden*', '*walking along the hilltop*', '*looking up at the stars at night and wondering*', '*walking on the beach*', '*listening to classical music*'.[5] In natural religion and popular spirituality the encounter with God is mediated via creation and not through Jesus. In other words, salvation comes through encountering God in and through the created world; it does not come explicitly through Jesus.[6] Nature mysticism also apprehends God in and through the natural world and examples of nature mysticism can be found in the work of the Romantics. Wordsworth, in one of his poems, calls nature mysticism 'natural piety', differentiating it from the piety derived from reading the Bible (Chesnut 1984: 57). As we have already seen, the majority of the sample do not spend time reading the Bible, but they do happily spend time '*walking the dogs*' or '*out in the garden*' (and going to worship, of course) and this is where they '*find God*'. Natural piety as opposed to scriptural piety seems to be the preferred option for many and their belief in God appears to be grounded largely, but not exclusively, in natural religion, as the following extracts illustrate.

---

[5] On 'popular spirituality', see Spohn 2003: 33–4; cf. Heelas 2002; Heelas and Woodhead 2004.

[6] I am only too aware that the terms natural religion, popular spirituality, and God are all being used in ill-defined ways here, and that popular spirituality would not name its 'object' as God. My point here is merely to draw attention to the fact that salvation is mediated via sources other than Jesus.

Tom

'You can't go out on a clear night and not look up and believe.'

Ben

'I suspect that belief in God is worldwide. That's why I feel that different religions are a form of expression of one's belief.'

'[Everyone has] *at some stage wondered and I think that is the starting point. You know, you are sitting there at night, looking up into the universe and you can't help but say, "I wonder."'*

Elizabeth

'I think it is something ... you feel it more in certain situations than you can in others ... you can sometimes feel that there is something there ... I'll tell you where I always feel near to God and that's the garden. I always think you are communing with him somehow out there. It's, well, you can see nature and God's creation ... things growing ... and it's all God.'

Kathleen

'Religion is a gut feeling with a lot of us isn't it. Primitive people were worshipping. It is a need within people to worship.'

The assumption here is that religion is a basic human constant, that the various religions are different expressions of a common religious experience and that this experience is the main reason for belief in God. These assumptions are the foundation for Christian theology in the liberal tradition presented by such as Wiles, for whom 'Christianity has roots in a religious sense of awe and wonder that seems to be a fundamental aspect of almost all human experience' (Wiles 1999: 80). This assumption has come under criticism in the academy, but it is alive and kicking here in rural Anglican religion. Religious experience and *'the feeling that God is there'* is clearly of prime importance for many in the sample, and in the case of their religiousness, which is centred on God, on *'something bigger'*, revealed religion may not play the major part. Jesus may not be all that important. In the attitude that says, *'When I say the creed I can stick with "I believe in God" and can do without the rest'*, revealed religion is only of secondary importance.

It is '*a hook on which to hang belief from ... which in our case is Christianity. In other people's cases it can be any one of many religions ... Christianity happens to be the way that we come to God*'. Belief in God is more important than the 'hook', that is, the network of beliefs and practices that go to make up a particular religion.

As we have seen already, the majority of the sample have a theocentric not a Christocentric faith. God is at the centre, not Jesus. These data therefore challenge the a priori assumption that for Christians, Jesus is the central object of worship, adoration and wonder. For the majority of the sample, he clearly is not. God is. God is the object of faith – with a qualification. As Tom (who has a functional Christology) says, '*We cannot have Christianity without Christ. When I come to pray I'm thinking of Jesus as well*'. Or as Kuitert puts it, Christians have Jesus in mind when they say God and God in mind when they say Jesus (Kuitert 1999: 184–5). Most of the sample say that they go to church to worship and praise God the Father/God the creator. Just as they feel close to God in nature, they also feel close to God in church. They '*get a tremendous sense of God in church*', which is why churchgoing is important to them. The building, the music, the prayers all mediate a sense of the presence of God. They evoke '*the feeling that God is there*', just as a beautiful sunset or the birth of a child can. The liturgy acts as a vehicle, a channel for apprehension of and relationship with God, providing the opportunity for encounter with God and the chance to '*get plugged back into the mother-ship*'; to '*recharge your batteries*', '*have a time to sit and be quiet and actually put things in order*'; '*to contemplate and to think beyond the routine*'. Many report feeling '*a lot better for going*'. Churchgoing '*puts you right for the week doesn't it?*' It is restorative, healing and life-giving. In short, it is salvific. Golden Rule religion also emphasizes the sense of God's presence in Sunday worship, in nature and in critical moments in the life cycle such as births and deaths (Ammerman 1997: 207–8). And there are links here too with Celtic spirituality and creation-centred spirituality, both of which have a profound sense of God's presence and the goodness of creation. (Interestingly, Pelagius, whom we have come across already in relation to the Christology of the functionalists, is considered to be an early proponent of creation spirituality.) These spiritualities, like nature mysticism, emphasize salvation as living in God's presence, and knowing that in him we live and move and have our being and that 'our hearts are restless till they find their rest in thee'. From this perspective, salvation is no more and no less than living in the transforming presence and power of God.

So what of Jesus? What part does Jesus actually play in the salvation of the churchgoing theists? I cannot give any definitive answer to this question. It is not possible to excise Christology from the complex that is the Christian tradition and describe its impact with precision on churchgoing theists. My only aim here, in this closing chapter, is to propose that Jesus may not be as important for Christian spirituality as we (quite naturally) often suppose. Whilst the content of Christian faith may be dominated by the story of the life, death and resurrection of Jesus of Nazareth, it is clear that his story does not dominate the spirituality of every believer. In a spirituality that is firmly focused on the creator God, Jesus may not be that important. Gerard Zuidberg, in his empirical study of the spirituality of Roman Catholic pastors in the Netherlands, found that Jesus was not the centre of spirituality for the majority of pastors interviewed. 'The central point is God as ground of existence, as source of life, whereas Jesus is far more a figure who puts us on our way.' Jesus is important as an example and guide: 'Jesus is the way. He is not the center, nor the final point' (Zuidberg 2001: 127–31).[7]

The data also challenge the assumption that Christians are those who are committed to Jesus. It is not obvious that all are. Evidence of a personal commitment or devotion to Jesus is limited. The story of Jesus happens to be the story that Christians tell. It does not follow that all get caught up in it or absorbed into it. The story is listened to and remembered, but it can be largely ignored. The figure of Jesus does not have to be taken seriously. After all, once one knows that '*God is our loving heavenly Father who looks after us and answers our prayers and is always there when we need him*', or that '*God is always there as a sort of rock that I can lean on*', then why bother paying attention to Jesus? Jesus is not really needed. Churchgoing can be salvific without attending to the story of Jesus. Jesus can be superfluous to requirements: a mere cipher. When belief in God is what really matters, then Jesus can end up playing a subsidiary role, a minor part. It has to be concluded that for some Christians, Jesus is not really that important.

---

[7]   Cf. Hopkins' pilot study referred to earlier, in which ten out of the 30 women interviewed said that Jesus played no role in their lives. See Hopkins 1995: 17.

Learning From Ordinary Christology

One might (understandably) conclude from this that ordinary Christology has nothing to teach us. Surely any Christology that makes Jesus superfluous cannot be taken seriously. But can ordinary Christology be so summarily dismissed? In this final section I want to consider how we might respond to ordinary Christology and what we might learn from it.[8]

I will begin by returning to the question with which I began: who do ordinary believers say that Jesus is and what significance do they attach to him? As we have seen, the majority of ordinary believers in this sample (evangelicals and some traditionalists excepted) do not say either that Jesus is God, or that his significance resides primarily in his atoning death. They do not adhere to Christological norms (as defined in Chapter 1). The majority of the sample can do without the doctrine of the immanent Trinity or the doctrine of the incarnation (traditionally understood) or any doctrine or theory of atonement. They do not need them for their religion/ spirituality. Right doctrine is clearly not that important for their Christology. (While the traditionalists will say that right belief *is* important, for them it is the fact of believing rather than the content of that belief that seems to matter most.) How should we respond to these findings? Should these ordinary Christologies be rejected (and then corrected) because they are deemed to be inadequate versions of Christianity? Or should they be critically embraced as having something to teach us about what it is to be Christian? It should come as no surprise that I favour the latter response. This does not mean that I think ordinary Christology should be accepted *in toto*, far from it. Clearly, not all aspects of ordinary Christology are acceptable and it deserves to come under criticism, not least when it sidelines Jesus and fails to believe in him. But its failings should not blind us to the lessons it may also have to teach us.

One thing we learn is that in matters Christological, ordinary believers only take what they need. That they do not need much conceptual theology is perhaps not surprising. What is surprising is that they do not need Jesus to be God or to have saved the world through his atoning death. These findings remind us that

---

[8] On the issue of responding to ordinary theology, see Astley 2002: chapter 5; Astley and Christie 2007: 21–7. Cartledge prefers to talk of rescripting ordinary theology. See Cartledge 2010.

Christology is always governed by soteriology, which in turn is governed by religious needs. Many in the sample seem to have no felt need for an atoning saviour, and therefore they simply bypass what I have called the traditional theology of the cross as irrelevant to their religious needs. These findings have clear missiological implications, for if the traditional stories of how Jesus saves have lost their power for many churchgoers, then what about those outside the churches? There have been many voices in recent years calling for the re-enchantment of the Christian story, particularly the story of atonement, and new ways of telling the old story are now being told in some contexts.[9] Ordinary soteriology teaches us to do the same. It invites us to tell new stories of how Jesus saves – stories that are on a par with peoples' lives and that enable storied connections to be made – so that Christianity can once again be heard as 'good news' in our contemporary context. More controversially, ordinary soteriology also suggests that such stories may not require Jesus to be God in the ontological sense that orthodoxy has demanded. The majority of this sample clearly do not need Jesus to be God in this way for him to function as saviour. For them Jesus saves as exemplar and revealer and he does not need to be ontologically God, in the sense required by orthodoxy, to do this. For the majority of the sample it is enough to claim that Jesus is 'as-if-God' for them. As we have seen, most have a functional not an ontological Christology. They do not make the momentous move from 'God was in Christ' to 'Christ is God', for they recognize no soteriological reason for doing so. So the data might be said to call into question the requirement for people to make the move from functional (biblical) to ontological (ecclesial) Christology. The data also challenge the necessity of continuing to speak of Jesus as the only way of salvation or of Christianity as the one true religion. The believers in this sample experience God's salvation through Jesus but most do not conclude, and it does not follow, that God only saves through Jesus. So ordinary Christology also invites us to reconsider whether salvation for the whole world does in fact *depend* on Jesus.

One might argue, in the light of these reflections, that the Christological norms which have governed the interpretation of Jesus for so long need to be widened and the legitimacy of a multiplicity of Christologies recognized. Clearly not any and every interpretation of Jesus will do. There has to be some continuity between what the New Testament says about Jesus and what we say about Jesus today. But

---

[9]   See, for example, Green and Baker 2003; Baker 2007; Lassalle-Klein 2011.

insisting upon one norm – that of orthodoxy – to which all are expected to conform is at best unhelpful and at worst divisive, and besides it does not *work*, as this study has shown. Christological orthodoxy canonizes one Christology (namely incarnationism) as *the* Christology. But, as Tilley observes:

> No story about Jesus can be elevated to the status of THE story about Jesus. When a single story is taken as final and absolute, it becomes an idol. When a single story is taken as *the* key to the canon, the others are degraded to a lower status. The multiplicity of stories of Jesus prevents this idolatry and degradation. When one story is raised above all others, it should be 'jostled' out of place by others in the tradition. If Christians could have and tell the final and absolute story about Jesus, they could understand his person and his significance. But the presence of many stories in the New Testament warrants the traditional claim that no human story will be fully adequate to tell of him. (Tilley 1985: 141)[10]

Ordinary Christology reminds us that all Christology, be it canonical, ecclesial, liturgical, academic or ordinary, is both selective and perspectival, and therefore limited. It cannot be otherwise. Most of this sample appear to have selected a fragmented synoptic Christology. They do not appear to have a Christology that has been shaped in any substantial way by either the gospel of John or the Pauline corpus. (As has already been stated, the majority of the sample do not adhere to orthodox incarnational Christology, which has its roots in the gospel of John, or interpret Jesus' death as an expiatory sacrifice, an interpretation that is prominent in the Pauline epistles, but not in the synoptic gospels.)

Ordinary Christology puts the stories of Jesus, not doctrines about him, at the centre of Christology. It shows that Christology at its core is an ongoing hermeneutical process not a doctrinal system, and that *what matters most in Christology is not right doctrine but letting Jesus' story have its way with us.* It shifts the emphasis in Christology away from right belief (orthodoxy) to right practice (orthopraxis). An over-emphasis on orthodoxy can lead to the perception that what is really important in Christianity is right belief, in which mental assent to a set of propositions becomes *the* criterion for deciding who is/is not Christian.

---

[10] Sallie McFague makes the same point about theological multi-model discourse more generally. See McFague 1982: 139–44.

But if adherence to Christological norms is used as the criterion for what counts as Christian, then the majority of this sample of faithful churchgoers and concerned Christians would fall outside the category of Christian. If, however, Christianity is not primarily a set of propositions to be believed, but a way of life, then disciples can follow Jesus as the Way without having to give assent to (or even understand) the Christological doctrines of the Church. After all, all the biblical models of discipleship predate there being a set of doctrines about him. If being a Christian is essentially about commitment and devotion to this person/story/Way then what is made of Jesus doctrinally becomes less important. Perhaps this is the most important lesson ordinary Christology has to teach us. If so, then maybe the most important question to ask of ordinary believers, is not who was/is Jesus or what did/does he do, but *do you follow him*? Does his story shape your story? For at the centre of Christology 'is not an idea to which one must assent, but a story, not an entertaining story but rather a dangerous one, a story not only to be told but to be lived' (Metz 1985: 7).

Bibliography

Abelard, Peter, 'Exposition of the Epistle to the Romans', in *A Scholastic Miscellany: Anselm to Ockham*, vol. X, ed. and trans. Eugene R. Fairweather (London: SCM Press, 1956), 276–87.

Ahern, Geoffrey, *The Triune God in Hackney and Enfield: 30 Trinitarian Christians and Secularisation* (London: Centre for Ecumenical Studies, 1984).

Ahern, Geoffrey and Grace Davie, *Inner City God: The Nature of Belief in the Inner City* (London: Hodder and Stoughton, 1987).

Ammerman, Nancy T., 'Golden Rule Christianity: Lived Religion in the American Mainstream', in David D. Hall (ed.), *Lived Religion in America: Toward a History of Practice* (Princeton, New Jersey: Princeton University Press, 1997), 196–216.

Astley, Jeff, *The Philosophy of Christian Religious Education* (Birmingham, Alabama: Religious Education Press, 1994).

Astley, Jeff, 'The Role of Worship in Christian Learning', in Jeff Astley, Leslie J. Francis and Colin Crowder (eds), *Theological Perspectives on Christian Formation: A Reader on Theology and Christian Education* (Leominster: Gracewing Fowler Wright; Grand Rapids, Michigan: William B. Eerdmans, 1996), 244–51.

Astley, Jeff, 'Non-realism for Beginners?', in Colin Crowder (ed.), *God and Reality: Essays on Christian Non-Realism* (London: Mowbray, 1997), 100–13.

Astley, Jeff, *Choosing Life? Christianity and Moral Problems* (London: Darton, Longman and Todd, 2000).

Astley, Jeff, *Ordinary Theology: Looking, Listening and Learning in Theology* (Aldershot: Ashgate, 2002).

Astley, Jeff, *Exploring God-Talk: Using Language in Religion* (London: Darton, Longman and Todd, 2004).

Astley, Jeff, 'Connecting Religion and Morality', *Dialogue* 23 (2004), 32–5.

Astley, Jeff and Ann Christie, *Taking Ordinary Theology Seriously* (Cambridge: Grove Books, 2007).

Austin, John L., *How To Do Things with Words* (Oxford: Oxford University Press, 1962).

Avis, Paul, *God and the Creative Imagination: Metaphor, Symbol and Myth in Religion and Theology* (London: Routledge, 1999).

Avis, Paul (ed.), *Public Faith? The State of Religious Belief and Practice in Britain* (London: SPCK, 2003).

Badham, Paul, 'The Religious Necessity of Realism', in Joseph Runzo (ed.), *Is God Real?* (London: Macmillan, 1993), 183–92.

Bailey, Edward, 'The Folk Religion of the English People', in Paul Badham (ed.), *Religion, State and Society in Modern Britain* (Lampeter: Edwin Mellen Press, 1989), 145–58.

Bailey, Edward, *Implicit Religion in Contemporary Society* (Kampen, Netherlands: Kok Pharos; Weinheim: Deutscher Studien Verlag, 1997).

Bailey, Edward, *Implicit Religion: An Introduction* (London: Middlesex University Press, 1998).

Bailey, Kenneth D., *Methods of Social Research* (New York: The Free Press, 4th edn 1994).

Baillie, Donald Macpherson, *God Was in Christ: An Essay on Incarnation and Atonement* (London, Faber and Faber, 3rd edn 1961).

Baker, Mark D., 'Freed to Be Human and Restored to Family: The Saving Significance of the Cross in a Honduran Barrio', in Brad Jersak and Michael Hardin (eds), *Stricken by God? Nonviolent Identification and the Victory of Christ* (Grand Rapids, Michigan: William B. Eerdmans, 2007).

Barr, James, *Escaping from Fundamentalism* (London: SCM Press, 1984).

Barrett, Charles Kinglsey, *The Gospel According to St John: An Introduction with Commentary and Notes on the Greek Text* (London: SPCK, 1965).

Barth, Karl, *Church Dogmatics*, vol. III/4, trans. A.T. Mackay et al. (Edinburgh: T&T Clark, 1961).

Barth, Karl, *Protestant Theology in the Nineteenth Century: Its Background and History*, trans. Brian Cozens and John Bowden (London: SCM Press, 1972).

Bausch, William J., *Storytelling: Imagination and Faith* (Mystic, Connecticut: Twenty-Third Publications, 1984).

Bellah, Robert N. et al., *Habits of the Heart: Individualism and Commitment in American Life* (Berkeley: University of California Press, 1985).

Bernsten, John A., 'Christian Affections and the Catechumenate', in Jeff Astley, Leslie J. Francis and Colin Crowder (eds), *Theological Perspectives on Christian Formation: A Reader on Theology and Christian Education* (Leominster: Gracewing Fowler Wright; Grand Rapids, Michigan: William B. Eerdmans, 1996), 229–43.

Bloom, Harold, *The American Religion: The Emergence of the Post-Christian Nation* (New York: Simon and Schuster, 1992).

Borg, Marcus J., *The God We Never Knew: Beyond Dogmatic Religion to a More Authentic Contemporary Faith* (New York: HarperSanFrancisco, 1997).

Borg, Marcus J. and Tom Wright, *The Meaning of Jesus* (London: SPCK, 1999).

Borg, Marcus J., *Jesus: Uncovering the Life, Teachings, and Relevance of a Religious Revolutionary* (New York: HarperCollins, 2006).

Braithwaite, Richard B., 'An Empiricist's View of the Nature of Religious Belief', in Basil Mitchell (ed.), *The Philosophy of Religion* (Oxford: Oxford University Press, 1971), 72–91.

Brown, Callum, *The Death of Christian Britain: Understanding Secularisation 1800–2000* (London: Routledge, 2001).

Brown, Joanne Carlson, and Rebecca Parker, 'For God So Loved the World?', in Joanne Carlson Brown and Carole R. Bohn (eds), *Christianity, Patriarchy and Abuse: A Feminist Critique* (Cleveland, Ohio: The Pilgrim Press, 1989), 1–30.

Brown, Raymond E., *Jesus, God and Man: Modern Biblical Reflections* (London and Dublin: Geoffrey Chapman, 1968).

Browning, Don S., *A Fundamental Practical Theology: Descriptive and Strategic Proposals* (Minneapolis, Minnesota: Fortress Press, 1991).

Brümmer, Vincent, *Theology and Philosophical Inquiry: An Introduction* (London: Macmillan, 1981).

Brümmer, Vincent, *Speaking of a Personal God: An Essay in Philosophical Theology* (Cambridge: Cambridge University Press, 1992).

Buber, Martin, *Israel and the World: Essays in a Time of Crisis* (New York: Schocken Books, 2nd edn 1963).

Buckler, Guy and Jeff Astley, 'Learning and Believing in an Urban Parish', in Jeff Astley and David Day (eds), *The Contours of Christian Education* (Great Wakering, Essex: McCrimmons, 1992), 396–416.

Bultmann, Rudolf, 'The Christological Confession of the World Council of Churches', in *Essays Philosophical and Theological* (London: SCM Press, 1955), 273–90.

Bultmann, Rudolf, 'New Testament and Mythology', in Hans-Werner Bartsch (ed.), *Kerygma and Myth*, trans. Reginald H. Fuller (London: SPCK, 1962), vol. I, 1–44.

Cartledge, Mark J., *Charismatic Glossolalia: An Empirical-Theological Study* (Aldershot: Ashgate, 2002).

Cartledge, Mark J., *Practical Theology: Charismatic and Empirical Perspectives* (Carlisle: Paternoster Press, 2003).

Cartledge, Mark J., *Testimony in the Spirit: Rescripting Ordinary Pentecostal Theology* (Farnham: Ashgate, 2010).

Chesnut, Glenn, *Images of Christ: An Introduction to Christology* (Minneapolis, Minnesota: Seabury Press, 1984).

Church of England Doctrine Commission, *Christian Believing: The Nature of the Christian Faith and its Expression in Holy Scripture and Creeds* (London: SPCK, 1976).

Church of England Doctrine Commission, *We Believe in God* (London: Church House Publishing, 1987).

Christie, Ann, 'Ordinary Christology: A Qualitative Study and Theological Appraisal' (unpublished PhD thesis, University of Durham, 2005).

Christie, Ann, 'Who Do You Say I Am? Answers from the Pews', *Journal of Adult Theological Education*, 4: 2 (2007), 181–94.

Christie, Ann and Jeff Astley, 'Ordinary Soteriology: A Qualitative Study', in Leslie J. Francis, Jeff Astley and Mandy Robbins (eds), *Texts and Tables: Explorations in Empirical Theology* (Leiden: Brill, 2009), 177–96.

Common Worship: Services and Prayers for the Church of England (London: Church House Publishing, 2000).

Cook, Michael L., SJ, *Christology as Narrative Quest* (Collegeville, Minnesota: A Michael Glazier Book, Liturgical Press, 1997).

Crisp, Oliver D., 'Incarnation', in John Webster, Kathryn Tanner and Iain Torrance (eds), *The Oxford Handbook of Systematic Theology* (Oxford: Oxford University Press, 2007), 160–75.

Crites, Stephen, 'The Narrative Quality of Experience', in Stanley Hauerwas and L. Gregory Jones (eds), *Why Narrative? Readings in Narrative Theology* (Grand Rapids, Michigan: William B. Eerdmans, 1989), 65–88.

Crowder, Colin (ed.), *God and Reality: Essays on Christian Non-Realism* (London: Mowbray, 1997).

Cullman, Oscar, *The Christology of the New Testament*, trans. Shirley C. Guthrie and Charles A.M. Hall (London: SCM Press, 1959).

Cupitt, Don, 'Jesus and the Meaning of God', in Michael Goulder (ed.), *Incarnation and Myth: The Debate Continued* (London: SCM Press, 1979a), 31–40.

Cupitt, Don, *The Debate About Christ* (London: SCM Press, 1979b).

Cupitt, Don, *Taking Leave of God* (London: SCM Press, 1980).

Davies, Douglas J., *The Mormon Culture of Salvation* (Aldershot: Ashgate, 2000).

Davies, Douglas J., *Anthropology and Theology* (Oxford: Berg, 2002).

Davis, Stephen T., 'Jesus Christ: Saviour or Guru?', in Stephen T. Davis (ed.), *Encountering Jesus: A Debate on Christology* (Atlanta: John Knox Press, 1988), 39–76.

Douglas, Mary, *Natural Symbols: Explorations in Cosmology* (London: Barrie & Jenkins, 1970).

Dunn, James D.G., *Christology in the Making: A New Testament Inquiry into the Origins of the Doctrine of the Incarnation* (London: SCM Press, 1980).

Dunn, James D.G., *The Theology of Paul the Apostle* (London: Continuum, 2003).

Edwards, Jonathan, *Select Works, Volume III: Treatise Concerning the Religious Affections* (London: Banner of Truth, 1961).

Ely, Margot et al., *Doing Qualitative Research: Circles within Circles* (London: Falmer Press, 1991).

Endo, Shusaku, *The Samurai*, trans. C. van Gessel (New York: Harper & Row/ Kodansha International, 1982).

Erricker, Clive, 'Phenomenological Approaches', in Peter Connolly (ed.), *Approaches to the Study of Religion* (London: Cassell, 1999), 73–104.Farley, Edward, *Theologia: The Fragmentation and Unity of Theological Education* (Philadelphia: Fortress Press, 1983).

Farley, Edward, *The Fragility of Knowledge: Theological Education in the Church and the University* (Philadelphia: Fortress Press, 1988).

Farley, Edward, and Peter C. Hodgson, 'Scripture and Tradition', in Peter C. Hodgson and Robert H. King (eds), *Christian Theology: An Introduction to Its Traditions and Tasks* (Philadelphia: Fortress Press, 1982), 35–61.

Ferré, Fredrick, 'Metaphors, Models and Religion', *Soundings* 51 (1968), 327–45.

Fiddes, Paul S., *Past Event and Present Salvation: The Christian Idea of Atonement* (London: Darton, Longman and Todd, 1989).

Fiddes, Paul S., 'Salvation', in John Webster, Kathryn Tanner and Iain Torrance (eds), *The Oxford Handbook of Systematic Theology* (Oxford: Oxford University Press, 2007), 176–96.

Fisher, Elizabeth, Jeff Astley and Carolyn Wilcox, 'A Survey of Bible Reading Practice and Attitudes to the Bible among Anglican Congregations', in Jeff Astley and David Day (eds), *The Contours of Christian Education* (Great Wakering, Essex: McCrimmons, 1992), 382–93.

Francis, Leslie J., 'The Pews Talk Back: The Church Congregation Survey', in Jeff Astley (ed.), *Learning in the Way: Research and Reflection on Adult Christian Education* (Leominster: Gracewing, 2000), 161–86.

Francis, Leslie J., Mandy Robbins and Jeff Astley (eds), *Fragmented Faith: Exposing the Fault Lines in the Church of England* (Milton Keynes: Paternoster, 2005).

Francis, Leslie J., Mandy Robbins and Jeff Astley (eds), *Empirical Theology in Texts and Tables: Qualitative, Quantitative and Comparative Perspectives* (Leiden: Brill, 2009).

Frei, Hans W., *Theology and Narrative: Selected Essays*, ed. George Hunsinger and William C. Placher (New York and Oxford: Oxford University Press, 1993).

Frost, David L., *The Language of Series 3* (Bramcote: Grove Books, 1973).

Fuchs, Ottmar, '"Priest-mothers" and "God-mothers": Qualitative Empirical Approaches to Research and the Human Image of God', in Hans-Georg Ziebertz, Friedrich Schweitzer, Hermann Haring and Don Browning (eds), *The Human Image of God* (Leiden: Brill, 2001), 231–48.

Gadamer, Hans-Georg, *Truth and Method*, ed. and trans. Garrett Barden and John Cumming (New York: Crossroad, 1982).

Gardner, Howard, *Frames of Mind: The Theory of Multiple Intelligences* (London: Heinemann, 1984).

Geertz, Clifford, *The Interpretation of Cultures* (London: Hutchinson, 1975).

Gellner, David N., 'Anthropological Approaches', in Peter Connolly (ed.), *Approaches to the Study of Religion* (London: Cassell, 1999), 10–41.

Gillham, Bill, *The Research Interview* (London: Continuum, 2000).

Glaser, Barney D. and Anselm K. Strauss, *The Discovery of Grounded Theory* (Chicago: Aldine, 1967).

Goulder, Michael (ed.), *Incarnation and Myth: The Debate Continued* (London: SCM Press, 1979).

Green, Joel B. and Mark D. Baker, *Recovering the Scandal of the Cross: Atonement in New Testament and Contemporary Contexts* (Carlisle: Paternoster Press, 2003).

Groome, Thomas H., *Christian Religious Education: Sharing Our Story and Vision* (San Francisco: Harper & Row, 1980).

Gunton, Colin E., *The Actuality of Atonement: A Study of Metaphor, Rationality and the Christian Tradition* (Edinburgh: T&T Clark, 1988).

Gutierrez, Gustavo, 'Liberation Praxis and Christian Faith', in Rosino Gibellini (ed.), *Frontiers of Theology in Latin America*, trans. John Drury (London: SCM Press, 1980), 1–33.

Habgood, John, *Confessions of a Conservative Liberal* (London: SPCK, 1988).

Haight, Roger, SJ, *Jesus: Symbol of God* (Maryknoll, New York: Orbis, 1999).

Haight, Roger, SJ, *Dynamics of Theology* (Maryknoll, New York: Orbis, 2nd edn 2001).

Hammersley, Martin, *Reading Ethnographic Research: A Critical Guide* (London: Longman, 1998).

Hay, David and Kate Hunt, *Understanding the Spirituality of People Who Don't Go to Church: A Report on the Findings of the Adults' Spirituality Project at the University of Nottingham* (Nottingham: University of Nottingham, 2000).

Hebblethwaite, Brian, *The Incarnation: Collected Essays in Christology* (Cambridge: Cambridge University Press, 1987).

Hebblethwaite, Brian, 'The Impossibility of Multiple Incarnations', *Theology* CIV 821 (2001), 323–34.

Hebblethwaite, Brian, *In Defence of Christianity* (Oxford: Oxford University Press, 2005).

Heelas, Paul, 'The Spiritual Revolution: From "Religion" to "Spirituality"', in Linda Woodhead, Paul Fletcher, Hiroko Kawanami and David Smith (eds), *Religions in the Modern World* (London and New York: Routledge, 2002), 357–77.

Heelas, Paul and Linda Woodhead, *The Spiritual Revolution: Why Religion is Giving Way to Spirituality* (Oxford: Blackwell, 2004).

Heitink, Gerben, *Practical Theology: History, Theory, Action Domains*, trans. Reinder Bruinsma (Grand Rapids, Michigan: William B. Eerdmans, 1999).

Hick, John, *God and the Universe of Faiths* (London: Macmillan, 1973).

Hick, John, 'Jesus and the World Religions', in John Hick (ed.), *The Myth of God Incarnate* (London: SCM Press, 1977), 167–85.

Hick, John, *Problems of Religious Pluralism* (London: Macmillan, 1985).

Hick, John, *An Interpretation of Religion: Human Responses to the Transcendent* (London: Macmillan, 1989).

Hick, John, *The Metaphor of God Incarnate* (London: SCM Press, 1993).

Hick, John, 'A Pluralist View', in Dennis Okholm and Timothy R. Phillips (eds), *Four Views on Salvation in a Pluralistic World* (Grand Rapids: Zondervan, 1995), 29–59.

Hick, John, 'Response to Clark H. Pinnock', in Dennis Okholm and Timothy R. Phillips (eds), *Four Views on Salvation in a Pluralistic World* (Grand Rapids: Zondervan, 1995), 124–8.

Hodgson, Peter C., *Winds of the Spirit: A Constructive Christian Theology* (London: SCM Press, 1994).

Hodgson, Peter C., *God's Wisdom: Toward a Theology of Education* (Louisville, Kentucky: Westminster John Knox Press, 1999).

Hogan, Richard M., *Dissent from the Creed: Heresies Past and Present* (Huntington, Indiana: Our Sunday Visitor, 2001).

Hoggart, Richard, *The Uses of Literacy* (Harmondsworth: Penguin, 1957).

Holmer, Paul L., *The Grammar of Faith* (San Francisco: Harper & Row, 1978).

Holmes, Stephen R., *The Wondrous Cross: Atonement and Penal Substitution in the Bible and History* (Milton Keynes: Paternoster, 2007).

Hooker, Morna D., *The Message of Mark* (London: Epworth Press, 1983).

Hooker, Morna D., *Not Ashamed of the Gospel: New Testament Interpretations of the Death of Christ* (Grand Rapids, Michigan: William B. Eerdmans, 1994).

Hooker-Stacey, Morna, 'Disputed Questions in Biblical Studies: 2. Jesus and Christology', *The Expository Times* 112, 9 (2001), 298–302.

Hopewell, James F., *Congregation: Stories and Structures*, ed. Barbara G. Wheeler (London: SCM, 1987).

Hopkins, Julie, *Towards a Feminist Christology: Jesus of Nazareth, European Women, and the Christological Crisis* (London: SPCK, 1995).

Hornsby-Smith, Michael P., *Roman Catholic Beliefs in England: Customary Catholicism and Transformations of Religious Authority* (Cambridge: Cambridge University Press, 1991).

Houlden, Leslie, 'The Creed of Experience', in John Hick (ed.), *The Myth of God Incarnate* (London: SCM Press, 1977), 125–32.

Hull, John M., *What Prevents Christian Adults from Learning?* (Philadelphia: Trinity Press International, 1991).

Inbody, Tyron L., *The Many Faces of Christology* (Nashville: Abingdon Press, 2002).

Jenkins, David E., *God, Miracle and the Church of England* (London: SCM Press, 1987).

Jenkins, Timothy, *Religion in English Everyday Life: An Ethnographic Approach* (New York and Oxford: Berghahn Books, 1999).

Johnson, Elizabeth A., 'Jesus and Salvation', *Proceedings of the Catholic Theological Society of America* 49 (1994), 1–18.

Jones, Paul Dafydd, 'The Atonement: God's Love in Action', in Tom Greggs (ed.), *New Perspectives for Evangelical Theology: Engaging with God, Scripture and the World* (London: Routledge, 2010), 44–62.

Kaufmann, Gordon D., *Systematic Theology: A Historicist Perspective* (New York: Charles Scribner's Sons, 1968).

Kay, William K. and Leslie J. Francis, 'The Seamless Robe: Interdisciplinary Enquiry in Religious Education', *British Journal of Religious Education* 7, 2 (1985), 64–7.

Keck, Leander E., *A Future for the Historical Jesus: The Place of Jesus in Preaching and Theology* (London: SCM Press, 1972).

Keck, Leander E., *Who is Jesus? History in Perfect Tense* (Columbia, South Carolina: University of South Carolina Press, 2000).

Keller, Ernst and Marie-Luise Keller, *Miracles in Dispute: A Continuing Debate*, trans. Margaret Kohl (London: SCM Press, 1969).

Kelly, John N.D., *Early Christian Doctrines* (London: Adam & Charles Black, 4th edn 1968).

Kelly, John N.D., *Early Christian Creeds* (Harlow, Essex: Longman, 3rd edn 1972).

Kelsey, David H., *To Understand God Truly: What's Theological about a Theological School* (Louisville, Kentucky: Westminster/John Knox Press, 1992).

Kerr, Fergus, 'Religious Language' in Adrian Hastings, Alistair Mason and Hugh Pyper (eds), *The Oxford Companion to Christian Thought* (Oxford: Oxford University Press, 2000), 608–10.

Knitter, Paul F., *Jesus and the Other Names: Christian Mission and Global Responsibility* (Maryknoll, New York: Orbis, 1996).

Knox, John, *The Humanity and Divinity of Christ: A Study of Pattern in Christology* (Cambridge: Cambridge University Press, 1967).

Kreig, Robert A., *Story-Shaped Christology: The Role of Narratives in Identifying Jesus Christ* (New York: Paulist Press, 1988).

Kuitert, Harminus Martinus, *Jesus: The Legacy of Christianity*, trans. John Bowden (London: SCM Press, 1999).

Küng, Hans, *On Being a Christian*, trans. Edward Quinn (London: Collins, 1977).

Küng, Hans, *Credo: The Apostles' Creed Explained for Today*, trans. John Bowden (London: SCM Press, 1993).

Küschel, Karl-Josef, *Born Before All Time?: The Dispute Over Christ's Origin*, trans. John Bowden (New York: Crossroad, 1992).

Kvale, Steinar, 'The Qualitative Research Interview: A Phenomenological and a Hermeneutical Mode of Understanding', *Journal of Phenomenological Psychology* 14, 2 (1983), 171–96.

Kysar, Robert, *John, the Maverick Gospel* (Atlanta: John Knox Press, 1976).

Lampe, Geoffrey, 'The Holy Spirit and the Person of Christ', in Stephen W. Sykes and John Powell Clayton (eds), *Christ, Faith and History* (Cambridge: Cambridge University Press, 1972), 111–30.

Lampe, Geoffrey, *God as Spirit* (London: SCM Press, 1977).

Lassalle-Klein, Robert (ed.), *Jesus of Galilee: Contextual Christology for the 21st Century* (Maryknoll, New York: Orbis Books, 2011).

Lash, Nicholas, *Believing Three Ways in One God: A Reading of the Apostles' Creed* (London: SCM Press, 1992).

Lee, James Michael, *The Content of Religious Instruction: A Social Science Approach* (Birmingham, Alabama: Religious Education Press, 1985).

Lindbeck, George A., *The Nature of Doctrine: Religion and Theology in a Postliberal Age* (London: SPCK, 1984).

Lindbeck, George, 'Spiritual Formation and Theological Education', in Jeff Astley, Leslie J. Francis and Colin Crowder (eds), *Theological Perspectives on Christian Formation: A Reader on Theology and Christian Education* (Leominster: Gracewing Fowler Wright; Grand Rapids, Michigan: William B. Eerdmans, 1996), 285–302.

Loughlin, Gerard, *Telling God's Story: Bible, Church and Narrative Theology* (Cambridge: Cambridge University Press, 1996).

Lossky, Vladimir, *In the Image and Likeness of God*, ed. John H. Erickson and Thomas E. Bird (London and Oxford: Mowbray, 1975).

McFague, Sallie, *Metaphorical Theology: Models of God in Religious Language* (Philadelphia: Fortress Press, 1982).

McGrath, Alister E., 'Doctrine and Dogma', in Alister E. McGrath (ed.), *The Blackwell Encyclopaedia of Modern Christian Thought* (Oxford: Blackwell, 1993), 112–9.

McGrath, Alister E., *Christian Theology: An Introduction* (Oxford: Blackwell, 1994).

McGrath, Alister E., *The Genesis of Doctrine: A Study in the Foundations of Doctrinal Criticism* (Grand Rapids, Michigan: William B. Eerdmans, 1997).

McIntyre, John, *The Shape of Christology: Studies in the Doctrine of the Person of Christ* (Edinburgh: T&T Clark, 2nd edn 1998).

McLeod, John, *Doing Counselling Research* (London: Sage, 1994).

Mackey, James P., *Jesus: The Man and the Myth* (London: SCM Press, 1979).

Mackey, James P., *The Christian Experience of God as Trinity* (London: SCM Press, 1983).

Macquarrie, John, *God-Talk: An Examination of the Language and Logic of Theology* (London: SCM Press, 1967).

Macquarrie, John, *Principles of Christian Theology* (London: SCM Press, revised edn 1977).

Macquarrie, John, *Jesus Christ in Modern Thought* (London: SCM Press, 1990).

Macquarrie, John, *Christology Revisited* (London: SCM Press, 1998).

Malley, Brian, *How the Bible Works: An Anthropological Study of Evangelical Biblicism* (Walnut Creek, California: AltaMira Press, 2004).

Marshall, I. Howard, *The Gospel of Luke: A Commentary on the Greek Text* (Exeter: Paternoster Press, 1978).

Martin, Bernice and Ronald Pluck, *Young People's Beliefs: An Exploratory Study Commissioned by the General Synod Board of Education of the Views and Behavioural Patterns of Young People Related to their Beliefs* (London: General Synod Board of Education, 1976).

Martin, Bernice, 'Beyond Measurement: The Non-Quantifiable Religious Dimension in Social Life', in Paul Avis (ed.), *Public Faith? The State of Religious Belief and Practice in Britain* (London: SPCK, 2003), 1–18.

Martin, David, *The Breaking of the Image: A Sociology of Christian Theory and Practice* (Oxford: Blackwell, 1980).

Martin, Dean M., 'Learning to Become a Christian', in Jeff Astley and Leslie J. Francis (eds), *Critical Perspectives on Christian Education: A Reader on the Aims, Principles and Philosophy of Christian Education* (Leominster: Gracewing, 1994), 184–201.

Merriam, Sharan B. et al., *Qualitative Research in Practice: Examples for Discussion and Analysis* (San Francisco, California: Jossey-Bass, 2002).

Metz, Johann Baptist, 'Theology Today: New Crisis and New Visions', *Proceedings of the Catholic Theological Society of America* 40 (1985), 1–14.

Migliore, Daniel L., *Faith Seeking Understanding: An Introduction to Christian Theology* (Grand Rapids, Michigan: William B. Eerdmans, 1991).

Miles, Matthew B. and A. Michael Huberman, *Qualitative Data Analysis* (Thousand Oaks, California: Sage, 2nd edn 1994).

Moltmann, Jürgen, *The Trinity and the Kingdom of God: The Doctrine of God*, trans. Margaret Kohl (London: SCM Press, 1981).

Momen, Moojan, *The Phenomenon of Religion: A Thematic Approach* (Oxford: Oneworld, 1999).

Moore, Gareth, *Believing in God: A Philosophical Essay* (Edinburgh: T&T Clark, 1988).

Moustakas, Clark, *Phenomenological Research Methods* (Thousand Oaks, California: Sage, 1994).

Nellas, Panayiotis, *Deification in Christ: Orthodox Perspectives on the Nature of the Human Person*, trans. Norman Russell (Crestwood, New York: St. Vladimir's Seminary Press, 1997).

Nichols, Bridget, *Liturgical Hermeneutics: Interpreting Liturgical Rites in Performance* (Frankfurt am Main: Peter Lang, 1996).

Nichols, Kevin, *Refracting the Light: Learning the Languages of Faith* (Dublin: Veritas, 1997).

O'Collins, Gerald, SJ, *Interpreting Jesus* (London: Mowbray, 1983).

O'Collins, Gerald, SJ, *Christology: A Biblical, Historical, and Systematic Study of Jesus Christ* (Oxford: Oxford University Press, 1995).

Ogden, Schubert M., *Is There Only One True Religion or Are There Many?* (Dallas, Texas: Southern Methodist University Press, 1992).

Oppenheim, Abraham N., *Questionnaire Design, Interviewing and Attitude Measurement* (London: Pinter, 1992).

Pannenberg, Wolfhart, *Jesus – God and Man*, trans. Lewis L. Wilkins and Duane A. Priebe (London: SCM Press, 1968).

Pattison, George, unpublished paper given at Artists and Theologians Colloquium, University College, Durham, 5 September, 1995.

Pattison, George, *The End of Theology – And the Task of Thinking about God* (London: SCM Press, 1998).

Pelikan, Jaroslav, *The Christian Tradition: A History of the Development of Doctrine: 1 – The Emergence of the Catholic Tradition (100–600)* (Chicago and London: The University of Chicago Press, 1975).

Pelikan, Jaroslav, *Jesus through the Centuries: His Place in the History of Culture* (New Haven: Yale University Press, 1999).

Percy, Martyn, *Shaping the Church: The Promise of Implicit Theology* (Farnham: Ashgate, 2010).

Phillips, Dewi Z., *Faith after Foundationalism* (London: Routledge, 1988).

Pinnock, Clark H., and Delwin Brown, *Theological Crossfire: An Evangelical/ Liberal Dialogue* (Grand Rapids, Michigan: Zondervan, 1990).

Pittenger, Norman W., *The Word Incarnate: A Study of the Doctrine of the Person of Christ* (London: James Nisbet, 1959).

Price, Henry H., *Belief* (London: George Allen and Unwin, 1969).

Quinn, Philip L., 'Abelard on Atonement: "Nothing Unintelligible, Arbitrary, Illogical, or Immoral about It"', in Eleonore Stump (ed.), *Reasoned Faith* (Ithaca and London: Cornell University Press, 1993), 281–300.

Rahner, Karl, *Theological Investigations*, vol. IV, trans. Kevin Smyth (London: Darton, Longman and Todd, 1966).

Rahner, Karl, *Theological Investigations*, vol. VI, trans. Karl-H. and Boniface Kruger (London: Darton, Longman and Todd, 1969).

Rahner, Karl, *Theological Investigations*, vol. IX, trans. Graham Harrison (London: Darton, Longman and Todd, 1972).

Ramsey, A. Michael, *God, Christ and the World: A Study in Contemporary Theology* (London: SCM Press, 1969).

Ramsey, Ian T., *Religious Language* (London: SCM Press, 1957).

Richard, Lucien, 'Theology and Belonging: Christian Identity and the Doing of Theology', in Jeff Astley, Leslie J. Francis and Colin Crowder (eds), *Theological Perspectives on Christian Formation: A Reader on Theology and Christian Education* (Leominster: Gracewing Fowler Wright; Grand Rapids, Michigan: William B. Eerdmans, 1996), 146–65.

Richter, Philip and Leslie J. Francis, *Gone But Not Forgotten: Church Leaving and Returning* (London: Darton, Longman and Todd, 1998).

Ricoeur, Paul, *The Symbolism of Evil*, trans. Emerson Buchanan (Boston, Massachusetts: Beacon Press, 1967).

Ricoeur, Paul, 'Philosophy and Religious Language', *Journal of Religion* 54, 1 (1974), 71–85.

Robinson, John A.T., *The Human Face of God* (London: SCM Press, 1972).

Root, Michael, 'The Narrative Structure of Soteriology', in Stanley Hauerwas and L. Gregory Jones (eds), *Why Narrative? Readings in Narrative Theology* (Grand Rapids, Michigan: William B. Eerdmans, 1989), 263–78.

Ruether, Rosemary Radford, *Sexism and God-Talk: Toward a Feminist Theology* (Boston, Massachusetts: Beacon Press, 1983).

Ruether, Rosemary Radford, 'The Western Religious Tradition and Violence against Women in the Home', in Joanne Carlson Brown and Carole R. Bohn (eds), *Christianity, Patriarchy and Abuse: A Feminist Critique* (Cleveland, Ohio: The Pilgrim Press, 1989), 31–41.

Ruether, Rosemary R., *Introducing Redemption in Christian Feminism* (Sheffield: Sheffield Academic Press, 1998).

Runia, Klaas, *The Present-Day Christological Debate* (Leicester: InterVarsity Press, 1984).

Schleiermacher, Friedrich, *The Christian Faith*, ed. Hugh R. Mackintosh and James S. Stewart (Edinburgh: T&T Clark, 1928).

Schleiermacher, Friedrich, *On Religion: Addresses in Response to its Cultured Critics*, trans. Terrence N. Tice (Richmond, Virginia: John Knox Press, 1969).

Schneiders, Sandra M., *The Revelatory Text: Interpreting the New Testament as Sacred Scripture* (Collegeville, Minnesota: A Michael Glazier Book, Liturgical Press, 2nd edn 1999).

Schreiter, Robert J., *Constructing Local Theologies* (Maryknoll, New York: Orbis, 1985).

Schreiter, Robert J. (ed.), *Faces of Jesus in Africa* (Maryknoll, New York: Orbis, 1991).

Schüssler Fiorenza, Elisabeth, *Bread Not Stone: The Challenge of Feminist Biblical Interpretation* (Boston, Massachusetts: Beacon Press, 1984).

Schüssler Fiorenza, Francis, 'Critical Social Theory and Christology: Toward an Understanding of Atonement and Redemption as Emancipatory Solidarity', *Proceedings of the Catholic Theological Society of America* 30 (1975), 63–110.

Schwarz, Hans, *Christology* (Grand Rapids, Michigan: William B. Eerdmans, 1998).

Schweitzer, Don, *Contemporary Christologies* (Minneapolis, Minnesota: Fortress Press, 2010).

Schweitzer, Friedrich, 'Distorted, Oppressive, Fading Away? The Dialogical Task of Practical Theology and the Human Image of God', in Hans-Georg Ziebertz, Friedrich Schweitzer, Hermann Haring and Don Browning (eds), *The Human Image of God* (Leiden: Brill, 2001), 177–91.

Sherry, Patrick, *Images of Redemption: Art, Literature and Salvation* (London: T&T Clark, 2003).

Slee, Nicola Mary, 'The Patterns and Processes of Women's Faith Development: A Qualitative Study' (PhD thesis, University of Birmingham, 1999).

Slee, Nicola, *Women's Faith Development: Patterns and Processes* (Aldershot: Ashgate, 2004).

Smart, Ninian, *The Phenomenon of Religion* (London: Macmillan, 1973).

Smart, Ninian, *Dimensions of the Sacred: An Anatomy of the World's Beliefs* (London: HarperCollins, 1996).

Smith, Christine M., *Preaching as Weeping, Confession, and Resistance: Radical Responses to Radical Evil* (Louisville, Kentucky: Westminster/John Knox Press, 1992).

Smith, Graeme, 'If You Can't Beat 'em', *Church Times*, 8 March 2002, 15.

Sobrino, Jon, *Christology at the Crossroads: A Latin American Approach*, trans. John Drury (Maryknoll, New York: Orbis, 1978).

Spohn, William C., *Go and Do Likewise: Jesus and Ethics* (New York: Continuum, 2003).

Stiver, Dan R., *The Philosophy of Religious Language: Sign, Symbol, and Story* (Oxford: Blackwell, 1996).

Stringer, Martin D., 'Situating Meaning in the Liturgical Text', *Bulletin of the John Rylands University Library of Manchester* 73, 3 (1991), 181–95.

Stringer, Martin D., *On the Perception of Worship: The Ethnography of Worship in Four Christian Congregations in Manchester* (Birmingham: University of Birmingham Press, 1999).

Surin, Kenneth, *Theology and the Problem of Evil* (Oxford: Blackwell, 1986).

Surin, Kenneth, *The Turnings of Darkness and Light: Essays in Philosophical and Systematic Theology* (Cambridge: Cambridge University Press, 1989).

Sykes, Stephen, *Christian Theology Today* (London and Oxford: Mowbray, 1971).

Sykes, Stephen, 'The Incarnation as the Foundation of the Church', in Michael Goulder (ed.), *Incarnation and Myth: The Debate Continued* (London: SCM Press, 1979), 115–27.

Sykes, Stephen, *The Story of Atonement* (London: Darton, Longman and Todd, 1997).

Talbert, Charles H. (ed.), *Reimarus: Fragments*, trans. Ralph S. Fraser (London: SCM Press, 1971).

Tanner, Kathryn, 'Theological Reflection and Christian Practices', in Miroslav Volf and Dorothy C. Bass (eds), *Practicing Theology: Beliefs and Practices in Christian Life* (Grand Rapids, Michigan: William B. Eerdmans, 2002), 228–42.

Taylor, John V., *The Christlike God* (London: SCM Press, 1992).

Thatcher, Adrian, *Truly a Person, Truly God: A Post-Mythical View of Jesus* (London: SPCK, 1990).

Thiselton, Anthony C., *The Two Horizons: New Testament Hermeneutics and Philosophical Description with Special Reference to Heidegger, Bultmann, Gadamer, and Wittgenstein* (Exeter: Paternoster Press, 1980).

Tilley, Terrence W., *Story Theology* (Wilmington, Delaware: Michael Glazier, 1985).

Tillich, Paul, *Systematic Theology*, vol. I (London: James Nisbet, 1957).

Towler, Robert, *Homo Religiosus* (London: Constable, 1974).

Towler, Robert, *The Need for Certainty: A Sociological Study of Conventional Religion* (London: Routledge and Kegan Paul, 1984).

van der Ven, Johannes, *Practical Theology: An Empirical Approach* (Kampen, Netherlands: Kok Pharos, 1993).

Village, Andrew, *The Bible and Lay People: An Empirical Approach to Ordinary Hermeneutics* (Aldershot: Ashgate, 2007).

Volf, Miroslav, 'Theology for a Way of Life', in Miroslav Volf and Dorothy C. Bass (eds), *Practicing Theology: Beliefs and Practices in Christian Life* (Grand Rapids, Michigan: William B. Eerdmans, 2002), 245–63.

Wakeman, Hilary, *Saving Christianity: New Thinking for Old Beliefs* (Dublin: The Liffey Press, 2003).

Wallis, Ian G., *Holy Saturday Faith: Rediscovering the Legacy of Jesus* (London: SPCK, 2000).

Wainwright, Arthur W., *The Trinity in the New Testament* (London: SPCK, 1962).

Ward, Keith, *Divine Action* (London: Collins, 1990).

Ware, Timothy, *The Orthodox Church* (Harmondsworth: Penguin, 1963).

Weaver, J. Denny, *The Nonviolent Atonement* (Grand Rapids, Michigan: William B. Eerdmans, 2nd edn 2011).

Whaling, Frank, 'Theological Approaches', in Peter Connolly (ed.), *Approaches to the Study of Religion* (London: Continuum, 1998), 226–74.

White, Vernon, *Atonement and Incarnation: An Essay in Universalism and Particularity* (Cambridge: Cambridge University Press, 1991).

Whitehouse, Harvey, *Modes of Religiosity: A Cognitive Theory of Religious Transmission* (Walnut Creek, California: AltaMira Press, 2004).

Wiles, Maurice, *The Remaking of Christian Doctrine* (London: SCM Press, 1974).

Wiles, Maurice, 'In Defence of Arius', in *Working Papers in Doctrine* (London: SCM Press, 1976), 28–37.

Wiles, Maurice, 'Myth in Theology', in John Hick (ed.), *The Myth of God Incarnate* (London: SCM Press, 1977a), 148–66.

Wiles, Maurice, 'Christianity without Incarnation?', in John Hick (ed.), *The Myth of God Incarnate* (London: SCM Press, 1977b), 1–10.

Wiles, Maurice, 'A Survey of Issues in the *Myth* Debate', in Michael Goulder (ed.), *Incarnation and Myth: The Debate Continued* (London: SCM Press, 1979), 1–12.

Wiles, Maurice, *Explorations in Theology 4* (London: SCM Press, 1979).

Wiles, Maurice, *God's Action in the World* (London: SCM Press, 1986).

Wiles, Maurice, *Reason to Believe* (London: SCM Press, 1999).

Williams, Delores S., *Sisters in the Wilderness: The Challenge of Womanist God-Talk* (Maryknoll, New York: Orbis, 1993).

Wilmer, Haddon, 'Forgiveness', in Adrian Hastings, Alistair Mason and Hugh Pyper (eds), *The Oxford Companion to Christian Thought* (Oxford: Oxford University Press, 2000), 245–7.

Wilson, Andrew N., *Jesus* (London: Sinclair-Stevenson, 1992).

Winter, Michael, *The Atonement* (London: Geoffrey Chapman, 1995).

Wittgenstein, Ludwig, *Philosophical Investigations*, trans. G. Elizabeth M. Anscombe (Oxford: Blackwell, 1968).

Woodhead, Linda, 'Should Churches Look Inward, Not Outward?', *Church Times*, 31 December 2004, 5.

Wright, Tom, *Who Was Jesus?* (London: SPCK, 1992).

Wright, Tom, *Jesus and the Victory of God* (London: SPCK, 1996).

Young, Frances, 'A Cloud of Witnesses', in John Hick (ed.), *The Myth of God Incarnate* (London: SCM Press, 1977), 13–47.

Young, Frances, *The Making of the Creeds* (London: SCM Press, 1991).

Zahl, Paul F.M., *A Short Systematic Theology* (Grand Rapids, Michigan: William B. Eerdmans, 2000).

Zuidberg, Gerard, *The God of the Pastor: The Spirituality of Roman Catholic Pastors in the Netherlands* (Leiden: Brill, 2001).

Index